For the
Sugar Hill Child
Museum

With respect and
gratitude for this
wonderful project.

Wishing every
success,

Wendy Johnson

August 28, 2015

A DANCER IN THE REVOLUTION

A DANCER IN THE REVOLUTION

STRETCH JOHNSON, HARLEM COMMUNIST AT THE COTTON CLUB

HOWARD EUGENE JOHNSON
WITH WENDY JOHNSON

Empire State Editions

An imprint of Fordham University Press

New York   2014

to Martha

Contents

Foreword by Mark D. Naison   ix

Acknowledgments   xv

Timeline   xxi

Part I

1 Early Days   3

2 Harlem and the Cotton Club   26

3 Moving Up   37

4 Show Biz   46

5 Joining the Party   53

Part II

6 The Young Communist League   65

7 The War Years   79

8 Back Home   99

9 *La Lucha Continua*   112

Part III

10   Starting Over   135

11   *Malimvu*   155

12   The Cotton Club Revisited   160

13   Martin Luther King Day in Hawaii   162

14   Paris to Texas and Home Again   166

Notes   169

Further Reading   175

Map of Harlem Nightclubs in the 1930s and '40s   176–77

Howard E. Johnson's Curriculum Vitae   179

Index   183

Photographs follow page 48

Foreword

This long-awaited memoir of Howard "Stretch" Johnson, former Communist Party leader and pioneer in the Black Studies movement, is a welcome addition to the rapidly growing literature on the role of the communist left in launching challenges to racism and white supremacy well before the civil rights movement of the 1950s and 1960s. Books like Glenda Gilmore's *Defying Dixie*, Danielle McGuire's *At the Dark End of the Street*, and Erik McDuffie's *Sojourning for Freedom* each highlight the experience of African American activists who were in or close to the Communist Party from the early '30s in creating movements around issues ranging from lynching and sexual assault to labor organizing and voting rights.[1] Johnson, who had a major role in a number of the initiatives highlighted in these books, has a unique perspective on the Communist Party's involvement in civil rights activism, both as a party member for more than twenty years and as a scholar and teacher trying to make sense of those experiences with the wisdom of hindsight. But what makes his memoir all the more fascinating is the path that led Johnson to communism. Johnson was the ultimate "insider" in the cultural and political life of the Black community in northern New Jersey he grew up in and his adopted community of Harlem. An athlete, star student, and NAACP youth leader who never met a party he didn't like, Johnson ended up getting work as a dancer at Harlem's world-famous Cotton Club and also danced on Broadway. When he was recruited to the Young Communist League in the mid-'30s, he was able to put the full range of his personal contacts, who included

bandleaders, ministers, professional athletes, and people in the underground economy, at the movement's disposal. Throw out your stereo-
types of the communist as grim-faced ideologue and disciplinarian.
While Johnson accepted party discipline, sometimes to his own and the
movement's detriment, he also was incredibly effective at bonding with
people, motivating people, and creating alliances between communist
organizations and a cross-section of Black community institutions, all of
which make his story exceptionally informative and intriguing.

But this memoir, which was completed by his daughter Wendy more
than ten years after his death, is not just about Johnson's life in the Communist Party. It is also about Johnson's odyssey growing up in a near–
middle-class Black family whose experiences in a racially hierarchical
society left it both with a strong residue of frustration as well as a high
level of race pride. Everyone on both sides of his family was racially
mixed. His father's family, originally from the South, had Native American and European as well as African ancestry, and his mother's family
came from a much-maligned, racially mixed group from New Jersey
known as the Ramapo Mountain People. Johnson and his siblings grew
up near-white in appearance in New Jersey towns that did not draw the
color line in schools but did so in many other aspects of life, especially
the job market. This forced multitalented "men of color" like Johnson's
father to have multiple sources of income, some on the other side of
legality, to support themselves and their families and left them with an
extremely cynical and unflattering view of white people. A professional baseball and basketball player and sometime professional gambler
who could "recite Shakespeare by the yard," Johnson's father instilled
in him a love of learning, a love of sports, a love of the arts, and a powerful conviction that Black people, however you defined them, were as
good as white people in most things, and better than them in most.

This race pride, or high self-esteem—however you want to describe
it—allowed Johnson to have a childhood and adolescence filled with
sports and music, romance and intrigue . . . and more than a little academic success. He was a star in the schools he attended, a star in his family,
and a star in the Black middle-class world of northern New Jersey. Although he had white friends, his most meaningful friendships were
with African American young people in his own and adjoining towns
who had their own distinctive and quite vital, social, and political lives.
Johnson describes an adolescence filled with ball games, parties, plays,
church socials, NAACP meetings, and fun-filled "road trips" during
which a hint of romance was in the air for the dashing and glamorous

Black teenagers Johnson hung out with. Although portions of Johnson's odyssey parallel those of Malcolm X's—childhood in a predominantly white northern community, immersion in the nightlife and cultural life of the Harlem community, followed by politicization—the story Johnson tells here, honed by his keen sociologist's eye, is very different from the one Malcom X told about his experiences in Michigan.[2] Not only did Johnson, unlike Malcolm, grow up in a vibrant, intact family, he was surrounded by strong Black institutions and Black people who were confident and economically stable, although their paths to economic stability were not always conventional or legal.

But though Johnson's childhood and adolescence were filled with excitement, joy, and opportunities to hone his intellect and artistic and athletic talents, the realities of living in a racist society still cast a shadow over his experience. The jobs he could get, such as working on the kitchen staff of summer camps for wealthy whites, all were in the service sector. High-paying blue-collar jobs as well as office work in corporations or government agencies were off limits to an African American teenager, even one as talented and charming as Johnson. Nowhere was this more true than in Harlem, the cultural capital of Black America, where Johnson's family moved in the early 1930s, following his sister Winnie, a glamorous and talented dancer and chorus girl at the Cotton Club. Winnie, strikingly beautiful, dated, married, or was otherwise involved with some of the best-known Black men of her era—among them Bill "Bojangles" Robinson, Stepin Fetchit, and Joe Louis—and Johnson got to meet all of them. Unlike Malcolm X, Johnson came to Harlem with contacts who could ease his entry into the top levels of the African American entertainment world, of civil rights advocacy, and of sports and the underground economy. But despite this cultural capital, Johnson found himself dependent on whites to find employment and advance his performing career. Some of the most powerful and chilling passages of the book describe the white underworld characters who controlled the Cotton Club and the upper-class whites who came to Harlem for all kinds of illicit thrill-seeking, people whom Johnson found himself needing to please, or manipulate, if he wanted to find any kind of work as an entertainer.

In one of the most honest and revealing portions of the memoir, Johnson pulls the cover off a powerful thread of homoerotic tourism in Harlem's nightlife that some African American men could parlay into income. In matter-of-fact prose suggesting his behavior was hardly unusual, Johnson describes opportunistic sexual encounters with men that got him a job in a Broadway show, as well as additional encounters that provided him with spending money. The Harlem milieu Johnson was in was pervaded with a free-wheeling eroticism that blurred sex and gender boundaries while reinforcing racial ones. Like Malcolm X, Johnson describes white thrill-seekers in Harlem as people whose nighttime intimacies with Blacks rarely translated into daytime friendships, much less effort to shatter racial barriers.[3]

However, there was another group of whites in Harlem whose behavior was markedly different, and that was the communists. White communists, who came to Harlem in force once the Great Depression struck, were not there to fulfill secret sexual fantasies under the cover of night; they were out in force, in broad daylight, to prove you could unite the working class only if whites fought for racial equality and practiced it every day in their personal and political relationships with Blacks. By the time Johnson came to Harlem to live in 1932, communists, white and Black, were a visible presence in the neighborhood, moving back the furniture of families who had been evicted from their apartments; marching through the neighborhood demanding freedom for the Scottsboro Boys, nine Black youngsters who had been sentenced to death in Alabama on a bogus charge of rape; leading hunger marches on private charities and city agencies; and sponsoring "interracial dances" to highlight the party's full support of social equality between Blacks and whites, up to and including interracial marriage.[4] Given Johnson's political background, his exposure to socialist ideas—via a high school history teacher—and the humiliations he experienced from whites on jobs inside and outside the entertainment industry, it is not surprising that Johnson gravitated to the Communist Party and its youth group, the Young Communist League. The book doesn't describe exactly how he was recruited, something that could have been added had he been alive when it was being prepared for publication, but it does provide a compelling portrait of the atmosphere of the communist youth movement in Harlem in the late 1930s and '40s when Johnson was part of a group of very talented African American intellectuals and students.

The second section of the book is less a narrative history than a series of vignettes dealing with different dimensions of Johnson's twenty-year life in the Communist Party. While it left me with many questions that I would have loved to discuss were "Stretch" still alive, it covers some new ground that will have historians of American radicalism scouring the archives and may result in some great theses and dissertations. First of all, Johnson gives us what is essentially a Young Communist League's organizing manual for Harlem that could be productively consulted by any group trying to build a base in an African American urban community. At its high point, Johnson points out that the YCL had members drawn from church kids, college students, nationalist activists, up-and-coming musicians and writers, and neighborhood gang kids. They were able to do this because they combined an emphasis on issues that hit home for working-class Harlemites, like unemployment and police brutality, with a strong anti-lynching platform, a call for the liberation of Black people living under colonial control, and a celebration of Black culture. Johnson's genius as an organizer was to know that "culture"—especially music and sports—reaches people where they live, and he includes a wonderful section on the Young Communist League's protest campaign to integrate major league baseball.[5] Some of the most famous cultural figures in Black America—Joe Louis, Duke Ellington, Jackie Robinson, Billie Holiday—make appearances in Johnson's story, reflecting the influence the communist movement had in Harlem during the peak years of its activity.

Other valuable sections include Johnson's wartime experiences in a segregated Army, which cover experiences at Army camps North and South, and service in the military in Italy, his postwar organizing with the United Negro and Allied Veterans of America, his trips to Mexico and Cuba to meet with Latin American communists, and his movement into the Communist Party underground during the McCarthy era. Many of these sections are unforgettably eloquent, with brilliantly drawn portraits of key individuals he interacted with, along with chilling descriptions of how racism poisoned life for African Americans in every section of the nation, especially the South, sometimes with murderous consequences, and created tensions even for those trying to challenge those injustices. Johnson is also brutally honest about the strains being a communist put on his marriage and family, his own bouts with alcoholism, and the refusal of most communists to acknowledge, much less grapple with, the murderous qualities of Stalin's rule until well after the Soviet leader's death. Johnson's candor about issues in his personal life that many people are reluctant to talk about gives his reflections on the political milieu he was in added authenticity and credibility. Among the many memoirs of American communists I have read, this is one of the few that admit to the author's human frailty in dimensions not strictly political. Portions of it are painful to read, but it makes for a work whose insights are etched in the reader's memory.

The final section of the book is about Johnson's experiences after he left the Communist Party in the late 1950s and his efforts to rebuild a life outside a movement shattered both by internal and external forces. And this section is downright inspirational. Here is a man beset by a train of tragedies, disappointments, and defeats that would crush most people, who goes back to get his high school equivalency, finds work as a printer, and pursues an undergraduate degree at Columbia's School of General Studies, making such an impression on his professors that they get him positions, first in the Upward Bound program at Fieldston, and then in the Sociology Department and Black Studies program at SUNY New Paltz. In both of those positions, Johnson not only thrived, he excelled! When I met and interviewed Johnson in 1977 for my book *Communists in Harlem During the Depression*, he had already achieved near-legend status in Black Studies for the inspirational quality of his speeches, his popularity among students, and the community partnerships he built for his university with Black organizations up and down the Hudson Valley.

The book does these experiences justice. It is every bit as eloquent, thoughtful, and memorable as the person who wrote it.

Mark D. Naison
Brooklyn, New York
June 5, 2013

Acknowledgments

Every story has its genesis, and this one, of course, would never have come into the world without Stretch. He lived the story before the first word was ever on the page, and Martha Sherman Johnson lived it with him. When I told her that the title of the book was *A Dancer in the Revolution*, she responded, "But your father wasn't a dancer and we didn't get our revolution." It made me think that Stretch, who would always tap dance at the first occasion, must have loved those brief moments as a "Demon Dancer" and that people remembered him for that. Perhaps his dancer's style and carriage even helped him draw crowds as a dedicated communist standing on a street corner in Harlem. While it was also true that he never got his revolution, he was—until the end—a revolutionary, fighting and marching throughout his lifetime. Even after he quietly left the Communist Party of the United States of America, he continued as a "communist with a lower case *c*" to live his life as a fierce opponent of racism, the "market economy," and the forces oppressing poor folks everywhere.

I met Maxine Gordon—scholar, researcher, and archivist—during one of her trips to Paris, thanks to David and Joanne Burke, filmmakers, reputed for their welcoming dinners. Maxine has been writing the biography of her late husband, Dexter Gordon, the great tenor saxophone player. We hit it off immediately and shared copiously about our respective projects. I told her about Stretch's manuscript and that I wanted to find the right publisher for his story. She read it and agreed that it needed to be published. Maxine sent the manuscript to

Mark Naison, professor of history, chair of the African American Studies Department at Fordham University, and activist. He had known my father and interviewed him for his own book *Communists in Harlem During the Depression*. Mark read Stretch's manuscript before Maxine and I were to see him at his office in the Bronx. At this meeting, right in front of us, Mark called the director of Fordham University Press, Fredric Nachbaur, saying, "Fred, I have a book for you to publish. It's a slam-dunk."

This is when I knew that Stretch, who adored basketball and used that expression himself, had his "dream team." Maxine, despite being busy with her own book, gave without counting of her time and has helped me every step of the way. My deepest thanks go to Maxine. She stood ready to help at all times.

Mark has given of himself to make this dream come true, and I have benefited from his deep sense of commitment. With his more-than-generous offer to write the foreword to Stretch's book, putting it on today's map, he has drawn a big circle of solidarity and bridged the divide between past and present. I can never thank him enough.

At this stage I have also to thank Henry Louis Taylor Jr., professor, Department of Urban and Regional planning at Buffalo University and founding director of the UB Center for Urban Studies. His enthusiastic and supportive recommendation was another determining factor that led to the publication of Stretch's book.

Joining Stretch's dream team as development editor is Paul Buhle, professor emeritus at Brown University; founder of the Oral History of the American Left at Tamiment Library, New York University; and lifetime activist himself. He has been an enthusiastic member of the team who early on was a strong supporter of publication. He has always encouraged me to keep the ball moving. Stretch's book is so fortunate to have had the benefit of Paul's experience as editor at *Radical America* and other publications. His project to bring Stretch to life in a pictorial biography version to be part of his Black History opus is an exciting venture that should reach many young people of all ages. My thanks go out to you, Paul.

Thanks to all the people at the Tamiment Library who helped me with a travel grant so that I could come to New York and conduct research there. This is a wonderful institution and a veritable treasure-trove of radical archives. I felt in such good company with the papers of the Young Communist League and the Jefferson School, where Stretch had taught, and also the James and Esther Cooper Jackson Archives.

I also owe a great deal to Barbara Falk, associate professor, Canadian Forces College, who gave me tremendous support and many invaluable research suggestions.

Deep thanks go to Vanessa Agard Jones, who was my initial research assistant. Her enthusiasm and generosity of spirit helped me start on the road to a more rigorous academic approach for Stretch's manuscript. Vanessa's guidance in the early stages gave me the momentum to carry on.

I am very grateful to Kem Crimmins, my amazing research editor. He is a dedicated and tireless researcher and has never ceased to surprise me with his scholarship, thoroughness, and caring. It has been a joy to know him, and I have come to cherish the telephone "visits" with Kem that were not only effective in our advancing of the work but also a precious break from the loneliness all writers must sometimes experience. His viewpoint highlighting how younger generations might receive Stretch's writing has been all-important in the process of getting Stretch out of the box, off the page, and into the world of today.

Finally, it is Fredric Nachbaur, director of Fordham University Press and founder of Empire State Editions, who made the publication of Stretch's book possible. He has shown me that the publishing world can indeed have a very human face. He has with great kindness been a key player in Stretch's dream team and supported my work over the past two-and-a-half years. With every phone call or meeting his special magic has been to give of his time and attention in such a way that I would think I was the only author being published by him. I owe a tremendous debt of gratitude to him.

I wish to thank all the people who knew my father and granted me interviews during which they brought him into the room with us, thereby making it possible to weave a strong link between the man who once lived and our present times. The three obstacles that for a while seemed insurmountable—the unfinished manuscript, my father's death, and the time that had passed since that day—faded away with their accounts of meeting him and knowing him.

Unfortunately, Delilah Jackson, jazz historian who specialized in the Cotton Club and at times seemed to know more about my own family than I did, is no longer with us, and the copy of the book I promised her will now be for her family. Jean Bach, who was a producer at CBS and made the film *Great Day in Harlem*, regaled me with the vivid story of when and how she first met Stretch. I imagine that her reaction to such masculine beauty was shared by many. I remembered Jean, at my father's tribute. She knew him and remained his friend for nearly seventy years.

Bruce Hopewell co-founded the National Black Network, a minority-owned and -operated radio network, and founded LBH Associates, one of the only minority-owned and -operated theatrical / film talent agencies in New York. Bruce and Mary, his wife, are now key actors in the Napa Valley Jazz Festival. They both gave generously of their time and searched high and low for letters that Stretch had written them. Bruce's interview took me back to my childhood in Harlem, where, when I was walking down the street in our neighborhood with my father, Stretch would stop and say hello to almost everyone. Bruce and Stretch had been close friends, and his perceptions of Stretch were invaluable.

My next debt of gratitude is to Herb Boyd, journalist, educator, author, and activist. His articles appear regularly in the *New York Amsterdam News*, and he teaches Black Studies at the City College of New York and the College of New Rochelle. He received me at the offices of the *Amsterdam News* and gave a stunning account of how he met Stretch and was mentored by him. Herb explained that Stretch had been a forerunner in the realm of jazz teachings and that he had laid the groundwork for generations to come in the fields of jazz history and the sociology of jazz. He said that Stretch, much interviewed and footnoted in many books, deserved "a book of his own."

Barbara Scott, a former professor at SUNY New Paltz, magnanimously offered me a full day of her presence in New York and gave extensive interviews, making it possible for me to relive the days she shared with "HJ," as she called my father. Partner and staunch supporter of his struggles during his SUNY days, she helped bring alive that period.

Ann Anthony, my father's partner of many years, shared militancy with him and helped tremendously with the Hawaii years and documents from that time. She told me about Stretch's marching with the Rainbow Coalition and the then-governor of Hawaii to achieve a Martin Luther King Day holiday in that state.

Kay Takara, publisher in Hawaii, interviewed Stretch at length and made it possible to retrieve much of how he perceived his years in Honolulu. Lou Rosoff, comrade and friend, gave an interview that moved me deeply when he shared how Stretch had regretted not being old enough to join the Lincoln Brigade and fight for the Spanish Republic. It was then I realized that above all else, my father was a soldier. Jarvis Tyner, also comrade and friend, offered to host Stretch's publishing party at the Communist Party headquarters in New York. Over a great lunch we spoke of many other militants my father worked with in the days before the civil rights movement of the '60s.

Jess Pinkham, photographer, tirelessly transcribed pages and pages of the Stretch interviews. She made it possible to salvage for generations to come the priceless first-account witnessing of those who knew Stretch and lived through the same times. I am grateful to her for this all-important contribution, bringing oral history to written words that can be saved for the future. These interviews are now part of the Howard Johnson Archives at Columbia.

I am deeply indebted to Robert O'Meally, the Zora Neale Hurston Professor of English and director of the Center for Jazz Studies at Columbia University, who has been an inspiration to me. His invitation to join the Paris Jazz Seminars at Columbia University Reid Hall has shown me a stellar example of creative teaching. It has been a privilege to know Dr. O'Meally, here in Paris.

Morgan Fletcher and Anneke Gronke, who were students in Professor O'Meally's class in Paris, helped me organize the Howard Johnson Archives and created a database during afternoons filled with dust, discoveries, good food, and fun. My gratitude for their work and their friendship continues. Michael Lewis, a young man living in Paris, also helped organize the archives.

I especially want to thank Farah Jasmine Griffin, professor of English and Comparative Literature and African-American Studies and director of the Institute for Research in African-American Studies at Columbia University. She gave me time and attention and introduced me to Michael Ryan, head librarian of the Columbia Library for Rare Books and Manuscripts. Michael made the decision to house Stretch's papers and subsequently provided the funding for the research work necessary to finalize the book. Without him, it would not have been materially possible to finish Stretch's book. Thank you, Michael.

I am grateful to all the men and women of Alcoholics Anonymous who helped my father find the sobriety that enabled him to continue his activism into the dawn of the twenty-first century. My thanks go out to all the friends who gave me support on both sides of the Atlantic Ocean, too numerous to name here—you know I am deeply appreciative of the encouragements that kept me going.

To my family, always right by my side, I am forever grateful.

My sisters, who are my dearest friends, Wini and Lisa Johnson, saved our father's papers and shipped them to me. We would never have had the manuscript and research documents needed for the book without their patience and love. My Paris brother, Jake Lamar, well-published author, has helped me in so many ways.

My cousin David Appel rescued Stretch's first draft of his memoir from the confines of cyberhell. Without David, we would not have had Stretch's version of the manuscript. I thank him for this crucial contribution.

My daughter, Eve, and her husband, Paul Oxby; my son, Martin Boutilié; and my granddaughters, Léa and Lou Boutilié and Elise Oxby, who wanted and needed to hear the story of their great-grandfather, are the family members who have kept me going through fair weather and foul. They have at times even kept the boat afloat. Without Martha and Stretch there would be no story, and without my children and my children's children there would be no pressing imperative to tell it. Beyond the duty of transmission for them, there is a duty to history. Now is our time. We are living at a period when our stories are being told. I share Stretch's story, his legacy of activism, with all of you, thanks to all those who made it possible and in the hope that one of our lesser-known everyday heroes will continue to be of use to folks and that Stretch will be with us for generations ahead as we "keep on keepin' on."

Timeline

1893	Stretch's paternal grandmother meets Frederick Douglass at the World's Columbian Exposition
1896	In the case of *Plessy v. Ferguson*, 163 U.S. 537, the U.S. Supreme Court sustains the constitutionality of a Louisiana statute that required railroad companies to provide "equal but separate" accommodations for white and Black passengers and prohibited whites and Blacks from using railroad cars that were not assigned to their race
1899	Edward Kennedy "Duke" Ellington—whose first-known composition, "Soda Fountain Rag," appears in 1914—is born
1909	Stretch's Uncle James Anderson founds the *Amsterdam News* in Harlem
1915	Stretch is born
	Germans announce U-boat blockade of Britain
	German submarine torpedoes the British ocean liner *Lusitania* off the southern coast of Ireland, resulting in the deaths of 128 Americans
	Ku Klux Klan revival occurs in Georgia
	D. W. Griffith releases Ku Klux Klan–sympathetic film *The Birth of a Nation*

1916	United States enters World War I
	Congress passes Selective Service Act
	War Industries Board and War Revenue Act give war effort economic support
	Congress passes Espionage Act (revised by Sedition Amendment in 1918)
	NAACP leads silent march in New York City to protest racial violence
	Start of Russian Revolution prompts Russia to withdraw from World War I
1918	President Woodrow Wilson announces "Fourteen Points" plan, promoting self-determination, liberalism, democracy, free trade, and establishment of a League of Nations
	Overman Act grants President Wilson unprecedented, wide-reaching wartime powers
	Armistice ends World War I combat
	Eugene V. Debs is imprisoned for denouncing U.S. government actions under the Espionage Act and Sedition Amendment; he is released in 1921
1919	Treaty of Versailles calls for heavy reparations, German disarmament, and creation of a League of Nations
	Eighteenth Amendment to the U.S. Constitution (Prohibition) outlaws purchase, sale, and transport of alcohol
	Race riots erupt in twenty-five cities, most notably Chicago, where thirteen-day riot results in nearly forty deaths and hundreds of injuries
1920–40 and beyond	The Harlem Renaissance—originally called "The New Negro Movement"—described by Black philosopher Alain Locke as a "spiritual coming of age" wherein artists, intellectuals, writers, and musicians created a cultural explosion, with such leaders as James Weldon Johnson, Zora Neale Hurston, Langston Hughes, Claude McKay, Duke Ellington, Louis Armstrong, Robert Riggs, Aaron Douglas, and many others, takes place

1931	Nine Black teenagers (the Scottsboro Boys) are accused of rape in Alabama
1932	In New York City, the Independent Subway opens with its "A" train to Harlem
1933	Franklin Delano Roosevelt becomes president of the United States and Adolf Hitler comes to power in Germany
1935	Great Harlem Riot takes place on March 19
1940	The Alien Registration Act of 1940 (Smith Act), enacted June 29, sets criminal penalties for advocating the overthrow of the U.S. government and requires all noncitizen adult residents to register with the government
1941	The Soviet Union suffers a surprise attack and is invaded by the Nazis in June, precipitating the Soviets' official entry into World War II against Germany
	The Empire of Japan attacks the U.S. naval base at Pearl Harbor; the United States enters World War II
1945	World War II ends in Europe
1949	The Smith Act trials take place
1950–57	Senator Joseph McCarthy (R.-Wisc.) heads a witch hunt against American progressives, a period now known as that of McCarthyism
1951	With the decolonization of Libya, a twenty-five-year period of liberation of African countries from colonial rule begins
1953	Julius and Ethel Rosenberg are executed after being convicted of espionage
1956	Nikita Khrushchev delivers "secret speech" revelations on Stalin at the Twentieth Congress of the Communist Party
1961	Affirmative action is first created from Executive Order 10925, signed by President John F. Kennedy and requiring that "government employers not discriminate against any employee or applicant for employment because of race, creed, color or national origin and take affirmative action to ensure that applicants are

	employed"; it gradually developed over a period of forty years to include the admission of students to universities and is still being challenged today
1964	The Civil Rights Act is signed into law
1965	Malcolm X, religious leader and Black nationalist, is assassinated at the age of thirty-nine in the Washington Heights section of Manhattan
1966	Bobby Seale and Huey P. Newton found the Black Panther revolutionary party
1968	Dr. Martin Luther King Jr. is assassinated in April in Memphis, Tennessee
	Senator Robert F. Kennedy (D.-N.Y.) is assassinated in June during his campaign for the presidency
1970	Angela Davis is arrested in October; later, in 1998, she writes the article "Masked Racism: Reflections on the Prison Industrial Complex"
1972	The Equal Rights Amendment is passed by Congress (but fails to achieve ratification by the 1982 deadline)
1973	Landmark U.S. Supreme Court decision in *Roe v. Wade* furthers the reproductive rights of women
1980s	In the Reagan area, a backlash against affirmative action begins; progress made begins to erode
1989	Martin Luther King Day is recognized in Hawaii after a successful campaign by a coalition led by Stretch
1992	Los Angeles riots over police brutality and the acquittals of police officers in the beating of Rodney King
1994	Nelson Mandela becomes the first Black president of South Africa on May 10, after more than three centuries of *apartheid*
1995	Demonstrations led by Julia Wright, daughter of Richard Wright, and Stretch in Paris in front of the American Embassy attempt to save Mumia Abu-Jamal, on death row for thirty-one years
2000	Stretch passes away in May after more than sixty years of activism

Part I

It don't mean a thing if it ain't got that swing.

—Duke Ellington

1

Early Days

Orange, New Jersey
January 30, 1915

While I was the first-born, I was not the first son, according to my father. He told me, during one of our man-to-man chats after I had become one of his favorite drinking buddies, that my mother had previously had an abortion of a baby boy about a year before I was born. For some reason I felt pre-empted. I was no longer the first son, one of the few things about which I felt good. I hadn't realized that one of the hooks that bolstered my self-esteem was being the first-born. By the same token I could understand the emulation, respect, jealousy, and even, sometimes, deference that my brothers, Bobby and Wesley, expressed to me at various times. Later, when I needed to have proof of age to enter the Army in September 1943, I wrote the Orange, New Jersey, city clerk for my birth certificate and received it a week later. It was a document stating that I'd been born at Orange Memorial Hospital on January 30, 1915. My name on the document was Baby McGinnis. Apparently, my father had not claimed me as his child. I had never seen a marriage certificate around the house, nor had my parents ever celebrated a wedding anniversary, but I had never added that up to being a "bastard," according to the mores of our neighborhood. It did not throw me; in fact, it added to my romantic notions about being a deviant, an outcast, a revolutionary, unbound by the prescriptions of a bourgeois and decadent society. No evidence of a legal marriage document has ever surfaced for my mother and father. For both of them it was a long marriage in the common law bound by a love relationship that was regarded as ideal among our friends and acquaintances.

Our family was of multiclass/multiethnic origins. In a six-generation span the family embraced the socioeconomic brackets from slave owner to "street nigger," fed by a fertile mix of Dutch, Irish, Cherokee, Iroquois, African, West Indian, French, and perhaps everything but Czech and "double-Czech" American, as Paul Robeson sang in his stirring rendition of Earl Robinson's "Ballad for Americans."

My father's father was George Gaither, a gambler, pool shark, and man-about-town who enlisted in Teddy Roosevelt's "Rough Riders," fighting in the Spanish-American War of 1898. Because of his veteran's status on discharge, he was able to secure a position in the Bureau of Engraving in Washington, D.C. He never returned to New Jersey. How we got the surname Johnson is something of a saga in itself. My grandfather's "cut buddy" was Eugene Johnson, also a gambler, and a hustler who specialized in dealing cards for big stakes. When my grandfather went off to war, he asked Eugene to look out for his woman—my grandmother Lethia Goode—and his kids. He did so with such love and affection that my father grew to love him and named me Howard Eugene after himself and the man he considered his stepfather. My father did not know that a Junior had to have exactly the same name as the Senior, so I was incorrectly called Howard Junior.

My father was a genius in all directions. Anything he attempted to do, he did well, at least; he oftentimes did things exceptionally well, and he was my role model for many years. I always strove to emulate him. Among his friends, I was known as "Little Monk." My father's nickname was established as "Monk" based on his agility on the basketball court and on the baseball diamond. I was known as "Little Monk" until I became significantly taller than my father at the age of twelve. I was already 5'10" at the age of eleven, and by the time I was fourteen I had grown to six feet. By that time, my father's buddies were jokingly saying, "That's a mighty thick piece of spit" or "Monk, he can eat peanuts off your head." The affectionate appellation "Little Monk" died a natural death as a result of the Mendelian behavior of height genes that skipped my father from my grandfather, who was 6'4", to me, at 6'5".

Whatever he lacked in height, my father compensated for in physical dexterity. His blinding speed, hair-trigger reflexes, coordination, and accuracy of throwing arm led him to stardom on such Black baseball nines as the McConnell Giants from Montclair, the Grand Central Red

Caps, and the Lincoln Giants. The Lincoln Giants later became the Black Yankees.[1] On the basketball court, those same athletic qualities allowed him to dazzle audiences all up and down the East Coast with the St. Christopher's, the Independents, and the Puritans, who were later to form the nucleus of the world-famous Renaissance. "Fats" Jenkins, "Pappy" Ricks, George Fiall, and "Fats's" younger brother, "Legs" Jenkins, were the members of this team. My father didn't make the Renaissance team because of a conviction that put him in Sing Sing Penitentiary at a time when he should have been playing basketball. Bob Douglass, the manager of the team, was a West Indian entrepreneur who had come to Harlem about the same time as Marcus Garvey, sharing the same basic philosophy of bourgeois nationalism. He owned the Renaissance Ballroom, the Renaissance Basketball Team, and the Renaissance Theatre. All of these names were inspired by the term for the period after World War I called the Renaissance. It represented the belief among Blacks of that time that the defeat of the Triple Alliance in the war "to make the world safe for democracy" would result in a renaissance of the aspirations and hopes of African Americans that had been so rudely crushed in the post-Reconstruction overthrow of the Civil War gains over slavery.

Romeo Dougherty, the best-known Black sportswriter of that time, wrote many columns in the *New York Amsterdam News* and, later, in the *Pittsburgh Courier*, describing Monk's exploits on the sports fields. The prison sentence responsible for my father's not getting selected for the Renaissance team was never mentioned. Black athletes were not highly paid in those days, and my father's transference of his skills into other, what he thought would be more lucrative, pursuits backfired on him.

In the 1920s, only a handful of Blacks had access through the rigid "Jim Crow" segregation of American society to more than a subsistence-level income. This caused many of the most talented, not-to-be-denied African Americans to move into various survival tactics known in our community as "hustles." The general term for such people was "hustlers." Monk had been prepared for this eventuality by his father and "stepfather," who, hustlers themselves, took great pleasure in passing on their pool-playing, card-dealing, crap-shooting, and other skills of the *demi-monde* to the quite eager, apt, and talented Monk at a very early age. Monk became a great billiards and pool player. He was often called upon to take on out-of-town traveling cue stick artists when the betting reached high stakes. The local players would support him in the hope of winning back money they had lost to the out-of-town hustlers.

Monk was steely-nerved and would rarely lose when the stakes were high. He prided himself on being a "professional," and I was often witness to games in which a hundred dollars or more was riding on the outcome. Even under that stress, he could calmly and effortlessly run off fifty or sixty balls with tournament-level concentration to the incredulous consternation of the formerly arrogant visiting "pro." He was considered to be in a class with the greatest Black pool hustler of all time, James Evans, who had once beaten the legendary Willie Hoppe in an exhibition match.

I can recall, after we moved to New York, walking into neighborhood poolrooms and finding all of the best local players refusing to play him for money. He was also a masterful manipulator of a deck of cards; in the card players' argot, he was a first-rate mechanic. That meant he could do about anything he wanted to do with a deck of cards. As they said, "He could make a deck do everything but talk." He could deal "seconds"—that is, withhold the desired card for himself at the top of the deck and deal the inferior cards underneath to his opponents. He could shuffle a deck so that all the aces would come up for him.

He could cut the deck exactly in half and then riffle-shuffle the cards so that they would be spread out in alternative sequence from each half of the deck. When times got really tight during the Depression, he would augment his own expertise with prepared decks. These specially prepared decks would have the desired cards, such as aces, sanded imperceptibly so that they would never come up in a cut. The cards could also be marked in a microscopic way so that only the dealer or his confederate could understand the marks which indicated the value of the card so that they could be read from the back. These cards were a type called "readers." To my youthful astonishment, my father took me to a gamblers' factory in New York City in the '30s. The factory was located around 53rd Street and Tenth Avenue—right in the heart of Hell's Kitchen, a territory that had once been the turf of the gang known as the Hudson Dusters. Owney Madden, one of the top chiefs of the Cotton Club mob, had been the most notorious leader of the gang. I now suspect that my father learned about this factory through his friendly connections with the Cotton Club owners when he was a waiter there. He and Madden had both done time in Sing Sing.

The factory was a veritable warehouse of gamblers' "cheats"—wholesale, retail, and custom-made to individual gamblers' specifications. While there was a spectacularly displayed array of phony cards, crooked roulette wheels, weighted cue balls that would not roll straight in big-money matches, brass knuckles, blackjacks (also called saps), bullet-proof vests, holsters, pistols, and switchblade knives, it was the dice section that dazzled me most. Bust-outs, six-ace flats, roll-forevers, and other dice would make endless passes at the expense of unsuspecting "marks." Bust-outs were dice that would automatically roll seven. They would be slipped into the game after an opposing bettor would establish a point and force him to lose his bet.

One of the arts much practiced by professional gamblers was the knack of substituting the crooked dice for the regular dice at the crucial moment of the big bet and then replacing the regular dice as soon as the crooked dice had performed their function or, at least, at some time before the "mark" had grown suspicious. Six-ace flats were dice that had two sides shaved so that the six and ace would roll up a larger percentage of times than any other numbers. The prescribed bets for the percentage player were "don't come" bets based on the much higher number of craps that would be thrown (double sixes and double aces). The roll-forevers were dice with only fours, sixes, and fives on their six sides, meaning that a seven could not be thrown. The recommended procedure when these dice were in was to start out with a high bet and parlay, or double, the bet with each roll so that the stakes could be rapidly escalated for the quick impoverishment of the "mark." Uncle Leon, my father's brother, informed me some time after my father died that much of the lore of gambling had been passed down to the two brothers by my "hustling" grandfather George Gaither and his pal Eugene Johnson.

The same expertise demonstrated in the pool hall, the gaming room, or on the crap table was available on the sports field. Monk was often on the Black all-star nines that played postseason games with barnstorming white major league all-star teams, including Babe Ruth and others of his stature. The Black teams often won, thus dispensing with the argument that Blacks did not have the skill to make it on the ball field. I needed little convincing that Blacks were not an inferior species. Hearing my father recite Shakespeare by the yard, I became quite skeptical, at a very early age, of the prevailing idea that whites were the intellectual superiors of Blacks. Contrary to all the sociological studies on so-called Black lack of self-esteem, I was never ashamed of being Black. Frustration, anger, and rage were more often the feelings. We knew we were as good, but our talents were circumscribed by the rigidly imposed walls of segregation, even in a northern town like Orange, New Jersey. Even as late as 1941, Blacks were not allowed to sit in the orchestra of the local movie house, the Colonial Theater on Main Street.

On my grandmother's side—that is, my paternal grandmother, Lethia Johnson—the family history is somewhat obscure. There must have been a mix of African, Cherokee, and European because of her walnut color, high cheekbones, ample lips, and muscular stride. When she had time to sit down and talk to me, she revealed her proudest moment: a visit to the World's Columbian Exposition in 1893. She was just twenty-two years old then. I recall her mementos on the sideboard in her dining room—a pennant with the words "Chicago World's Fair" emblazoned on it, a silver serving tray, and a glass paperweight with "Columbian Exposition" printed on the underside of it so that you could read the legend through the glass.

For many years she peppered her conversation with comments such as "Douglass would have said this" or "Douglass said that" or "Douglass wouldn't have stood for that." I used to wonder who this man she was referring to was, because the only Douglass I knew didn't appear capable of the wisdom her Douglass espoused from time to time. It was only after many years of research and study on the life and activities of Frederick Douglass that I made the connection. Douglass's last public speech was given at the World's Columbian Exposition, and Lethia had been there to hear him in the flesh! That instruction during my early adolescence probably accounts for my longstanding identification with Frederick Douglass. I recall that she often spoke with scathing contempt for those she termed "Booker T. Washington Negroes." She had nothing but scorn for some of our local Black leaders, who entered her books as "Toms." And the way she emphasized the "T" in "Booker T" led me to believe she considered that it stood for TOM in no uncertain terms. She chose sides very early in the debates that raged between W. E. B. Du Bois and B. T. Washington after Washington's Atlanta Compromise speech called on African Americans to put aside the struggle against segregation and focus exclusively on economic betterment.[2]

Grandmother Lethia was part of an enterprising family from Greenville, South Carolina. She had three brothers, each of whom made his mark in his chosen field. The oldest was George Goode, who became a headwaiter at the Palmer House hotel in Chicago. The second brother was James, who changed his name to Anderson because of his respect and admiration for a man who had raised him. The youngest brother was John, who became a barber and owned one of the most popular barber shops in Harlem during the '20s near the corner of 117th Street and Seventh Avenue.

Uncle James left home at the age of fifteen to go to sea, then came to New York to live in what was then the San Juan Hill area around 64th Street and Tenth Avenue, a stone's throw from what is now Thelonious Monk Place. He started a small mimeographed newspaper that he hawked for pennies on the subway. The paper prospered and continued as the *Amsterdam News*, named after Amsterdam Avenue, which is the name of Tenth Avenue after it reaches 59th Street. His editorials condemned segregation, supported the NAACP, protested lynching, defended Du Bois, and characterized the African American people as a developing nation as early as 1915, at least a decade before the Communist International had its debates on the character of the "Negro Question" in the United States. He hired Cyril Briggs as an alternate editorial writer, strengthening the radical orientation of the paper. Cyril, while at the *Amsterdam News*, joined with Harry Haywood and Harry's brother, Otto Huiswood, to form a Black Marxist organization known as the African Blood Brotherhood. This organization existed before Harry Haywood was to sit with Joseph Stalin in the meetings that led to the Comintern Resolution on "The Negro Question as a National Question."

The charge that the American communists imported their position on "the Negro Question" from Moscow had no significance to me, because I knew the role of Black radicals in the United States in developing the party line in this area. Cyril Briggs told me about my great-uncle's leading discussions on the Negro nation years before Harry introduced the concept in the Comintern meetings.

Uncle James became prominent in the Republican Party, served as an Exalted Ruler of the Oddfellows, and was also a Mason. His wife, Hattie, whom he loved very much, died in 1919, and he began to drink heavily. During that period he came under the influence of his secretary, Sadie Warren. Sadie married a racetrack tout and pimp named Charlie Davis, at whose direction she convinced Uncle James to turn over the management and ownership of the *Amsterdam News* to her. He did so, much to the chagrin of my father and grandmother, about a year before he died in 1925 of the combined ravages of cancer and acute alcoholism. Later I came across a picture of Uncle James sitting next to W. E. B. Du Bois with a group of Black leaders who had assembled as a committee in 1913 to celebrate in Harlem the fiftieth anniversary of the Emancipation Proclamation. Uncle James had on a morning coat and a starched collar with ascot tie and looked quite the dandy. It presented a very startling contrast to my recollection of him sitting while looking hopelessly out of my grandmother's living room window in an alcoholic haze. He had to come to Orange, New Jersey, to literally drink himself to death.

My father had a sister, Corinne, ten years younger, who died of alcoholism in a basement in the Bedford-Stuyvesant section of Brooklyn. Only many years later did I discover that alcoholism was a family disease and I was to inherit it in deadly proportions from both the paternal and maternal sides.

My mother's name was Gertrude. On her side, the family history is well documented, though the documentation is studded with racist theoretical explanations of that history, for generations going back to 1791. Albert Payson Terhune's novels about dogs (later the basis of the *Lassie* series on TV), set in the Pompton Lakes area of New Jersey, contained frequent references to the "Jackson Whites" or the "Jackson Blacks" and more frequently to the "blue-eyed niggers." My mother told me when I started reading about the "blue-eyed niggers" that Terhune was referring to our relatives, and I always had a burning curiosity about that part of the family. More recently, a scholarly work based on a doctoral dissertation by David Stephen Cohen was published under the title *The Ramapo Mountain People*. The book names the DeGroats as one of the stable families of the group.[3]

My mother's mother was Henrietta DeGroat. The DeGroats were considered one of the four most important and longstanding families among the Ramapo Mountain People, dating back to pre–Revolutionary War days.

My mother's father was Frank McGinnis, a rough-hewn, heavy-drinking Irishman, who was exercise boy for the world-famous trotter Dan Patch, holder of the world's mile record for many years, now enshrined at the Trotter's Museum in Goshen, New York. I recall him coming home and beating my grandmother until she cried. I don't remember her ever smiling. I think it must be then that I resolved never to drink, not knowing at the time that the family curse would catch up with me later.

Among the other families that formed the core of this people, called "tri-racial isolate groups," were the "Van Dunks" (a corruption of the Dutch "Von der Doncken"; Adrian Von der Doncken was a member of the first New York state legislature), the DeFreeces or DeFreeses (an Anglicization of DesVries), and the Manns, who represented the British strain. There was some dismay on my part to discover that one of my ancestors, James DeGroat, was a slave owner, listed in the 1790 census. He was also identified as Negro, indicating or suggesting that there must have been interracial cohabitation among the Dutch and the runaway slaves who used this area as a refuge. However, James DeGroat could have been the progeny of a free Black woman and a Dutch man, though the possibility would have been unlikely. The Native American strain is not so easily traced, but there was much reference to our "Indian blood" at family "pow-wows." They are still held every Thanksgiving in Hillburn, New York. This discovery of James DeGroat as a Black slave owner dismisses a myth that plagues writings on the "Jackson Whites" or "Blacks." This literature is riddled with the assumption that an interracial heritage is a handicap. This fiction of the "tragic mulatto" occupied a central place in much of the literary production of the *fin de siècle* period when Jim Crow was riding high among Black as well as white writers. As the assumption is transferred from the literary medium to films, it crystallizes into a "given" and Hollywood presents us with obligatory stock characters, the renegade "half-breed" who can do no good or the Peola character of films like *Imitation of Life*, where the tragedy is that of a light daughter of mixed ancestry with a Black mother.

The influence of this mythology extends across disciplinary lines into the fields of anthropology and sociology, where high rates of alcoholism, incest, and other deviant behavior are accepted as givens also. So-called objective studies have fastened tendentiously on negative trends among the Ramapo Mountain People, excluding their success stories. Those who have climbed out of poverty and made it in America despite the obstacles that confront people of interracial extraction are conveniently overlooked. The norm has been accepted in our culture that racial purity is healthy—but such a norm, particularly after the experience of the Holocaust, is demonstrably pathological. Despite David Stephen Cohen's effort to override previously established racist assumptions about the Ramapo Mountain People, his study shares this racism in no small dimension.

As sweeping as Cohen's study would appear to be, he makes no mention of the fact that a Howard DeGroat was the president of Cortland State University College on the southern tier of New York state, an area to which many Ramapos migrated. Other rather significant omissions are the failure to mention the leadership of the struggle of the NAACP Hillburn chapter that led to a desegregated school system eleven years before the *Brown v. Board of Education* decision of 1954. That struggle was led by a Van Dunk. No mention is made of my sister Winnie

Johnson, a Cotton Club dancer who later went on to sing with the Duke Ellington Orchestra. Nor are the community activities of "Pooch" Van Dunk and Vivian DeGroat, leaders of a community action housing program, or Terry Jackson, radio station commentator in Kingston, New York, considered worthy of notice. Because so few members of any family rise to prominence in our pyramidically structured society, it takes only a few omissions of this kind to build up a picture that is quite dismal. It is encouraging to know that a college-educated DeGroat is constructing a family history that will unearth the buried positives that Cohen and others, blinded by racism, have missed.

The Ramapos could very well be considered an Appalachian people, and I recall when I was a youngster in Orange that we called our cousins from the Ramapos "hillbillies." My mother was quite proud of her ancestry and told us many stories about her relatives, quite a few of them laced with songs and sayings that had the flavor of the Pennsylvania Dutch, not to mention the expertise in the kitchen associated with them. Our favorite dessert was called "pig in a blanket"—cooked apples in a big boiled blanket of dough that were topped with a mound of delicious sauce.

My mother had three brothers, Albert, Theodore, and Sanford, and two sisters, May and Helen. She also had some first cousins, Bertha (Bea), Tina, Sarah, Peter, and John Marsh. Sarah was a stunningly beautiful woman who died at an early age. Bea, Tina, and Pete were heavy drinkers who used to visit us on Saturdays. They would spend their winters in Florida and their summers in Saratoga during the racing season. Often, after they had made big money at the track, they would come by the house to party, sometimes winding up dancing on the table to all our merriment with dresses uplifted and appeals from my mother to "please put your dresses down" while my father chuckled at her embarrassment. Pete was a tough customer when he was three sheets to the wind. He often got together with another relative named "Swat" Milligan. Milligan Alley in Orange was a dead-end street running off Hill Street between Center Street and Oakwood Avenue. The whole area has been wiped out by a throughway, part of the urban renewal evacuations of the '60s. But at that time, when Pete and Swat had had a few, they were known to beat up policemen who dared to come into their turf on Milligan Alley—named, by the way, after Swat's family. In fact, Milligan Alley was inhabited almost exclusively by Milligans, Marshes, Van Dunks, and Manns, all extensions of the Ramapos. This aspect of family tradition is continued in the borough of Ringwood on the street named DeGroat Lane.

My mother's oldest sister, May, and their cousins Bea and Tina moved to New York during the post–World War I migration to Harlem, and I recall our family's visiting Aunt May in her elegant apartment at 2424 Seventh Avenue in 1924 or 1925. Seventh Avenue, now Adam Clayton Powell Boulevard in Harlem, was a dazzling wayfare at that time with the most richly dressed people strolling up and down the avenue in clothing and with style that filled us small-towners visiting from the "sticks" with awe. It was the beginning of the Harlem Renaissance, and a spirit of creativity, optimism, and confidence filled the atmosphere with pace-setting artists like Paul Robeson, Countee Cullen, Langston Hughes, Aaron Douglas, Bruce Nugent, Zora Neale Hurston, James Weldon Johnson, J. Rosamund Johnson, Rose McClendon, Claude McKay, Louise Thompson, and a host of others generating currents that rippled through every African American community in the nation.

Claude Winfrey, my Aunt May's boyfriend, had a "seal brown" complexion, and he was usually smoking a Havana cigar of the same shade. Aunt May adored him and was instrumental in getting my mother and father to name my sister Winnie after him. Claude Winfrey was transposed to Winifred Claudia. My Aunt May was living a sort of dual existence at the time—during the day she was white, working as a hostess in a quite middle-class restaurant called Alice MacDougald's, and at night, after a forty-five-minute ride uptown on the Fifth Avenue Coach Company's double-decker bus, the Fifth Avenue–Edgecombe Avenue #2 line, she rejoined the Black community as one of Harlem's elite "high yellers." Aunt Tina and Aunt Bea also worked at Alice MacDougald's as they too were able to "pass" because of their straight hair and light skin. Being light enough to "pass" didn't faze them as far as being Black was concerned. They always spoke with some contempt about the racism that was openly expressed to them on the job by fellow employees who didn't suspect that they were from the "enemy camp" (as they sardonically put it). In fact, my impression was that they enjoyed being part of the Black community more than the average Black because they experienced the coldness, greed, and competitiveness of white society first-hand. If they had any sense of superiority because they were light-colored, they compensated for it by usually having the darkest men in our social circle as their lovers.

I often heard them quote an old saying with a kind of erotic relish, "the blacker the berry, the sweeter the juice." Aunt Tina went with both Willie "the Lion" Smith, from Goshen, New York, and James P. (J. P.) Johnson, who often came to Orange to transcribe piano rolls for the QRS piano roll company, which had recording studios there. Orange was a center of that sort of activity because of the impact of Thomas Edison and his "talking machine." The Edison Laboratories were in West Orange, adjacent to Orange.

Willie the Lion was a little lighter than Uncle Claude, a walnut shade. J. P. Johnson was about the color of blackstrap molasses, and if the saying had any validity then he must have been an awfully sweet man! Aunt Helen, my mother's younger sister, had married Jim, a handsome man about the shade of Jackie Robinson, complemented by a mouthful of brilliant gold teeth, every one of them, and when he smiled there was so much gold you almost felt that a second sun was shining. Much importance was attached to shades of skin; we even referred to each other as "shades."

All in all, my early environment was color-coded in a far more complex variety of colors than that of the white world, which might be described as a simple, one might say simplistic, Manichean world of good whites and bad Blacks. The multihued familial heritage of the Ramapo Mountain People and the additional multiethnic associations of my father—whose closest friends were a Jew, Joe Cash; an Italian woman, Chris D'Amato; and our barber, who was the most political Black person I had ever met in my life—prepared me very early for integrated living, and I never felt a moment's discomfort in the presence of whites—yes, anger at their racism, but never any sense of being inferior to any group of whites on a personal level. In the financial realm, the feeling was different, but we knew that had nothing to do with talent. However, we were not immune to the pervasive racism that saturated our society. Racism infiltrated the Black community despite its being sealed off on the social level from the white community. My mother and father sometimes made jokes about darker folks than we, and, as I grew up with some darker schoolmates who were my closest buddies, I began to be embarrassed by the prejudice my parents demonstrated. Later, when I was an adult, an experience with hypnotic regression revealed even greater depths to my embarrassment.

My goal during the hypnotic regression was to go back in time as far as I could to attempt to recall the first time I felt anger. It took several efforts, the first attempt highlighting my becoming an atheist because I thought God had forsaken me when he caused, as I thought, my grand-mother to die on my fifteenth birthday. The second attempt took me back to the age of six when I saw my father being stabbed, with blood running down his arm, in a street fight with a local bully and drunk who had abused my maternal grandfather in a barroom brawl. My third try took me back to the age of four, when my Uncle Sanford, coming back from the Army, stroked my head while calling me a "nappy-head little nigger." That episode may have been completely conjured up in my desire to cooperate with my hypnotist, but it had the feeling of unchallengeable authenticity. That may be how most Black males de-velop a fairly universal antipathy to someone's touching their heads and, more particularly, their hair. I still have an automatic "head-jerk" reac-tion when a white person touches my head. Even though I have had many welcome caresses during amorous encounters with white women, the aversion endured for many years. These hypnotic episodes revealed to me the early onset of racial feelings. They also told me that racism has a penetration into the American social fabric that is difficult to overestimate.

As the family grew, each new member added his or her voice to the complex interactions within the family circle. My first sibling was my previously mentioned sister Winnie, born December 3, 1917. Bobby (Robert Quentin) followed on January 27, 1921; Wesley Williams was born on March 26, 1923; and my youngest sibling, Shirley Gertrude, wound up the parade of Johnsons on November 23, 1925.

Bobby's middle name came from a visiting nurse, Miss Quentin, who played an important role in teaching my mother many construc-tive things about hygiene, nutrition, and balanced diet that were to play a major role in the exceptional good health, drive, and energy of all the members of the family. Wesley was named after the son of a man who was greatly respected by my father, his supervisor, Chief Williams, when he was a "red cap" at Grand Central Terminal. Chief Williams's son, named Wesley Williams, became the first Black battalion commander in the New York City fire department. With Shirley having our mother's first name, Gertrude, as her middle name, I imagined that this was a signal putting an end to the further extension of the family.

In the desire to advance our family, my mother aggressively searched out the various religious institutions in our community. In hindsight, I believe she disapproved of my father's buddies. We never heard an argument between them, but two different lifestyles were being placed before us. My father's activity contrasted with and was sometimes overshadowed by my mother's silent effort to achieve upward social mobility via the route of what might be called "denominational progression" in the churches of Orange. We started at tent meetings on the corner of Hill and Center streets, not far from the old Krueger's brewery. I remember little about the tent meetings except for the music, which was loud, rhythmic, and highly persuasive, especially the rattling rustle of the tambourines. Our next stop on the church route to better days was Reverend Watkins's Ebenezer Baptist Church. Reverend Watkins was a huge Black man who used to preach sermons that rang the rafters. Sometimes, as the good reverend got carried away with the emotions aroused by his own preaching, his juices would flow to such an extent that the spray from his mouth would baptize everyone in the first two rows of pews. I was only about eight years old then and dreaded sitting too close to the pulpit. We moved from Hill Street to South Street into a building owned by a Mr. San Giacomo behind which was a huge rag-and-junk warehouse with all the accompanying rats and smaller animal life. Down the street in the direction of Oakwood Avenue was St. Paul's AME Zion Church, our next step upward on the church ladder. The only thing I recall about St. Paul's was a Sunday school program in which I was to recite a poem or sing a song. Oh, yes, it was a song! I rehearsed and rehearsed it only to get up on that Sunday and break out crying in fright before I could finish the second line of "Jesus loves me this I know for the Bible tells me so." That was to be my last public recitation until high school.

The final step in our journey of upward social mobility through the denominational route landed us in what I later learned was the top of the heap in our restricted and segregated Black community, the Episcopal church of Reverend George Plaskett, the Church of the Epiphany, on Taylor Street at the corner of Center not far from Orange Memorial Hospital, where I had been born. Reverend Plaskett was a vigorous, highly organized West Indian with a slight British accent and a very progressive outlook that enabled him to get the Church of the Epiphany to become a ward of Trinity Church in New York City. The reverend and his church were playing an important role in our exposure to ideas and cultural influences beyond our small town of Orange. He felt that what was happening in New York was something we should be exposed to, so he arranged for a busload of us to go to New York to see a Broadway matinee and in the evening to hear Harry T. Burleigh, whose magnificent voice was sensational. Some of the tunes he sang that night are still among my favorites. I was fortunate to have Reverend

Plaskett soon take me under his wing. I became an acolyte and was given the honored assignment of reading the Psalms at Sunday evening services. Among the regular acolytes were Freddie Peniston, whose father was partial owner of Titan Hall, where my father had played basketball and where I was to reach semi-pro level with the Titan Junior Five. Freddie and I became buddies and I'll always remember the Sunday dinners prepared by his mother during which the table really groaned under the weight of the delicious meals she used to prepare, especially the rich and crusty apple pies. Emerson Johnson was another of this handsome group of acolytes. Somewhere at one time there was another very tall six-footer about whom Carolyn Plaskett and I were to have an uproarious laugh over the simple fact that his name, Kerchival Messick, was so unusual.

Among the girls who graced the choir were Carolyn and Harriet Hardy. Their father was the director of the "colored" YMCA in Newark, and their mother played the church organ and directed the choir. Other choir members were Florence Rhodes, a second cousin of mine; Bea Sparrow (who was the natural daughter of the town's leading physician, Dr. Walter G. Alexander, and whose brother, also a natural offspring, Albert, was called the bad boy of Epiphany); and Constance Calloway, whose family worked for the Dwight Morrows in Englewood. (The Morrows' daughter, Anne, married Charles Lindbergh, and the tragedy involving the kidnapping and death of their infant son was to occupy our conversations for weeks.) Bea and her family often rode up to church services in what seemed like a half-block-long Packard, as if they were the Morrows themselves. A platoon of older men in the congregation provided us boys with role models of serious and successful men: Lawrence Sparrow; William Fenton; Albert Tilary, the organist; and Dan Wing, assistant pastor, who took us on a field trip to New York. The trip included a Broadway show (my first, *Roberta*, with Bob Hope in his first Broadway appearance) and the Episcopal church St. George's, where we heard the great Black baritone Harry T. Burleigh, the regular soloist with the St. George's choir, sing works by J. Rosamund Johnson and James Weldon Johnson.

My mother had certainly made the right choice in providing us with an instructive and inspiring environment. Reverend Plaskett not only had a fine congregation, he saw to it that the best minds in the Black community of the United States were brought in to share their wisdom with us. I recall listening in transfixed astonishment to figures such as Dr. W. E. B. Du Bois, Paul Robeson, and William G. Pickens of the

NAACP speak to our Sunday evening services. I have no doubt that the scholarly rationality of Dr. Du Bois, the mellifluous voice of Paul Robeson, and the oratory directed against racism quite often laced with side-splitting comic asides by W. G. Pickens got through to me and influenced the development of my social and socialist vision, though, at the time, I certainly had little comprehension of much that they were talking about. But soon after a year at Epiphany, some of us formed a Sunday morning discussion group, in which my cousin Linton and I were the prime movers, to exchange ideas on what we called the fundamental problems of the world. In time the group crystallized into an organization called the JBS (the Junior Bachelor Society), all young men who were from the Church of the Epiphany. They were Teddy Moore, Prince Terrell, Joe Parker, Harvey Blount, Rennie Silvera, Burditt Stith, Emerson Johnson, William Sparrow, Cyril Riley, Linton (Marsh), Clement Smith, and I. As was probably to be expected with a group of hot-blooded adolescents, over time we lost sight of our original purpose of Sunday morning discussions on philosophy and the social problems of the globe and gradually became a Saturday night carousing group determined to score with a bountiful crop of beauties who were North Jersey's claim to fame on the eastern seaboard in the Black community.

We did carouse as JBSers, but our Sunday group had evolved in two directions, both marked by an operative structure and a set of different activities. The first group, the JBS, was loosely formed with no designated by-laws, leadership, or officers. The leadership was ad hoc and transitory. The structure was nonexistent and its political outlook was anarchic in a very elementary sense. The JBS, as I said, was the group that had become a springboard for our girl-hunting all over the North Jersey terrain, which we called our happy hunting ground. The second group had more structure and provided most of the leadership for the Junior Branch of the NAACP of North Jersey's Essex County. Our inspiration, organizer, and advisor was Mrs. Bertha Randolph, the portly, tall, and beautiful wife of the leading African American lawyer of Newark, Oliver Randolph. One Sunday a month, we met at Mrs. Randolph's home in Newark to plan and carry out all the necessary work for the monthly meeting of the Junior Branch of the NAACP. The meetings usually had a program on Black culture and history, and we studied whatever aspect of the African American experience we could. This was not easy in the '30s, with only a few stalwarts like Carter G. Woodson, Arthur Schomburg, J. A. Rogers, and W. Hansberry mixing the pitifully few exposed veins of the enormous but underground Black history.

One of the unforgettable moments in our experience was a second trip to New York. We had a joint meeting scheduled with Mildred Johnson, who headed the Junior Branch of the New York NAACP. Mildred was the daughter of James Weldon Johnson, the executive director of the national organization. We met in an office and hall owned by the adult organization on Seventh Avenue in the landmark architectural gem of an entire block of buildings that had become known as Strivers' Row. To our utter delight, Mildred was able to arrange for her uncle J. Rosamund Johnson to come to the afternoon get-together and entertain us with his repertoire of show tunes and spirituals for which he and his brother, James Weldon, were already famous. It was my first time hearing the impressively melodic and moving tune "Lift Every Voice and Sing," which was to become the national anthem of the civil rights movement.

Mrs. Randolph was also a prime mover in another group of North Jerseyans in their twenties and thirties who were in touch with the cultural explosion in Harlem known as the Renaissance.[4] The group of North Jerseyans with which Mrs. Randolph was connected decided to open up the first year of the decade of the '30s with a major affair to be called the Beaux Arts Ball, the name taken from the famous Latin Quarter gathering on New Year's Eve in Paris. It was held in the largest ballroom in the state of New Jersey, the Mosque Ballroom, part of a huge complex of offices and meeting halls, with its centerpiece being the Mosque Theater, a huge and beautiful movie palace. Devotees of the Harlem Renaissance were called in to lend a hand to the organization of the Beaux Arts Ball, which was planned to be the biggest and most successful event—social and political—of the decade. Jules Greene, the artist, supervised all the art work; Rae Olley, later to become the wife of Judge Ed Dudley, choreographed the dances and directed our play. Dudley Hill gave us a professional example for our acting in the play based on a traditional African folk tale. The inspiration of the mother continent was very strong in our cultural outlook, reflecting the nascent national consciousness that the Renaissance was evoking and raising to a new level.

We in the JBS were called in by Mrs. Randolph to take part in all of the myriad preparations necessary for making the affair a dazzling success, working as solicitors for ads in the journal designed by Jules Greene, acting in the play with all the required rehearsals, learning the African dances that were an important part of the play, and encouraging the more talented in our ranks to come forward for solo numbers in the all-star show that was to be the centerpiece of the ball. I, between the play and dance rehearsals, worked as a solicitor and collected a respectable batch of paid ads for the journal from small-business men in Orange like Drs. Catlett and Bynum, who had the pharmacy at the corner of Parrow and Hickory streets; Mr. George Corrin, the Realtor; and the Mellingers, who were friends of my mother's and whose grocery store always had supplies for our family even when we could not come up with the cash. I also collected personal signatures that were to be scattered over the cover page at $1.00 per signature. In fact, James Weldon Johnson's signature so impressed me that I changed my handwriting style to resemble his close-knit finishing school hand.

Once our rehearsals were finished, the greatest excitement was the ball itself. As busy as we were with our preparations for our part in the festivities, it was obvious to us that this night was to be an unforgettable one. I was almost fifteen years old, and every pore of my being was open to the impact of the ideas, reflected in every aspect of the ball. Cars were pulling up as we went in the stage entrance of the Mosque Ballroom with our costumes, disgorging couples dressed to the nines in the latest fashions. The raccoon coat, the hip flask, spats, knee-high flapper gowns, bobbed hair—all the styles mentioned by F. Scott Fitzgerald in his *Great Gatsby* were there in force. With our African heritage as resource and inspiration, style was not something we had to learn from the white bourgeoisie. As a matter of fact, we were the originators of much of the style that later found its way downtown to Park and Fifth avenues.

We from the JBS with our girlfriends were to be the tribespeople in the African village, the *mise-en-scène* for the African folktale–based play. We had much sport kidding around in our tribal loincloths, practicing our tribal dance taught us by Rae Olley and Dudley Hill. We enjoyed "gunning" our girlfriends in their more revealing grass skirts, typical of the '30s style. Rennie Silvera, Linton Marsh (my cousin), Teddy Moore, Harvey Blount, Genevieve Green, Katherine Ashby, Connie Calloway, and Thelma Thompson were all part of the tribe—not to mention our own chief sex pot, Betty Duval.

Our play went on to an ovation at the stirring end, where the character played by Dudley Hill triumphs over the tribal enemies. It was the first half of the program with a lengthy intermission for the two or three thousand people having their drinks at the bar and indulging in the dance of the beginning of the decade, the Bump. The Bump was a furiously sensuous hip-to-hip, groin-to-groin, butt-rolling kind of dance with the primary movement a sex act–simulating, back-and-forth rocking motion that we called "dry fuckin'." After much "Bumpin'" and slow grinding, the dancing and drinking during the intermission came to a halt. Act Two opened up with an intimate revue-style entertainment, the high point of which for me was cousin Linton singing in his light baritone voice "New Sun in the Sky" with all the optimism that carried over from the Roaring '20s and that had not yet been wiped out by the crash of '29. Another cousin of mine, Gene Rhodes, did a ballroom dance with the incredibly sensuous beauty Laura Nichols. New Jersey and New York Renaissance luminaries such as Henry "Kid" Collins and his wife, Elizabeth; Lacy Brannick; Harold Majors; Lawrence Sparrow, our sepia Prince of Wales, with his English drape suit and British posture; Albert Tilary, our church organist; Elwood Dean; Helen Harden; Johnnie Silvera; Walter Frye; and Kenneth Woodruff made it an unforgettable and gala evening.

Of the three Silvera brothers, the closest to me was Rennie, the youngest. Rennie was also good at track, specializing in the one-hundred-yard dash and pursuing the ladies. He was one of the most daring and wildest of the JBSers. He had a Model A convertible Ford that became the "cruising" vehicle for the entire JBS. One night he passed a red light and the cops came after us. They chased us for blocks until we escaped with a mad turn into Orange Park, where the car rolled over with none of us being hurt and all dispersing in different directions—a miracle if there ever was one.

Another event that reflected the influence of the Harlem Renaissance on the culture of the Black community outside of Harlem was held in Montclair, which had a reputation for having the most beautiful girls on the East Coast. The budding impresario who staged the event was a handsome and most articulate young Montclairan named Ralph Lenard Baker (accent on the *nard*, *à la française*). Some of us, when we were emphasizing our European rather than our African origins, went beyond the very affected Oxford accent, an indisputable symbol of class, onto the continent itself to cultivate a French or a German accent. So here we were in the first year of the Depression and Ralph Baker came up with a song-and-dance show called "The Fun Revue." It was important to our family because it was the first time that my kid sister Winnie was to dance outside of Orange. Winnie did a beautiful tap number to the 1928 song "Doin' the New Lowdown," one of Bojangles' hit numbers. The choice was prophetic, because Winnie later danced to the same tune with the man himself, Bill Robinson, known as the world's greatest tap dancer, on the stage of the Alhambra Theater in Harlem.

All of this was manna from heaven for my omnivorous appetite for ideas, books, music, sports, and dance. My appetite seemed to grow the more it was fed. I was now in my sophomore year at Orange High School and was running on the track team, playing on the Junior Varsity basketball team and football teams, and was, at the same time— which was unusual then more so than now—making the honor roll as a top student in most courses of study. My closest rival on the monthly reports was Robert Hoffman, the son of a wealthy plumber of German extraction. He and I ran neck and neck for the best grades regularly. I was the kind of student who couldn't wait to take the books for all the subjects home to read them through from cover to cover by the end of the first week of the term. This made it possible for me to get through my classes without doing any homework except for written assignments. This also made it possible for me to play basketball with the Oakwood Avenue YMCA team as well as the Junior team of North Jersey's leading semi-pro team. Friday nights were a fantastic dream realized for my urge to play basketball. On Friday afternoons, our high school team usually played its games at 3:30, and then I would go home to eat and then return for the 8:00 P.M. games at the Y, then I would dash from the Y to Titan Hall, where the Titan Juniors would play the preliminary game before the Seniors. After the Seniors played, there was a dance, and despite the three basketball games, there was still enough energy to get out on the floor and do the Lindy Hop. I seemed to be inexhaustible. Whatever I asked my body to do was done without a second thought. My mentor and idol at the Titans was Jesse Miles, who had been one of the few Blacks to make the Orange High School Varsity. He was the manager and playing captain of the Titans. Jesse had always been a great admirer of my father as an athlete and moved on the court very much as my father did. He had his hair cut in the same way and had developed an unerring side court shot that bounced off the backboard and swished through the net at the same angle as the shot that was one of my father's specialties. Jesse also encouraged me, overlooking my awkwardness from having grown too tall too fast for my muscles to get accustomed to the size of my bones, but I played regularly at center on the JVs and we got plenty of scrimmage playing the Seniors that made my basketball development quite rapid.

"Do-Do" Raymond, a fast-as-lightning forward, and Burke Harris were my favorite co-players, and later Venerable Evans from the Orange High School Varsity became one of my best friends. We had teamwork on the court that was superb, and we rarely lost a game.

At school, my scholastic ability was being observed and Miss McGovern, my Latin teacher, whose legs I still fondly remember, selected me to give a speech to the high school Friday assembly on the subject of "The Planned Society." My assignment was to research the planning of Roman society under Julius Caesar and the Soviet Five Year Plan and compare them with American society in the '30s. Needless to say, with my already developed class consciousness, my reading on the Soviet Union and the impact of its stated objectives of transforming a backward agrarian society into a rival of the United States in industrial strength hastened the emergence of a strong socialist outlook on my part. I was also reading books like Jack London's *Martin Eden*, whose eponymous protagonist I identified with; he was the son of a poverty-stricken family who worked the longest hours to survive and send himself through college to become one of California's most powerful men without ever losing his early socialist perspective. By the time I had made my address to the assembly, fulfilling one of my freshman ambitions—that is, to emulate Cyril Riley, who was president of the high school debating society and one of the few Black students to address the assembly—I was saturated with ideas about the need for planning in the United States to avoid the kind of disruption of peoples' lives that a chaotic capitalist system brought in the crash of 1929.

But, paradoxically, one of my favorite activities was going to the East Orange Armory with Teddy Moore to see the regimental teams play polo. Teddy's mother's boyfriend was the cook at the armory, and we could get in for free. For me, it was an exotic and exciting episode. The sound of the horses' hooves on the turf, the squeak of the leather saddles as the horses made sharp turns, the thudding crack of the mallet on the ball and the centaur-like attachment of the riders to their horses even on the most difficult, twisting turns, and the fact that the periods were called "chukkers" rather than halves or innings—all of it exuded an aura of fantasy, particularly the costs of keeping ponies, tack, outfits, and the leisure time to acquire the skill.

Teddy and I quickly became satiated with the rich diet—hastened by the idea that this sport was something that would be forever an academic one for our conceivably limited budgets.

Another experience continued to raise my sense of class and race even higher. Alexander Williams, a chef and a poker-playing friend of my father's, needed an extra hand to work in his kitchen crew for ten weeks at a camp for wealthy white boys in Friendship, Maine. To my joy, I was selected to go—at a salary of $12.50 per week, which would be paid to me in one lump sum at the end of the ten-week stint. To my further joy, "Lanky" Jones, who had been a star on the Orange High School basketball team, which had gotten a statewide reputation for beating the Passaic High School Wonder Five, was going to be the first cook. Lanky had already graduated from Orange High and was playing intercollegiate basketball with the Morgan College team from Baltimore. I had seen his prowess demonstrated on the East Orange Armory court when Morgan played Lincoln and beat them soundly in what was an internecine rivalry. I looked in awe at Lanky and was soon to get the thrill of working out with him on the basketball court at the camp in Maine, Camp Wapello, during our breaks in thirteen-hour days in the afternoons. Lanky taught me his style of shooting and some moves that gave me quite an edge on my teammates when I returned to basketball practice in the fall.

But the work was terribly hard—long hours, peeling potatoes for a roster of 125 boys and staff of 50, all with the healthiest appetites sharpened by the cool breezes from the Atlantic Ocean that swept across the island that contained Camp Wapello. My responsibilities included setting the table, washing the silver and glassware, peeling potatoes and fixing other vegetables, and waiting tables during the meals. We really worked from sun-up to sun-down, actually; it was dark when we started and dark when we finished. Before I had gotten hardened to the routine, I wrote my family letters in which I transposed the address

Camp Wapello
Crotch Island
Friendship, Maine

to

Camp Mopello
Grouch Island
Hardship, Pain

All the labor, of course, was designed to make the camp experience of all these adolescent white boys a glorious one, and without ever having read Karl Marx at this point in my life, my class- and race-consciousness reached a very high level. It cost a family $300.00 to send their kids to this camp, plus clothing, for all aspects of camp life—transportation and so on. Some of the families had two or three sons enrolled, so to my Depression-educated mind on the value of a dollar, the expenses were astronomically high.

The highlight of the camp experience was the annual show, which was staged by a Hollywood director and screenwriter named Earl Baldwin, a friend of Glenn Stokes, the owner of the camp. Earl and his wife were driven by their chauffeur, who was Black, all the way from Hollywood in a Duesenberg that looked a block long. I later found out that the expression "It's a doozy!" was derived from the name of that vehicle, and then and only then did I appreciate the expression as symbolizing the utmost of the utmost. The show was top-flight entertainment with songs, dances, and witty and really funny skits written by Earl, and to my delight I was selected to appear in the show, doing an imitation of Louis Armstrong. One of the counselors, Bill Eberhardt, a Princeton University senior and jazz buff, had gotten wind of my interest in jazz and played some of his records for me, among which was my first listening to Satchmo's "I Surrender, Dear." I fell in love with the tune to the extent of singing along with Louie. I got the song together, sang it, and polished off my appearance with a crudely conceived version of some of the tap steps that I had seen my sister Winnie perform. It went over big and helped whet my appetite for the stage.

The next year when I returned to the camp, I was something of a celebrity and I began to participate in many of the activities of the campers—swimming, playing volleyball and Ping-Pong, and working out with the tennis rackets. Sometimes my involvement led me to forget to report for kitchen duty and I got called down, to my chagrin, by both Alex and Lanky for getting "too big for my britches." I now see this as a sign, anticipatory in its nature, of my rebellious character. The second year was also a sign of my growing up in another way. Being away from my close-knit family had given me a strong sense of self, and when my father looked for me to turn my pay over to him as I had done the first year, I said, "I think I should have my pay to spend as I want to. I earned it!" He shot his famous "drop dead" look at me and I realized I was no longer "Little Monk."

2
Harlem and the Cotton Club

The Cotton Club, New York
March 4, 1933

The first time I heard of the Cotton Club was in 1927, when the Duke Ellington Orchestra broadcast on a nationwide hookup on WABC. We couldn't wait to hear the strains of the Ellington theme song of that time, "The East St. Louis Toodle-o," gradually swelling as the voice-over of Ted Husing in an impeccable mellifluous baritone said, "and now from the Cotton Club—the aristocrat of Harlem—where Park Avenue, Broadway and Hollywood rub elbows . . . the Jungle Band of Duke Ellington!"

We didn't know at the time that the splendid sound of the Ellington organization was not jungle music but a creative form of irony that masked the commercial pandering to an upper-class white audience thrilled at the opportunity to witness and hear what it thought was genuine Black exotica. So, in our innocence, my friends Irving Overby and Robby Benjamin and I with four hastily recruited sidemen formed our replica of the Ellington orchestra, playing kazoos for brass, tissue paper folded over combs for reeds, and washboards and pots and pans with thimbles for rhythm and percussion. We played in the Overbys' cellar, where our "jungle" music would not bring the neighborhood down on us.

My next connection with the Cotton Club came through my sister Winnie, who danced at local affairs sponsored by social clubs that wanted a floor show, a "something more" than just the usual dance. Bill "Bojangles" Robinson had heard about Winnie's talent and offered her a week at the Alhambra Theater with him if she could do his routine. Winnie learned the routine in no time—she had what might be called a photographic memory in her muscles and could reproduce steps within two or three tries if they were complicated; once was enough for the simpler combinations—and she got the week's work. Elida Webb, choreographer and talent scout for the Cotton Club, heard about Winnie from Bill Robinson and hired her for the chorus of the revue "Flying Colors" from which she would go to the Cotton Club for more stable employment, Broadway shows being somewhat ephemeral.

However, "Flying Colors" went over big, what with Clifton Webb, Tamara Geva, Charles Butterworth, and Patsy Kelly as principals and a young team, Vilma and Buddy Ebsen (the latter of later *Beverly Hillbillies* fame), doing a captivating eccentric dance. Agnes de Mille did the choreography in her first shot at Broadway. One of her innovations was the production of a major number, "Smoking Reefers," the first time Black and white girls were to perform on stage as equals. I should say the first *admissible* time, because Black girls light enough to pass for white had made the Ziegfeld Follies and white girls bold enough to say they were Black had worked at the Cotton Club.

After "Flying Colors" closed, Winnie joined the Cotton Club chorus, and because this offered relatively steady employment, our parents had to make a big decision: Should the family pull up stakes and move to New York, or should my mother and Winnie continue to make the regular commute from Orange to Harlem? During the year 1932, the opening of the Independent Subway, especially the "A" train, had made commuting to Harlem easier; the fare was only five cents (!) and we wouldn't be as exposed to the dangers of New York night life. But, the Cotton Club was open seven nights a week, and there were two shows, 11:00 P.M. and 2:00 A.M., meaning very late traveling. At the same time, my father had lost his job as porter at the Embassy Theater and was surviving only as a "super" at a cluster of apartment buildings on Berwyn Street in exchange for free rent and a pittance of a salary. But we all finally said, "Let's go!" when Elida Webb informed us there was an apartment available next door to the Cotton Club at 646 Lenox Avenue—the club was at 642 on what is now Martin Luther King Boulevard at 142nd Street. We joked about the location, saying, "They want to make sure Winnie gets to work on time!" In fact, after we moved in, we were thrilled and tickled to hear the band playing the dance music before the show was to go on—and the band was Cab Calloway's. It was the "Minnie the Moocher" show.

During this period I was to get a postgraduate course in the complexities of class relationships in American society with the Cotton Club as the laboratory. The owners of the Cotton Club were white mobsters who had grown wealthy during Prohibition. They represented a band of the most vicious thugs and racketeers that has ever been produced in New York.

Up until he was killed in 1928, Arnold Rothstein, a big-time gambler whose greatest achievement was the rigging of the 1919 World Series, was a major figure in the Cotton Club management. The movie *Eight Men Out* with Charlie Sheen tells the story well. Rothstein's partners or successors were Owney Madden—overlord of the Hell's Kitchen section of the lower West Side, arrested fifty-seven times, convicted only twice, once for complicity in a gang killing involving the Gophers gang and the other for a minor traffic violation—and "Dutch" Schultz, a.k.a. Arthur Flegenheimer, boss of the numbers racket in Harlem. A "silent" partner was the Tammany politician Jimmy Hines, who was later sent to prison for his connection with the gang world. The cabal that operated the "club" also included a strong-arm man, Jerry Sullivan, and "Big Frenchy" De Mange, of the old New York gang the Hudson Dusters. This unscrupulous bunch exploited the Black entertainers and staff as if we were sharecroppers in the Deep South. The titular manager, Herman Stark, a front for the mob, had ties with the power structure—top police officials, politicians, judges, and corporation heads were frequently seen at ringside in the friendliest relations with the mobsters.

The bane of our existence was the constant benefits we had to play at Police Benevolent Association affairs on Sunday nights when there was only one show at the club. For this there was a wink of the eye by the police department for infractions of the law by the mob, but no pay for us. Our only pay was a free meal, thereby eliminating the usual exorbitant backstage prices. Conditions were such that many of us referred to the club as "Herman Stark's Plantation." The mob had no thought of any rights for us. Even among themselves, questions were often settled with brass knuckles or at gunpoint, rather than through more peaceful arbitration procedures. When negotiations over the "divvy" of the loot from the illegal beer industry broke down between Vincent "Mad Dog" Coll and Dutch, the latter offered $50,000 to any man who would kill Coll. Every freelance gunner in New York went after Coll. He was finally brought down with fifty submachine-gun bullets in a telephone booth on West 23rd Street near Ninth Avenue. That night, Dutch and the rest of the mob celebrated into the wee hours of the morning at the Cotton Club. The monopolistic control of the beer trade had been maintained, and the awesome power of the mob to police its own jurisdiction had been reaffirmed. This was history when we arrived at the Cotton Club.

The arrogance of the mob toward society in general was exponentially multiplied when it was mixed with white racist attitudes toward the performers. They had no respect for women in the show, except in the few instances where family members escorted chorines to work and back (there was a kind of underworld respect for the family as an institution). Usually, the mobsters or their visiting friends from out of town would point out a chorine to join them, as if at a slave market, for after-the-show drinks or raunchier entertainment. The bosses at the club had installed red velvet curtains that could be drawn over their private booths, and when that happened, we knew that the party was going to be no-holds-barred.

Lena Horne's stepfather, a Cuban refugee and radical ousted by the Batista regime for his political activities in Havana, once took issue when the mobsters refused to raise Lena's pay. He was beaten unmercifully, further contributing to the ubiquitous atmosphere of iron fist in velvet glove dictatorship that represented our working conditions. It is even ironic, in reference to the episode with Lena's stepfather, that the same mob which controlled the Cotton Club had a tacit alliance with Fulgencio Batista that controlled and made Havana "the whorehouse of the Western Hemisphere." I admired Lena's stepfather. He later told me that he was a communist. That had some influence on my thinking.

It is hard to understand how Ellington could produce a single creative musical sound in this setting. But it was similar sordid subject matter that provided the source material for Van Gogh's *Absinthe Drinkers*, Toulouse Lautrec's *Moulin Rouge*, Picasso's *Guernica*, and Gorky's *Lower Depths*. In a like manner, African American artists extracted vitality, emotional strength, and universal truths from the material conditions of life in the ghetto and the myriad ways in which they dealt with their own oppression. This relationship was often expressed in Ellington's music at the club. The sensitivity, lyricism, and beauty of Ellington's sound even when the band was "growling" made it clear that the jungle did not necessarily have to be African. Harlem was one of the feeding grounds for the mob—and the mob was only an illegitimate shadow of the larger predators from Wall Street who exploited the community.

Later, as my political education matured, I saw that the savages were not the stereotypical Blacks in loincloths in Hollywood's Tarzan-type thrillers. For me, they were the upper-class elites who sought vicarious "kicks" out of hob-nobbing with their underworld counterparts while fantasizing about their own libidinous urges for the Black performers. The mob controlled most of the entertainment in Harlem and the rest of New York, except for a few Black-owned night spots. The Black owners did not have the kind of capital to invest in the kind of spectacular shows mounted at the Cotton Club, but after the performers finished their chores for the white audiences, they would put on impromptu shows at the Black-owned spots for Black audiences that were unrivaled.

Most of these clubs commenced their activities at two or three in the morning when the white-owned clubs were through with the Black entertainers. Among these clubs were Jeff Blount's Lenox Club, Happy Rhone's Radium Club, the 101 Ranch (named after the famous New Orleans Club) on 138th Street with its bizarre transvestite and homosexual chorus line, and Pod's and Jerry's, where Billie Holiday improvised her first singing appearance after her dance act flopped. Some of the late spots that Blacks patronized after hours also catered to whites. Nowadays one of these, named Dickey Wells' Shim-Sham Club, might be called a crossover club in today's recording industry parlance for mixed audiences. The Shim Sham (Shimmy) was a dance invented by homosexuals from the chorus line at the 101 Ranch. The Shim was a condensation of the term *she-him*, and the Sham was a word serving the dual purpose of denoting the female role played by males and the shambling nature of the steps, particularly the first eight bars. The Shimmy was the combined hip and shoulder wiggle that was a part of the third combination, called the "tack Annie" step.

Dickey Wells was a former Cotton Club dancer–turned–pimp and entrepreneur. He ran his club on as economical a basis as possible, employing a "jug" band of musicians on kazoos, washboards, and jugs: The Shim-Shammers or Kenny Watts and His Kilowatts. Watts played the piano; Eddie Dougherty played drums; and Fletch Jahon, Eddie "Hawk" Johnson, Heywood Jackson, and Milton Lane played kazoos, making a sound somewhere between those of Red McKenzie's Mound City Blue Blowers and the Duke Ellington Orchestra. Carol Walrond, the brother of Renaissance poet Eric Walrond, was on bass. Fletch and Sammy Page did vocals and whistling, and the group was fronted by an extra-ordinary "hoofer" whose percussion rhythms afforded an unusually inspirational jazz dance. He was "Baby" Lawrence, a master of tech-nique, rhythmic flow, and continuous innovation.

"Virgie" was also a stellar attraction, doing a fast, "dirty" song like "I Want to Be a Yale Man," followed by an extra-sensuous "shake" dance during which she'd simulate copulation with folded dollar bills stuck out by customers on the edge of their tables. Her act would cli-max with a vigorous snatching of the bills with her genitals. Breakfast dances were held all over Harlem in the '30s. The topper was Small's Paradise (later bought by Wilt Chamberlain and whimsically retitled "Big Wilt's" Small's). At Small's, the breakfast dance started at 4:00 A.M. Monday and continued until 12:00 noon or 1:00 P.M. Hardly an enter-tainer, musician, sportsman, gambler, prostitute, or pimp functioning in Harlem missed the breakfast dance—it was a crossroads of the night life. Yet it was connected with the everyday life of the community be-cause the entertainment, gambling, and tourism industries in Harlem in the '30s employed more people in the various services connected with them than any other trade.

The other main employments were outside Harlem: domestic work obtained in the "slave markets" of the Bronx and Brooklyn for the women and hard, mostly unskilled labor for the men. The connection between the night and day life in Harlem is best illustrated in "kitchen mechanics' night" at the Savoy Ballroom. "Kitchen mechanic" was the name for domestic workers, mostly women, more likely to be employed than the men. Thursday night was free night for women, and a lonely male could be sure of getting a dance, a dinner, a date, or even a domi-cile for the most aggressive. But more than this heavy forerunner to what is called the singles action today was the sheer entertainment evoked through the music of the Savoy Sultans, and Chick Webb and his band with its most appropriate theme song, "Let's Get Together." Band battles that saw the best from downtown, like Benny Goodman, came up and fell by the wayside under the inspired attack of the Black musicians on their own turf, catering to the uninhibited dancing of the Black audi-ence. Later, they were joined by Lindy-Hopping white youth from the Bronx and Brooklyn who were hip enough to find the real jazz good-ies, free from the demands of the commercially oriented tastes of the upper-class tourists who would go up to Ellington and request Ferde

Grofe's "Grand Canyon Suite" or Guy Lombardo's "My Blue Heaven."
Cy Oliver was later to finish off that request with a satirical version of
"Heaven" that winds up in a heavy blues riff.

But back to the Cotton Club: It was the most prestigious, the classic
Black night club, the ideal for racist America—Black entertainers, white
underworld bosses, and white upper-class audiences. The mob, though
the club was in deep Harlem, did not admit Blacks unless they were
world-renowned celebrities like Stepin Fetchit, Bill Robinson, or Jack
Johnson.

The show following "The Minnie the Moocher Show" was designed
to be the very best. Harold Arlen and Ted Koehler were hired for music
and lyrics; Ethel Waters was the star, Avon Long the juvenile; and Swan
and Lee, the comics (Johnnie Lee was to later play Brother Crawford
on the TV *Amos 'n' Andy* show). The show broke records. "Stormy
Weather" became an international hit along with the Ellington band,
which had just returned from a road tour that had included a stopover
to make the film *Check and Double-Check* with Amos and Andy, one of
its many peaks as an organization. The Ellington sound had achieved
worldwide renown felt by many to express feelings that could not be
verbalized. The Aesopian language of titles gave the insiders in the
orchestra amusement, like "Skrontch," which meant "intercourse"; "TT
on Toast" stood for Tough Titty; and the sidemen's name for "Warm Valley" was "Call of the Clitoris."

I was in seventh heaven because I had passed the audition for chorus
boys, who were going to be added to the famous chorus girls to augment the impact of the line. Winnie had said to me, "Stretch, you've
got good rhythm and coordination from your basketball playing. If
you'll rehearse with me for the next week, you ought to be able to pass
the audition!" She added, "You're tall and good looking—light, bright
and out of sight—be sure to move big, wave your arms while you're
dancing, keep lookin' up and, above all smile!"

With that recipe, I passed the audition and started rehearsing. I was
not the world's greatest dancer by any means, and of the Ten Dancing
Demons, as we came to be known, I would rank myself about seventh
from the top among the ten. Walter Shepherd, whose sister Ethel had
some pull, was the tenth in talent and Jimmy Wright, a Harlem man-
about-town, was ninth, in my estimation. Billy Smith was almost my
equal. Walter had such a hard time keeping up with the routines that
he began to drink more and more as the show went on. Finally, one
night he came in staggering and was in such bad shape that he could

not get fully dressed for each number until we were coming off from
that number. It was both tragic and comic that he got fully dressed for
each number, but only by the time it was finished. He was dismissed
shortly after that. But I was never completely happy with my dancing.
I was never able to get the small muscle dexterity that close tapping
required, so I compensated with exaggerated movement, inspired by
the loose and big movements that I had seen Buddy Ebsen use so effectively in "Flying Colors," and of course Ray Bolger's style suited me
to a T. My eccentric moves and the enthusiasm and energy I put into
my performance added a dimension that kept me in the show. But I
always had a sneaking suspicion that being Winnie's brother had a lot
more to do with it. The best of the Ten Dancing Demons was Maxie
Armstrong. Maxie went on to develop a single that he wound up with, a
smash finale doing a show-stopping "circus one" tempo array of "mule-
kicks" to the tune "Chinatown, My Chinatown!" Fifty years later,
Henry LeTang told me of his sad experience trying out for the Dancing
Demons on the set of Francis Ford Coppola's film *The Cotton Club*. He
was a better dancer than any of us, becoming the greatest choreographer
Harlem ever produced, in my estimation. He was rejected because he
was too short. He said, "I went home crying, because I knew I was as
good as any of you who were hired, Stretch!"

But the *pièce de résistance* of the Cotton Club shows was the female
chorus! The women were handpicked from the best dancers and beauties in show business. For the 24th Edition of the Cotton Club Revue,
the array of beauty and talent would knock your eyes out—Anice Boyer,
Dolly MacCormick, Hycie Curtis, Edna Mae Holly, Lena Horne, Joyce
Beasley, Lucille Wilson, Arlene Marshall, Catherine Nash, Peggy
Griffith, Amy Spencer, Marie Robinson, and Una Mae Carlisle of "I
Walk Alone by the River" fame were just part of the cream of the crop
of tall, tan, and terrific chorines who graced the highly polished pine
boards. My sister Winnie was one of the most beautiful of the beautiful
array of feminine pulchritude. As a group, they had their choice of the
most eligible Black males on the planet. Anice was one of Bill Robinson's mistresses; Edna Mae married Sugar Ray Robinson; Joyce married Bobby Brown, one of Harlem's leading numbers bankers; and
Lucille married Louis Armstrong. Flo Ziegfeld had nothing on the
Cotton Club for female beauty. The legend over the backstage entrance
to the Ziegfeld Follies that boasted "through these portals pass the most
beautiful girls in the world" could well have been put over the entrance
to the Cotton Club!

Some of the women had multiple lovers. My sister Winnie numbered among her lovers, and sometimes husbands, Bill Robinson, Joe Louis, "Chuck" Green, Adam Clayton Powell, Canada Lee, Duke Ellington, and the penultimate husband before her last marriage to Dr. Middleton Lambright, the disastrous Stepin Fetchit. As Winnie's older brother, I was often the somewhat embarrassed but not completely reluctant recipient of favors that came my way from Winnie's suitors. They hoped that getting on my "good side" would open the doors for a date with Winnie. Joe Louis gave me a $100.00 ticket to see the Buddy Baer fight. I could never have afforded such a seat after I left show business. It was one of the greatest experiences I ever had in the fight game. For me, when Joe started chopping into Baer's ribs with his hammer blows, it was like watching a lumberjack chop down a tall tree.

Most important about the Cotton Club was that its location was not accidental. The mob chose to purchase the club from Jack Johnson because the Harlem Renaissance was just beginning. The year 1927, when *Opportunity* magazine gave Langston Hughes its literary award, is named by Alain Locke, Rhodes Scholar and dean of Black literary critics, as the beginning of the Renaissance.[1] The club had been acquired by the mob five years earlier. They knew that Harlem was becoming the most magnetic of locations with its reputation for sophistication, creativity, and excitement. The Renaissance in Harlem was a continual display of the extraordinary talent of poets, writers, playwrights, singers, dancers, and musicians who congregated there much as political exiles and creative people from all over Europe assembled in Paris in the first two decades of the twentieth century. The Hotcha, Small's Paradise, Dickey Wells, Clinton Moore's, the Jitterbug, LaMarcheri (dig the Parisian accent!), and the Red Rooster were some of the hot nightspots in Harlem of the Harlem Renaissance. While the gangsters who were located in Harlem may not have known all that went into the makeup of Harlem's attraction, they knew there was some money to be made in the ghetto. The Savoy, "The Home of Happy Feet," anticipated the discotheque. Pot was the preferred mind-alterer among the "hip." Kaiser's tea-pad on 133rd Street (212 West) had tables where off-the-street customers could sit down to the strains of Duke, Billie Holiday, or Fletcher Henderson on the jukebox, and order their dozen-for-dollar joints bathed in surrealistic red and blue lights.

These were Harlem's equivalents for Paris's Le Dôme Café, La Coupole, Les Deux Magots, and Le Flore. Harlem was a Montmartre in Mocha, the Latin Quarter in Rotogravure, the Seine in Sepia!

A cross-fertilizing process accelerated the fermentation of the arts and received steady impetus from the massive gathering of Blacks from every state in the Union, augmented by a continual stream of immigrants from the Caribbean, Central America, and Africa, the mother continent. Harlem became an international center, and one could walk down Seventh Avenue (the Black Champs-Élysées, to prolong the metaphor) on a Saturday night and hear Haitians speaking French, Jamaicans conversing in the broad A's of the British, mingled with the Spanish accents of the Afro-Cubans and Afro-Ricans, seasoned with the drawls and slurs of Delta folk from Mississippi, melodic tongues from Alabama and Georgia, not to mention the talk of the Geechies—direct transmission of the Gullah tongue to Harlem from west Africa via South Carolina.

The cultural hybridization produced by the continual multiethnic melanistic melange provided sounds that existed nowhere else in the world. The streets of Harlem anticipated the United Nations. For the musician more than any other group of artists, Harlem with its multitudinous tongues represented a linguistic paradise of sound that could be captured for instant translation into the universal language of music. It was this objective setting that created the basis for the Black musicians' becoming the best in the world. Hugues Panassié recognizes this in his second jazz book, *The Real Jazz*:

> I had the bad luck, in a sense, to become acquainted with jazz first through white musicians. . . . I did not realize until many years after the publication of my first book that, from the point of view of jazz, most white musicians were inferior to Black musicians.[2]

Of like significance is Marshall Steams's story, of Isham Jones's enthusiastically buying Don Redman's arrangement of "Chant of the Weeds" played at Connie's Inn at 132nd Street and Adam Clayton Powell Boulevard and his white musicians' not being able to play it.

This recognition of the superiority of the Black musician was later to be pejoratively labeled "Crow-Jimism," but, as they say in the streets, "Jack, the Jims really could crow!"

New Orleans may have played that role during the *fin-de-siècle* period, but by 1930 all roads led to Harlem. Besides this global mix of Blacks and browns, Harlem was host to a never-ending stream of tourists from all over the world who came to experience the lifestyle of an avant-garde community that was reputed never to sleep. If New Orleans was the cradle of jazz, Harlem was where it grew up. Harlem in the '30s was a preview of much that was to be characteristic of the counterculture which grew out of the radical upsurge of the '60s. The language of the street was a creative reservoir, the raw material for the musician like that of no other community in the world. This multicultural mix was augmented by the arrival of the best musicians from all over the country, seeking to find work in a community where the tourist industry created employment in the nightclubs, bars, and theaters for more than 2,000 musicians, waiters, bartenders, chorines, singers, dancers, and hustlers. The saying was, "If you can make it in New York, you can make it anywhere!"

3
Moving Up

Broadway, New York
June 1, 1936

One of the Harlem after-hours spots where some of the Cotton Club dancers hung out was Clinton Moore's Chez Clinton. It was a rendez-vous for the cosmopolitan and upwardly mobile creative and literary set. Its fame, or notoriety, increased nightly. By this time I knew the ropes, so to speak, and each of us had dreams of hitting it big in some way, because of the fame, money, and power that was represented in the downtown clientele of Chez Clinton. I knew that if I was going to go anywhere in show business, it would have to be through people like some of the whites who patronized Chez Clinton. I made it my busi-ness to be there as often as I could. One night when I walked in, Clin-ton Moore caught my eye as soon as I got through the door. He said, in his most Oxonian accent, with a hint of a lisp, "Stretch, there's a very important man here who is looking for talent for a show that's going to be on Broadway. You should get up and dance when the next piece is played. . . . I'll tell the trio to play something really hot." The trio, a stellar group, consisted of Carroll Boyd, Roland Smith, and Clarence Tisdale. They played at two different clubs on the same night, going from the swank Le Ruban Bleu down on the East Side to the Chez Clinton.

I said, "Who is he?"

Clinton replied, "It's the short, good-looking man sitting at the center table on the banquette, and I'll tell him to take a good look at you."

Clinton, by the way, was an unusually light homosexual from a wealthy Black family in Texas. Physically, he was an amazing prototype for Alfred Hitchcock. I was later to be startled by the sight of Hitchcock, particularly with his shrewd, measuring eyes and pouting lower lip, so much like Clinton Moore's. Clinton might have possibly been called a Black Elsa Maxwell; his extravagant parties and his red velour wall liners, brass lamps, and black velvet–covered divans in the large upstairs living room provided one of the "in" attractions for any moneyed people who really wanted to see the night life of Harlem. The room's notoriety was its Saturday night soiree where homosexuals from every part of the East Coast, more whites than Blacks, jammed in to do "touch dancing." It was quite a sight to walk into the room and watch forty to fifty men, its capacity, dancing cheek to cheek. Chez Clinton was down on the street level. It catered to anyone who could pay the stiff prices, but the upstairs room was limited to the cognoscenti or close friends of Clinton's from Harlem and the social register. Jimmy Wright and I had a permanent pass to the Saturday night soiree.

This night, however, when our Broadway impresario was buying drinks for the house, it was obvious that the crucial action was to be downstairs. The trio, on a signal from Clinton, broke into a nice, easy, danceable tempo and I moved out to the center of the floor to do my flash steps, high kicks and rubber-leg steps winding up with a faster trench, double-wing, and split. There was much applause. Many of the customers knew that something of an audition was going on, and I seemed to have struck the impresario's fancy as he joined in enthusiastically, shouting, "Attaboy, Stretch!" After the applause died down, I joined him and his party, during which time he asked me if I would be interested in becoming one of the principals in his forthcoming show; it was entitled *New Faces of 1936*. His two previous shows, both great successes, were *Garrick Gaieties* and *New Faces of 1934*, which had introduced Henry Fonda and Imogene Coca to Broadway. I said, "Certainly, but you'd be missing something if you didn't see my younger sister and brother." He agreed and we made a date for the three of us to come downtown for an audition. Winnie and Bobby got together with me and we rehearsed for hours getting something together for presentation.

We were hired as the Three Johnsons, so it was only through the fortuitous circumstance of being at Chez Clinton on a special night when a man of influence was there that the Three Johnsons could make it to Broadway overnight. What few knew, including my family, was that after he had seen me dance I had ensured the family success by spending the first night with him at his hotel appeasing his "gay" appetite. The casting couch was not for women only. However, we were a great success in *New Faces of 1936*, to such an extent that Van Johnson, who was a chorus boy in the show, called himself the Fourth Johnson. The show "rolled them in the aisles" and we had a nine-month run with the stellar cast that included Jack Smart, who was later to play "The Fat Man" on television; Tommie Rutherford, later of the movies; Imogene Coca; and Marian Pierce, a woman of great wealth who wanted to be on the stage as a kind of hobby to talk about with her social register friends. My mother became her maid and worked for her, both at the theater and the Hotel Pierre, Marian's permanent residence. Later, Rags Ragland and Gypsy Rose Lee were to give the show some spicy burlesque flavor. Regular show-stoppers were Billy Heywood and Cliff Allen, who became good friends of ours. In fact, we became such good friends that Billy and I started smoking reefers together on the fire escape in the back of the Vanderbilt Theater, and not long after, I was spending nights with Billy in her room at the Hotel Woodside. The Woodside was to become famous later through Count Basie's tune "Jumping at the Woodside." That tune was aptly named, because even before the hotel became a resting place for the Basie band, it jumped, and Billy and I jumped at the Woodside many a night after we finished our stint in *New Faces*.[1]

Backstage at *New Faces* was a gas. We lived a segregated life, and because we were Black, the white performers talked among themselves in front of us as if we were part of the furniture, so we often heard the rampant anti-Semitism expressed by non-Jewish performers who didn't care for the director's style. To tell the truth, he was extremely intense and it got worse as opening night approached. Of course, it had nothing to do with Judaism at all; it was show business.

One of the other favorite gay hangouts was Jimmy Daniels' place, where concerts were held over Tillie's Chicken Shack on Lenox Avenue. Among the downtown whites often seen at Jimmy's, the Donahues, Jimmy and Jack, heirs along with Babs Hutton to the Woolworth fortune, spent their money like water while movie stars like Cesar Romero, Hugh Sinclair, and Humphrey Bogart dropped in from time to time. Bogart had a favorite whorehouse over Fat Man's on Sugar Hill at the corner of 155th Street and St. Nicholas Avenue that he patronized frequently. His tastes were more "macho." The Stettheimers, patrons in a lavish way of many of the young talents who were introduced to them, often attended the Friday nights. Florine Stettheimer was most widely known, because of her sponsorship of the Metropolitan Museum of Art. Her crippled brother, Eddie, who came escorted in a wheelchair, rarely missed the galas on Lenox Avenue.

I, usually in Jimmy Wright's company, looked on all this as excitement and glamour while repelled by the cynicism and corruption that seemed to be an integral part of the whole scene. My repulsion was not strong enough to overcome my need for some cash, and under Jimmy's tutelage, I learned to be accommodating for a ten-spot. This was not bad for a fifteen-minute blow job being performed on me. Yet I knew from the beginning that this was not the proper use of my talents.

My indoctrination and participation in this fast-paced life (it was a "jet age" in tempo) lasted from my disemployment as a Cotton Club dancer until I began to collect a regular paycheck in *New Faces of 1936*. In fact, after it was discovered that I was not going to continue satisfying the sexual appetites of the producer, he agreed with Martin Jones, his partner at the Vanderbilt Theater, to let me go, thus breaking up the Three Johnsons. Because we were vulnerable and the Two Johnsons still brought in a good paycheck to the Johnson household, the family went along with the brutally imposed (in my self-centered mind) decision. Winnie and Bobby continued with *New Faces* through the summer. We didn't perform as the Three Johnsons again until we joined the Duke Ellington revue at the 125th Street Apollo in June 1937, though Bobby and I had done a double in burlesque through the good graces of Rags Ragland at the Eltinge Theater on 42nd Street. We did a hot song and dance to the tune of "Nagasaki" delivered in a corny beat that practically ruined our act with the poor rhythm and musicianship of the burlesque band. They seemed to play OK for the strippers, however, and I later wondered whether there was some racism in the musicians' uninspiring performance. We also had the trio booked into Victor's Lombardy Room at the Hotel Navarre on Central Park South, next door to the famous Essex House. We dressed in evening clothes, presenting a stunning trio in Black and white and *café au lait* to a "posh" audience using tunes from Fred Astaire's latest hits. I thought we had it made. It was to be eight months before we would get the Ellington assignment. When that news broke we were on cloud nine. Ellington asked us if we wanted to present something new, and we showed him some variations on the Susie-Q that we had developed from the dance introduced by Taps Miller, one of the most inventive and witty dancers in Harlem. Taps was later to become the permanent consort of Count Basie until his (Taps's) death. We hummed a riff to our steps that went Boom-da da-Boom-da! We called it "the Skrontch." In no time at all Duke had an arrangement on that riff that had the whole orchestra blasting out with "The Skrontch." The term itself, as I had told Duke, was a term we had used in the JBS to represent for us an "in word" for rollin' butt or the more vernacular expression "dry fuckin'"—*skrontch* or its other version *scraunch* a portmanteau of *screw* and *raunch*. Duke loved the etymology and the idea of making a "funky" folk term a hit so that the white folks would come up and ask at the dances, "Duke, how about some 'Skrontch'?" in complete ignorance of the hidden meaning of the term or the title. Anyway, it was the closest I ever came to a musical collaboration with the Duke.

But the most important part of the Duke Ellington engagement for me was the sheer joy of working in front of the Ellington organization; it was the closest thing to heaven for us. I had heard the Duke play at the Cotton Club for the shows in 1932 and 1933 before he left for Hollywood. And I had danced at ballroom dances to the Ellington sound. But for sheer ecstasy, there is nothing for a dancer like the lift that the Ellington band gives when he is molding the rhythm, pulsation, and beat of the orchestra to the dancers' movements.

The music itself seemed to lift us up off the floor of the stage in a cushion that supplied us with an additional energy that we did not have without the band. Our act used all Ellington tunes. We opened with the three of us singing "Drop Me Off in Harlem." Then Winnie went into her challenge, followed by Bobby, who was developing as a great tapper, with the haunting strains of "The Mystery Song," and I pranced to the bouncing rhythms of "Merry-Go-Round," with the three of us closing with "Showboat Shuffle." The act before us was Whitey's Lindy-Hoppers and they stopped the show cold with their high-flying acrobatic syncopation to the swinging Ellington jump tune "Stompy Jones." It is a difficult thing in show business to go on after an act that has stopped the show. It's like getting the audience to have a second orgasm, if you stop the show again. We did it despite the tough spot we were in, so I would say we had a class act to go on day after day behind Whitey's Lindy-Hoppers and get that second orgasm consistently.

That year was a most productive one of smash hits for the Ellington organization. The Apollo show was the spot where many of the great Ellington tunes were played for the public for the first time, at least for a Black audience. "Echoes of Harlem" with Cootie Williams, Rex Stewart doing his cornet masterpiece "Boy Meets Horn," "Caravan," crafted by Juan Tizol and there was always the medley of Ellington favorites "Mood Indigo, "Solitude," "It Don't Mean a Thing," "Sophisticated Lady," and "Harmony in Harlem." The traditional trio of Barney Bigard on clarinet, Tricky Sam on trombone, and Cootie Williams on trumpet did the first, Ivy Anderson did "Solitude" and "It Don't Mean a Thing," and Johnnie Hodges did "Harmony in Harlem." The great Harry Carney was the soloist with his baritone sax. It was while hearing such sessions that I grew to appreciate Duke in all his mastery of African American music. He defined it when he expressed his feelings about Blackness as a composer:

> If only I can write it down as I feel it. I have gone back to the history of my race and tried to express it in rhythm. We used to have, in Africa, a "something" we have lost. One day we shall get it again. I am expressing in sound the old days in the jungle, the cruel journey across the sea and the despair of the landing. And then the days of slavery. I trace the growth of a new spiritual quality and then the days in Harlem and the cities of the States. Then I try to go forward a thousand years. I seek to express the future when, emancipated and transformed, the Negro takes his place, a free being, among the peoples of the world.[2]

This came through in the inspirational impact of the Ellington music on us as performing artists. I shall never get over, and never would want to, the Ellington experience. One of the events that gave me an idea of the extravagant life style of the bourgeoisie was a party that Elsa Maxwell gave for Cole Porter's legs. He had broken them in a riding accident and was just being released from the hospital. Stars from all the Broadway shows and nightclubs were invited to participate. The show was to be held in the Persian Room on the roof garden of the Waldorf Astoria Hotel. Helen Lawrenson and Bernard Baruch were guests there that night. Helen came to my attention because we had seen her in the company of "Bumpy" Johnson, a leading Harlem gangster, at Small's Paradise in Harlem. She certainly covered the waterfront in her relationships! Lena Horne was one of the singers with the Noble Sissle Orchestra, which provided the music for the occasion. Lena had left the Cotton Club after her stepfather had been beaten. The family was shocked when Winnie showed up pregnant just before the engagement. She had been valiantly performing every night in *New Faces*, not knowing what to do about her ever-increasing girth as well as her heaviness in dancing, which both Bobby and I had gently complained about. Winnie made some irrelevant excuse about not eating right and kept making the *New Faces* performances with increasing difficulty. But by the time of the Elsa Maxwell party, she had become just too big. By this time the family knew what the problem was and Winnie had to have an abortion the night of the Waldorf affair. So we drafted our younger sister, Shirley, to learn Winnie's routine and she did quite well with it. She was a little thinner than Winnie but she was able to wear her costume. With Shirley looking something like Winnie, we looked pretty much like the Three Johnsons as they appeared in *New Faces*. As we looked through the curtains at the gala audience, we saw Cole Porter arrive in his wheelchair to the accompaniment of stormy applause and we knew that we were at a history-making party. Billy Heywood and Cliff Allen led off the *New Faces* contingent who were in the middle of the show, and they really broke it up with Billy's scorching rendition of "My Last Affair," one of the hit tunes from *New Faces*.

Well, the house lights had come down and it was our turn to go on. Shirley was quite nervous and as Bobby and I moved out onto the stage to our assigned positions, we saw a blank space where Shirley was supposed to be! Shirley had gotten such an attack of stage fright that she could not move. She was essentially paralyzed for a moment. Bobby and I improvised some movement to cover up her not being in formation, and after one brief moment of suspense Shirley unfroze and moved into her position so that the act came off as if nothing had happened.

What I did not explain was that we were earning a good piece of money for the engagement that we could not afford to turn down, otherwise Winnie could have just taken a night off. Rose Poindexter could have filled in for Winnie at the *New Faces* performance, but we could not substitute her for one of the Three Johnsons at the Elsa Maxwell party. It would not have been the same thing. We later heard that everybody in the Big Apple of any consequence had been at the Waldorf that night. No one ever wanted to miss one of Elsa Maxwell's parties.

Helen Lawrenson's book *Stranger at the Party* lists a large group of celebrities of the period as being at the Elsa Maxwell affair in addition to Bernard Baruch and herself.[3] Besides them, the Grand Duchesse Marie of Romania, Mrs. William Randolph Hearst, Clare Boothe and Henry Luce, Joseph Kennedy, and Ralph and Eddie Crowninshield had ringside tables. It was one of those "amazing coincidences" type of experiences for me to meet Helen's daughter, Joanna, at the Hudson River festival organized by Pete Seeger and the Clearwater group in 1982. Joanna was there with the late Abbie Hoffman, who was one of the invited speakers along with me. The collective topic at our panel was mass organizing. At our particular session, Abbie spoke after me and later told me he'd had to change most of his speech because I'd covered so well many of the points he wanted to make. I thought that was most gracious of him. Joanna was very interested in my remembrances of seeing her mother in the company of Bumpy in Harlem during the period of the Maxwell parties.

Another important experience in the shaping of my outlook was the organization of the Negro Peoples' Theater under the leadership of one of the greatest actresses of the American theater, Rose McClendon.[4] We used to call her "the Black Ethel Barrymore." My friend and neighbor Billy Owens, who was an active member of a very exclusive group of self-proclaimed men-about-town, Harry Henley's Osbiny Club, presenters of many outstanding affairs in Harlem, approached me with the proposition of joining the Negro People's Theater. Its sponsors were going to put on an all-Negro production of Clifford Odets's *Waiting for Lefty*. I was unemployed at the time and while having had little experience as an actor, I felt my stint as a chorus boy at the Cotton Club was sufficient preparation to join what I thought was essentially an amateur group of actors and actresses. That thought, I soon learned, was rather condescending because Chick Morris, Rose McClendon, Edna Thomas, Lionel Monagas, Percy Verwayne, and Viola Dean were all accomplished pros. They all had much experience with groups of longstanding professional accomplishment such as the Lafayette Players. I was selected to play the part of Sid, the taxi driver, and as I studied for the part, Clifford Odets's lines describing the Depression, class exploitation and the class struggle, and the need of the taxi drivers to organize penetrated my very soul, confirming, reinforcing, and augmenting ideas I had long carried in almost inarticulate, nonverbal form. I did not need any acting lesson as I repeated the lines in my scenes with Viola Dean. I felt every word as the truth. I took another leap forward, when, to my delight, the *Daily Worker* published in the theater section a large photo of Viola Dean and me as the young lovers. This was June 1935, shortly after the great riot of March 19, 1935. I didn't know that the play was being done as part of a huge rally at the Rockland Palace in support of Ethiopia and the Scottsboro Boys and for unemployment insurance.

As part of our preparation, we were taken downtown to meet the cast of *Waiting for Lefty*, which was playing on Broadway, and other members of the Group Theater, including Harold Clurman, Clifford Odets, Stella Adler, and J. Edward Bromberg, who were not in *Waiting for Lefty*. We got to see the performance of *Waiting for Lefty* and went backstage, where we met the performers and chatted with them about the roles.

Little did I realize that our performance was going to be on the stage at the Rockland Palace facing more than 3,000 people, two-thirds of whom were white. I almost fell through the floor when I first caught a glimpse of the multitude waiting to hear me recite my lines. My knees turned to jelly for a moment. It was only after summoning all my strength that I was able to get the lines out. What impressed me most besides the play itself was the quality of the audience. It was 66 percent white, which to my naïve political sensibility was bizarre given the fact that the meeting was on the north edge of Central Harlem. At one time, the hall had been a rallying place for the Garvey movement. I did not realize that the left could produce this kind of mobilization through concentrated effort. This power was one of the most impressive aspects of the left's activity in Harlem. The other thing about the audience was a kind of love and reinforcement that reached up out of the audience onto the stage and embraced all the performers and speakers. It was something I had experienced only in peak stage performances and I was no doubt immediately addicted to that embrace. In hindsight, I realize that I spent a great deal of time watching and studying top-quality speakers extract that warmth from the audience, unconsciously hoping to duplicate the experience for myself over and beyond whatever the cause I addressed.

4
Show Biz

The Black Cat—Greenwich Village, New York
September 1, 1937

After the Duke Ellington Revue at the Apollo, work in the theater seemed to dry up for the Three Johnsons. Our *New Faces* producer hired Winnie and Bobby for *New Faces of 1937* and they did a summer try-out at the beautiful Cape Cod Theater in Dennis, Massachusetts. He was still sore at my independent stance, and I felt that breaking up the Three Johnsons was his way of getting back at me. I also felt betrayed by my father, Winnie, and Bobby for collaborating, but my feelings were assuaged by the knowledge that I was not quite the dancer that either Winnie or Bobby was, and besides there was the Depression out there so maybe there was nothing they could do. Thus, my ambivalent feelings were depressed, compressed, and repressed. Moreover, the overall understanding I had developed from my reading and experience informed me that we were all, like Oedipus, the hero in a Greek tragedy, condemned to a fate we could not escape. We were all paralyzed prisoners of a system that cast us around quite without respect to person.

I was mollified by the family's inviting me along to stay at the Cape Cod Theater housing arranged for the performers. The Cape was gorgeous, and I felt great sibling pride seeing my kid brother and sister perform. Their skills were improving, and I began to appreciate them as a natural team. Ironically, the same agony of breakup was to hit Bobby when Winnie married Stepin Fetchit at my father's urging, primarily as a way out of poverty.

During that period back in Harlem, I was still connected with the set that hung out at Clinton's, and Jimmy Daniels, and was introduced to another group that played penny poker on Saturday nights at Cascar Bonds's home. The poker game was hectic, accompanied by continual gay dirt–dishing and/or eyeing of the new "chickens" that would appear on the scene. Countee Cullen and his lover, Harold Jackman; Embry Bonner, who was kept by Allan Priest, the curator of the Metropolitan Museum of Art; Holmes Morgan and Terry Carter; Max Stinnette and Edward Perry, big wheel with the Federal Theater Project; and Claude McKay with his cynically bitter comments on most things were frequent visitors, surveying the "trade" that was available. Most of the "trade" were white longshoremen, Teamsters, or sailors, usually big dudes who looked more than qualified to play pro football. The big guys were called "rough trade."

The poker game was always fast and furious, and my thing was to stand around hoping that one of the lucky ones would toss me a couple of bucks to sit in and "drive a tack," as the expression went, meaning try to increase through careful conservative betting one's small stake. I was a pretty good poker player, having learned many of the finer points of the game from the complete pro, my father. He had taught me, long before Professor Russell Birdwhistell at Temple University had developed his theories of kinesics, the importance of noting body language and other nonverbal forms of communication in the course of the game. The game at Cascar's was not a professional game, more a campy pursuit for diversion, and homosexuals there were far from restrained in expressing both verbally and nonverbally their reactions to their hands. This made it relatively easy for me to pick up the equivalent of one or two days' pay on a Saturday night without getting involved as "trade," the name for the heterosexual guys who tried to make a living from homosexual appetites for masculine types.

At one of these Saturday night soirees, Terry Carter introduced me to a writer named Enge Menaker, who was to have a great influence on my thinking. He came from a German socialist family and at the time was heavily involved in the support movement for aid to the Americans in Spain fighting against Franco's fascism in the Abraham Lincoln Brigade.[1] He spoke to me about Ralph Bates's book *The Olive Field*, André Malraux's *Man's Hope*, Thorstein Veblen's work *The Theory of the Leisure Class*, and about many other works and people who were urging fundamental social change. The Veblen work was most influential with its description of the sources, causes, and meaning of the phenomenon of conspicuous consumption. I was caught up in the spirit of Veblen's definition of the basic nature of capitalist society and was already a ripe candidate for some form of radical activity. Enge invited me up to his family's Camp Tohone, where I came into contact with an imposing group of left-wing folks like Lyman "Dick" Bradley, a professor at New York University, and his lovely wife, Francine Bradley. When my daughter Wendy was born, Francine was delighted to become her godmother. Edwin Berry Burgum from the English Department at NYU and the radical economist Victor Perlo were also among the people I met. Enge had two brothers: Pete, a most loyal communist, and Bob, a Trotskyist. Enge was ashamed of Bob's politics, and his discussion of the schisms in the family gave me an early impression of left-wing politics. Bob's wife, Mary Grace (Grace was her surname), was an editor at *Fortune* magazine. Mary had a brainy sister, Emily, who frequently visited the Soviet Union. Menaker, known as Frederick Engels, had a crush on Emily. If he had had his way, there might have been two radical Menaker brothers both married to two sisters from one of the top families of the capitalist world. The Grace sisters were of the Grace shipping line Graces.

It was at that level of my own radicalization when I learned that one of the subordinate factions of the mob that controlled the Cotton Club was going to hire singing and dancing waiters and waitresses to work at a new joint in Greenwich Village called the Black Cat. Those who were hired would be paid $1.00 per night plus tips. Jimmy Wright, Billy Smith, Maxie Armstrong, and I all went down to try, with Jimmy, Billy, and me trying to get jobs as waiters. The women were all former chorus girls or performing waitresses who had worked other clubs. Among them was Verna Smith, whom I had started to date when her husband, who played with Chick Webb's band, was out of town. Verna was a tall, Asian-looking beauty who rarely talked but whose psychic presence made a conversation superfluous. Florence Lee, an octoroon brunette beauty; Melba Moore; Wilma Sturkey from Detroit; and Rose Guillaume from the 1927 Cotton Club Revue were among the other performing waitresses. We were all like one big family, spending our hard-earned tips on good times after work as if there were no tomorrow. Our floor show, which was a razzle-dazzle poor man's version of the Cotton Club Revue, had as its driving force a fine band of young musicians, most of whom were going to be heard from in the international music world. The group was headed by Lonnie Simmons, a fine

Lethia, Stretch's
paternal grandmother

Howard Johnson Sr.
and his baseball team
(circa 1925–30)

Above: Howard Johnson Sr. and Gertrude McGinnis; *below:* Adelaide Hall and Ellington musicians (circa 1935)

Right: Stretch and his high kicks (circa 1935); *below:* Winnie and Stretch (circa 1935)

Left: Winnie (*left*), Stretch, and unknown performer (circa 1935); *below, left:* Bobby and Stretch dancing (circa 1936); *below, right:* Bobby Johnson (circa 1938)

Right: Stretch as a new father (1944); *below:* Stretch in uniform (1945)

Below: Rare picture of Sarah Vaughn (in fur) and Billie Holiday together, with Jimmy Jones (*left*) and Bobby Johnson (1946)

Above: Lena Horne and Stretch campaigning (1946); *below, left:* Stretch on
Seventh Avenue campaigning against lynching (1946); *below, right:* Stretch goes
from door to door (circa 1946)

Right: Stretch in
tuxedo (circa 1960);
below: Martha and
Stretch under
Charles White's
Gideon (circa 1959)

Right: Cab Calloway,
Edna Robinson, and
Stretch (circa 1970)

Stretch salutes us (circa 1960)

tenor sax man. The sidemen were Charlie Shavers on trumpet; Kenny Clark on drums (he had not yet refined his bebop techniques, but his inventiveness was already evident); Freddie Green on guitar, later to become one-quarter of the famous all-American rhythm section of the Count Basie Band; Jimmy Coco on bass; and Freddie Jefferson on piano. They really swung the show. I got to do a single song and dance on the tune "Running Wild," and Kenny would catch every move and nuance of a move in a way that pushed me to ever better performance. It was as if we were connected rhythmically as Siamese Twins are physically. I also danced with the foursome called the Black Cat Boys. We came on with a patter that went:

Ladies and gentlemen and others too!
We're here to shuffle a step or two.
We're the Black Cat Boys and we're raring to go,
We'll do our best to stop this show!

I had written the patter and was quite proud of my contribution. Jimmy Wright, Billy Smith, and Jimmy Thomas, our chief reefer supplier, were the rest of the Black Cat Boys, and we stopped many a show, even though the competition was keen, what with Amanda Randolph at the piano, Billy Daniels getting off on "That Old Black Magic," Rudolph Smith playing an extraordinary piano version of Gershwin's "Rhapsody in Blue," "Honeyboy" Thompson doing his "Way Down Yonder in New Orleans" and soft-shoe with plenty of "Uncle Tomming" that usually brought cascades of money thrown at him as he performed. I never saw a performer who could bullshit and "milk" a white audience as smoothly as he did. He didn't need a salary, because he collected $20 to $40 nightly from the money thrown his way.

Another of the acts that got rave reviews, particularly from the men, was Amy Spencer's fan dance, an anticipation of Sally Rand's imitation at the World's Fair two years later. Amy was a shapely redhead with the usual milky white skin that had once entranced Cab Calloway when she was in the chorus line in the 1933 Cotton Club spring show with the "Lady with the Fan" number. Amy was selected out of the chorus by Cab to be the lady with the fan. But it went beyond that because Cab found himself so taken with Amy that he arranged a date with her in a hotel room, not knowing that Amy had worked out her version of the Murphy game, an old confidence trick, with her lover, Neil, the swindler, arriving at the crucial moment to catch the victim, Cab, in flagrante delicto. He was taken for a bundle of money on that one and Amy disappeared from the Cotton Club line to surface at the Black Cat in the Village, as both the "Lady with the Fan" and also as a breathtaking nude in a special cabinet with a magnifying glass that gave you the opportunity to see Amy in her resplendent altogether in what resembled a goldfish bowl.

Every one of the sidemen in the Jimmy Lunceford Band went on to outstanding success: Freddie Green to the Count Basie Band, Charlie Shavers to the John Kirby Quintet, Lonnie Simmons to his own band at the Grand Terrace in Chicago, and Kenny Clark to the Edgar Hayes Blue Rhythm Band and from there to the small group that formed around Charlie Parker inventing bebop. I was hanging out smoking reefer with Kenny Clark the night he unpacked his new vibraphone at the Dewey Square Hotel at 117th Street and St. Nicholas Avenue. He asked me, "Would you like to hear some vibes, Stretch? I haven't heard this instrument myself, yet." My response was an eager YES. We took the subway uptown to 135th Street and a club where Kenny set the vibes up and played a number of tunes as if he had been at the instrument for years. Kenny was also very militant. He hated the system, and not long after became a Muslim. Our attraction to each other was based on our mutual militancy and love for music.

One of the episodes I got involved in had all my co-workers cracking up for weeks. Jack Monroe had caught me sleeping in the checkroom before the club opened one night. The opening time was 6:00 P.M. and I was napping on the premises so that I could catch up on some much-needed sleep after carousing after work the night before with a Harlem beauty who will be called simply Marva. He took a newspaper and hit me on the soles of my shoes, waking me up in the style of the police with vagrants on benches in Central Park. He must, however, have thought it was a good idea, because a few nights later, I came in for work and found him stretched out on the same chairs. I rolled up a newspaper and struck him on the soles of his feet, saying as he had said to me, "No sleeping on the job!" He jumped up, eyes red, looked at me in rage, and said, "You tend to your own business and get the hell downstairs."

Some of the other employees heard the whole incident and it was repeated time and time again as evidence of my crazy radicalism that made it possible to kid around with a white boss in this unorthodox manner. Many of the other employees thought surely that I would be fired, but I think Jack held his fire because he had known both my mother and father when they were porter and ladies' room attendant at the old HA HA Club on 52nd Street. Jack had been the bouncer at the HA HA Club at the same time and had a great deal of respect for them both. Matty Steiglitz, who had also worked at the HA HA Club, used to laugh at me every time I passed his cash register. I think he appreciated my puncturing Jack's pomposity, which had grown as he climbed the gangland ladder from lowly bouncer to nightclub owner. But the Depression's grip was slowly tightening on the nightclub business all over town, and within eighteen months the Black Cat was shut down.

One other little caper I was involved in with Marva took place at the Golden Grill, where we often drank stout. One of the very-moneyed guests at the Black Cat took a fancy to Marva and invited us out, not knowing that I was Marva's lover. We left the Cat at 4:00 A.M. to go up to our favorite hangout, the Golden Grill at the corner of 145th Street and St. Nicholas Avenue. Junie, the bartender, would let his friends in the back entrance where there were chairs and tables for dining, as opposed to the bar room, which was designed for serious stand-up drinking, after hours. New York City had a 4:00 A.M. closing law, so only the "privileged" were able to indulge their boozing after the legal hours when all the bars were shut down. Patsy, the Italian owner, had a mob connection that enabled him to "bend" the law. Marva and I and our "guest" entered to start our drinking seriously, with two objectives that night. The first was to get high ourselves, which was standard operational procedure. We could both drink an extraordinary amount, aided by the marijuana we usually smoked during our working hours because it "buffered" our alcoholic intake enough for us to maintain control. Our second objective was to get our guest high for two reasons: the first, to get him so high that any sexual interest he had in Marva would be dissipated, and the second, to get him to the point where his pockets could easily be picked. He had flashed at least a dozen $100 bills and Marva felt that she could take him if enough booze was consumed.

Our drink of choice was Black Velvet, a heady mixture of half Guinness stout and half Mumm's champagne. The contrast of the dark, smoky stout mixed with the bubbling, light champagne gave us a high that was a delight. The guest drank at least a quart of scotch before his eyes began to roll glassily while Marva began to hug him and kiss him while reaching for his pockets. Once she had successfully struck, she signaled to me and began to feign sickness as we had agreed. Our guest, just about on his heels and definitely *non compos mentis*, was really glad in a sense to be offered a cab ride home unharmed physically. He was totally unaware that our drinking party had cost him five $100 bills that Marva had relieved him of in addition to the $30 bill for the scotch, champagne, and stout we had consumed.

When we got home to Marva's place, I asked Marva for my share of the operation. I thought she would offer me at least two bills, but, with her usual eye-twinkle when she was really bullshitting someone, she smiled and handed me a $20 bill. It was equal to almost a week's pay, but I harbored a huge resentment and broke off seeing her after that escapade.

Enge Menaker had once exclaimed to me, when discussing my adventures in Harlem and those of my father, sister, and brother, "Your family is quite amoral." We rationalized without even a second thought that we were in a "dog eat dog" world and anything went in order to survive. Exploiting others seemed a reasonable way to live when you were constantly victimized by the more powerful whites who visited Harlem. Most of my friends did not even get to the level of considering the right or wrong of the matter. To them it was the only way. Eat or be eaten! That was the code for most of us—that is, the group around the entertainment and nightlife world.

5
Joining the Party

Harlem
March 19, 1938

As I look back, it was a perfectly logical step in my development to join the American Communist Party. Being Black and beginning to look for some solutions to the problem of survival, there seemed to be nothing else to do. American society had excluded us.

It was the last years of the Great Depression. Millions of hungry, unemployed, and desperate Americans had made American capitalism's claim to be the greatest society on Earth somewhat suspect. However, the dehumanizing effects of the Depression were not a new thing to the Black community. Where we lived, starting in 1930 there had been a long familiarity with being on relief, or what is now known as welfare. The Depression served only to throw a little more light on the whole Black condition.

While my employment at the Cotton Club had given me nine months' financial security, the fear and insecurity that struck me when we got notice there'd be no boys in the following show were a strong stimulus to radical thinking on my part. I wasn't fully aware of all the printed reports and statistics on Black unemployment, but I could see how bad the situation had become. There were days when we walked through our communities and it looked as though everybody was out of work, and most were. Later, I learned some of the statistics that described Harlem life. During the Depression the proportion of Black unemployed ranged from 30 to 60 percent higher than it was among whites.

This disproportionate unemployment, of course, led to the higher Black percentage on relief—in 1933 almost three times as high as the numbers of whites on relief. Those Blacks fortunate enough to be working, especially in skilled labor, lived in constant fear of being laid off to make room for jobless whites. Employed Blacks and the companies they worked for became the targets of fierce intimidation by unemployed white vigilante mobs. The threat of lynching for the Black employee and the destruction of the property of his white employer was real. Numerous reports of the National Association for the Advancement of Colored People indicated a sharp rise in the lynching of Black Americans during the Depression.

The usual response to any Black plea or demand for better conditions was, "What do you expect? White people are looking for jobs, too." This was precisely the point. We knew who would get the jobs—in good times or bad. The familiar Black cry of "last to be hired, first to be fired" was a grim reality that would become a nationwide protest slogan.

President Franklin D. Roosevelt had emerged as a legendary, charismatic personality. Many thought he was going to save America. But the Black community had no such father figure. The Horatio Alger myth fed to impoverished whites was meaningless to Black people. Most of us listening to Roosevelt's "fireside chats" just weren't sure he was including us. "How the hell can he help us and keep them rednecks happy?" At the same time we tried hard to trust Roosevelt. Who else was there? A Black national political leader, commanding respect and influence outside the Black community, was not visible. And most congressmen and senators, whether from the North or the South, were tenacious supporters of white supremacy, viewing our Black lawmakers as idiots.

There was protest then, and often it brought violence and bloodshed. One such protest was the Bonus Marchers of 1932. Twenty-five-thousand jobless veterans of World War I, with many Blacks among them, decided to march on Washington to demand immediate payment of the cash bonus promised them by 1945. They were met by the Army of General Douglas MacArthur and Colonel Dwight D. Eisenhower. Quickly and ruthlessly the small rebellion was put down. The reaction of the Black community to the stories of this bloodshed reflected a long-held awareness.

"If they do that to their own kind, Lord knows what'll happen if we holler."

We knew well what would happen. In Alabama in 1931, seventy Black citizens were killed in one month by rampaging lynch mobs.

Black frustration and anger kept spilling over anyway. In our communities, almost daily, there were small spontaneous outbreaks—often no more than a brick heaved through a white merchant's window and the shop looted. The conditions forced hundreds of Black youths to learn to become good shoplifters. It was the reaction of the police to many of these incidents that sometimes triggered larger and more violent protests. The Harlem riot of 1935 was typical. A Black youth, Lino Rivera, had been arrested for stealing in Woolworth's on 125th Street. The rumor spread like wildfire that the boy had been beaten by the police and was probably dead. Hundreds of people converged on the store and the precinct station, demanding to see the boy. The police refused this demand. Angry crowds gathered throughout Harlem, and the police began to disperse them in the manner too familiar in every Black community. And the riot was on. The anger that had swelled up over so many years exploded in all directions. Special attention was given to those establishments that discriminated. Stores that refused to employ Blacks, restaurants that refused service or employment to Blacks, public transportation that had no Black operators—these shops became the focal point of the full fury of the crowds and were destroyed by the angry protesters. It began to appear that the idea was to try, at once, to physically batter the wall of racism—to destroy the city itself. "You can bet on it, man. When we through here we goin' downtown!" That didn't happen. The main areas of disruption were surrounded by armies of police. And the exhortations of local Black spokesmen for calm prevented wholesale bloodshed.

"Are we crazy? . . . yuh can't fight guns with sticks! They just itchin' to kill us all!" It is interesting that the Cotton Club, which had never admitted Black patrons, was spared—possibly because it was some blocks uptown from the center of violence, and also because of its fortress-like exterior and the fact that it was above street level.

Despite the protests and violence, the suspicion and cynicism, the prevailing Black mood was that, one day, we would have equal opportunity and be able to put an end to racism under American democracy, as long as we made the right changes within this system. In the meantime we went about the business of struggling to survive. The old institution of the "rent party" gained a new vigor and kept many Black families from being evicted from their kitchenette "apartments." A typical invitation to a rent party would read:

"COME ONE, COME ALL . . . CHARLIE AND HATTIE
ARE HAVING A BALL . . .
Saturday June, Time: 9 until? . . .
At 2430 Seventh Avenue. . . . Bring your
bottle . . We have the fine food and
music . . . Adm. $0.75 per person." . . .

or

"There'll be brownskin mamas
High Yallers, too
And if you ain't got nothin' to do
Come on up to ROY and SADIE's
228 West 126th Street."

After sending out these written or printed invitations, the host or hostess was required to provide no more than indicated plus a reasonable amount of space for slow dancing. The announcements were never mailed. They were handed out, to friends and strangers alike, wherever the folks congregated—barber shops, beauty parlors, poolrooms, street corners, and churches. The admission charge varied, usually fifty cents to a dollar. Thus, with thirty or forty guests, the month's rent could be paid, often with something left over for the next week's food.

Volumes have been written by sociologists, psychologists, anthropologists, and political scientists in America. Not as much was written when we were young, but nobody had to tell us we were unique or how complex our lives were. We knew we were different from the accepted American "norm," but we had a certain pride in our difference (often reflected in a contempt for standards we considered white). There was a zest for living in our communities that few outsiders understood. We were young and enthusiastic participants in a lifestyle that was distinctly our very own. The fact that this lifestyle was a direct outgrowth of white supremacist rule wasn't the point. Our lifestyle was an adjustment to the impact of that rule. We were really inhabitants of a city within a city. Our communities weren't called ghettoes then, except by a few sociologists. The name Harlem was as well known nationwide as that of any major American city. The only reason we had to leave our areas was to travel to school or to work. We shopped, ate, drank, played, had our hair done, went to church or to the movies, visited friends—all this we did "among our own kind." In Harlem and other ghetto communities we even elected our own "mayors." Such elections were really no more than popularity contests, but they were participated in with no less enthusiasm than any presidential contest. We knew that the only place we could find any truths about Blacks was in Black newspapers.

We began to read and talk more and more about our life, our style, our culture—"Negro culture." There was little belief that such a culture, born of slavery and oppression, could make any positive contribution to white American society. I was not especially militant. I had, however, acquired an awareness that sometimes confused my parents and startled our friends. I knew of Adolf Hitler and the German Nazi oppression of the Jews. The anti-Semitic street shouts we heard in our communities against bigoted Jewish merchants about bringing Hitler here made me uneasy. We already had Congressman John Rankin and Senator Theodore Bilbo from Mississippi, along with the vigilante Ku Klux Klan. Who the hell needed Hitler? I had read about the German leader's refusing to shake the hand of the Black Olympic champion Jesse Owens, and I felt that there had to be some link between German and American racial policies. I didn't express it, but I was beginning to take on a worldview. This thinking, along with my feeling for art and music, began to give me a better understanding of my heritage. Many of us undoubtedly overestimated our own creative talents then, but our ambitions gave us a determination to know more about Black culture and its contributions to the struggle for true democracy. And perhaps we would find our place in the struggle. With this in mind, it was the constant white American put-down of Black culture that particularly embittered us.

Black cultural interpretations were seldom taken seriously in our country and were usually dismissed as "primitive." Black people had long recognized the genius of Duke Ellington when most white observers were still calling his music "jungle rhythm." Our music, generally, and our dancing, was looked upon merely as sensual entertainment. Our language was seen as further indication of our inability to absorb American life. (No one dreamed that thirty years later, an American president, Lyndon Johnson, would use one of the staples of Black talk, "Cool it," in a major speech.) Those years were the last stages of the Harlem Renaissance, a period that saw many Black writers and intellectuals gain some international recognition. But, in the United States, the vibrant color and strength of the work of Langston Hughes, Jacob Lawrence, Margaret Goss, Charles White, Richard Wright, and others

were largely categorized as "race" exceptions to all of this strong ste-
reotyping. However, artists such as Roland Hayes, Paul Robeson, Jose-
phine Baker, and Henry O. Tanner had to go abroad to receive their
early acclaim. Such exceptions, judged by white American standards,
were invariably viewed as freaks of some kind.

The United States had lived a long time with its teachings of Black
inferiority, and the Black community wasn't totally immune to this
continual brainwashing. So, the struggle to overcome, then, sometimes
meant embracing white morality. This, of course, meant accepting the
idea of white supremacy. Almost every Black can think of at least one
light-skinned friend who "passed," crossed the line, and disappeared
into the white world. To paraphrase the words of James Baldwin, some
of us tried hard not to "act like niggers." Whenever we took this
approach, though, it quickly became clear that, even given some chance
of equal opportunity, we couldn't be just like whites—we had to be
better. Whatever our endeavors we always had to jump the extra yard.
This was most obvious in sports. Our country was always super–jock
happy, and achievement in sports was the solid indication of manhood. The Black athlete, however, had to perform superhuman feats
in order to be recognized. If Jesse Owens had received only one gold
medal in the 1936 Olympics, instead of four, it would have been a
drag—the white press would have given him little mention. We couldn't
be ordinary.

In those days we had one universal Black hero, Joe Louis. From a
Detroit slum to heavyweight boxing champion of the whole world.
Unbelievable. A true miracle. Joe Louis was discussed in Black barber
shops and preached about from Black pulpits as if he was the second
coming of Jesus. Joe Louis was our manhood. And this heroic figure was
continually depicted as a humble, illiterate "credit to his race."[1]

The strongest political influence in our communities then was the
National Association for the Advancement of Colored People. Since its
formation in the early 1900s, it was viewed as the leader in the struggle
for Black liberation and human dignity. The association had never been
able to achieve active participation of a majority of Blacks, but, aside
from the church, it was the most staunchly supported organization in
our communities. By the time we came "of age" there began to be some
disenchantment, particularly among younger Blacks. The NAACP, with
its scholarly and college-trained leadership, along with its white board
membership, seemed to be removing itself from what we thought were
the real problems of average Blacks. It was not unusual in our young

circles to hear the association referred to as "The National Association for the Advancement of CERTAIN Colored People." Despite the many historic struggles it had led for civil rights, I could not shake my grow-ing feeling that the NAACP was a bourgeois-oriented organization.

We began to hear serious discussions about the Communist Party mainly because of the party's participation in the Scottsboro case. The case itself became a symbol of the whole Black liberation effort during the '30s. In 1931, nine Black youths were arrested in Scottsboro, Alabama, and charged with the rape of two white girls. Such a charge meant certain death. In those days, regardless of age, a Black male's attempting even the most casual and innocent conversation with a white female was dangerous. "Ahm tellin' you straight, Jim . . . if you walkin' down the street and there ain't nobody else on that street and you see a white chick comin' toward you, you better cross over, man . . . 'cause that chick could holler . . . for no reason . . . and you a dead nigger!" In one day, eight of the nine Scottsboro boys were tried, convicted and sentenced to die in the electric chair. "Legal problems" developed in the case of the ninth boy. Because he was only fourteen years old, the jury couldn't decide whether to recommend death or life imprison-ment. It was during the long years of struggle to save the Scottsboro boys that the Communist Party gained its early notice in our com-munities. The first exposure of the Scottsboro case as a frame-up ap-peared in the Communist Party newspaper the *Daily Worker.* The party began to be written about in Black newspapers almost as much as Black organizations. There were articles and editorials, sometimes warning the Black community against the Reds, but also praising the party for having the only whites who seemed to really believe in brotherhood and democracy.

We didn't know much about communism and there were some among us, usually our elders, who accepted the grotesque caricatures of communists as bomb-throwing maniacs. Although we had read some party literature, we certainly had no ideas about revolution or doing away with capitalism. Even so, some of the philosophy of the party, at least as we interpreted it, was being discussed and argued. And we became a part of much of that dialogue. "Listen, Jim . . . them Reds catchin' so much hell from Mr. Charley . . . got to be somethin' to what they sayin'." "Ahm hip . . . they talk about takin' from the rich and givin' to the poor . . . what the hell we got to lose?" "That's just what the Reds say, man . . . see, they don't look at us as a race, but as part of the workin' class and we all have to pull together." "Solid . . . now if they can just get them white boys to believe that." "I read where in Russia any kind of discrimination is against the law . . . damn if I can believe that!" "Shee-it . . . they just ain't got no niggers there."

Before I thought of joining the party, I didn't know many Black communists. Those few were seldom a part of our block-level discussions about politics, and they appeared aloof. In all fairness, they probably regarded us as no more than young nightlifers, not yet ready for any kind of serious struggle or commitment. And, admittedly, despite our bitter awareness of the nature of white society, we were dedicated to enjoying life—not just surviving. Also, influenced by the majority Black outlook, we had as our main concern about politics the struggle to get local white politicians to remember us as a force in our communities.

I can recall one Black communist, Angelo Herndon, whose name became well known in our communities and in much of the nation. Angelo Herndon was indicted in 1932, in Fulton County, Georgia, for attempting to incite insurrection. Older Black folks would talk about him with a mixture of wonderment, pride, and disbelief. Arresting a Black for anything so sophisticated was a little beyond comprehension. We were used to the usual charges of rape and robbery. The stories of Herndon held a kind of fascination for many Black youth. Angelo Herndon might very well have been the first modern Black militant. He was defended during his trial by a young Black law graduate, Benjamin J. Davis, who was later to become a member of the National Committee of the Communist Party and a New York city councilman. Davis, many years later, would put it that, ". . . I just had to meet this young Negro who was supposed to be trying to overthrow the government of Georgia . . . unbelievable." Hearing about Herndon's attitude during his trial exposed us to a different kind of defiance. At one point in the trial he rose and shouted, ". . . you can kill me, but you can't kill the working class!" Well, we knew about "the working class and white workers"—and often about them fighting each other. To hear a young Black talking about working people as a united group was a whole new thing, especially considering that many white workers probably thought of Herndon as just another "crazy nigger." Surely Angelo Herndon must have helped to broaden the outlook of many young Blacks. And more than a few of these young people came to the realization that there was something more to American racism than appeared on the surface. "Hate the niggers . . . lynch 'em." "Kill the kike Christ-killers." "Hate the spics, hate the wops, hate the greasers." Was it really "human nature" to have all that hate? A lot of people believed so, but we weren't sure. As bitter as we were, we couldn't buy the wholesale bigotry being peddled. As one friend would put it to me many years later, "I don't know one thing about this communism you talkin' about . . . but I DO know this fuckin' system is a bitch . . . it has got to go!"

Part II

There are times when . . . the demands of struggle made it difficult . . . to play fully the role of father and brother. There are times when commitment . . . created A WORLD APART, where full family life . . . became an ephemeral dream.

—Nelson Mandela's address at Joe Slovo's funeral

6

The Young Communist League

Seventh Avenue, New York
January 30, 1940

In 1940, the Young Communist League (YCL) of Harlem set out to consolidate the ties we had among Harlem youth. It was our adaptation of the united front against fascism set forth in Giorgi Dimitrov's work.[1] The new headquarters was located on the second floor of the building that Small's Paradise occupied at Seventh Avenue and 135th Street, now called, most appropriately, Adam Clayton Powell Boulevard. My idea was to use the headquarters as a convenient base for popularizing the Young Communist League of Harlem—appealing to the hundreds of young people who congregated regularly on the sidewalk outside of Small's. They were mostly fun-loving, unemployed youth looking for diversion on weekends, the "hangout" nights. We set up a schedule with a Friday night meeting for business, education, and some culture, followed by a Saturday night "shindig" that combined dancing, entertainment, and, quite often, a guest speaker. Most important were the music, refreshments, and spirit of friendliness and warmth, which I knew from my experience in the entertainment world were crucial to any group seeking public support.

The young communists were in an admirable position to do so, because our recruitment in 1938, 1939, and early 1940 had brought into our ranks young people from Wadleigh Junior High School, the Baptist Young Peoples Union (BYPU) of Abyssinia Church, the YWCA, the

Epworth League of the Episcopal Church of St. James, and the Catholic
Youth Organization of St. Charles Church. We also had in the membership of the Harlem organization students who were resident in
Harlem and held dual membership in Harlem and their Marxist or African American student organizations, such as the Meroe Society at
NYU, the Frederick Douglass Society at City College (CCNY), and
the Harriet Tubman Society at Hunter. Other student members held
leadership positions in general campus organizations. The student members were almost uniformly articulate, well versed in Marxist theory,
and well respected on campus as serious and committed people. Some of
them were editors of college papers, some earned excellent grades as
outstanding students, and others were stars on various athletic teams.
Len Bates, for example, was a member of our student club and a star on
NYU's football team; he was not allowed to play against Georgia Tech
because the racists there did not want a Black man on the field.

A number of students were very close friends of mine. My closest
friend was Louis Burnham, who lived in a brownstone on Strivers'
Row on 139th Street with his mother and brother, Charlie.[2] Louis was
our equivalent of a Renaissance man and a regular on the Dean's List at
CCNY. Though his mother owned the brownstone, Louis, like most
of us, was continually out of money, but he was able to develop a consistent source of income by doing papers for well-heeled middle-class
white students. I used to meet with Louis at his house quite often. He
was the executive director of the Harlem Youth Congress, and we
needed constant contact to monitor the day-to-day developments in
the youth movement.

Louis was one of the most lovable people I have ever met. He had a
mordant wit, always saw the humorous side to keep us all "cracked up,"
and could recite poetry by the yard. At the same time, he had an ability
to put words down on paper with a speed and precision that I never
experienced with anyone else. When I would go to meet him, I would
often find him pounding away at the typewriter. He'd ask me if I could
wait a few minutes until he finished a few pages of a thirty-page paper.
Out of curiosity I would ask him what he was working on, and he
would say nonchalantly, "Oh, this is a paper on the economics of the
period of Henry VIII in England," or "This is an analysis of the political role of small farmers and small businessmen during the period of
Jacksonian democracy." He had a far-above-average ability to marshal
his facts through well-documented research and translate his material
into well-written and convincing prose.

After World War II, Louis was to go south and organize for the Southern Negro Youth Congress (SNYC). His main base of operation was Birmingham, Alabama. At the time, the chief of police there was a rabid racist named Theophilus Eugene "Bull" Connor, and Louis would have us listening in rapt horror or amusement to stories of the encounters SNYCers had had with the police. It was almost destiny that Louis was assigned the responsibility for coordinating the activities of the left when the Montgomery bus boycott started. He came up with the idea of moving the Wednesday night meetings of all the participants in the boycott in a round robin from one church to another. This was a tactic designed to carry the spirit of the most militant rank-and-file boycotters into every church in Montgomery. Some of the more conservative or more fearful of the ministers were reluctant to involve their congregations in the boycott. But few could resist the offer to have the meeting in their church the following Wednesday. If they refused, they might find some of their members drifting off into the congregations where the bus boycott meetings were being held. Louis and his colleagues, of course, elaborately spelled out in the meetings what the dangers of nonparticipation were for recalcitrant ministers. All of this is simply to say that I was not surprised when Louis told me he was writing speeches for the young Black minister who was later to be awarded the Nobel Prize for Peace, Martin Luther King Jr.

While every one of the leaders of the Harlem Youth Congress had talent, it would be stretching the truth to say that they were all of the caliber of Louis Burnham; he was *sui generis*. But we had a collective leadership in which many diverse talents were pooled, creating our own brand of synergy. We were able to see the abstract principle of the united front dramatically brought to life in the concrete. Our unity was cemented on the basis of systematic day-to-day association in carrying through the practical tasks of the Youth Congress. The practical tasks might, for example, embrace organizing a delegation to go to Washington on a bus to present the voice of Harlem youth on the issues of collective security, world peace, defense of Ethiopia, or passage of an anti-lynching bill. At its peak the Harlem Youth Congress represented close to 200 youth organizations in Harlem. When we spoke on behalf of Harlem youth we were not talking about a paper constituency.

To use an anatomical analogy, as dangerous as it can be, we in the Young Communist League were akin to a spinal column in the body politic of the Harlem youth. We had members who were active in most of the youth organizations in the Harlem community. The first ingredient of unity was the establishment of clarity in our own ranks on what our main tasks for the week should be. Our cadre would meet in our various branches to have discussions on the most desirable strategies and tactics we should follow in each of the organizations in which we had members. So the first element that contributed to the unity of the youth was the general political unity within the ranks of the radical youth. That meant that in every youth organization in which there was a radical, the theme of unity of the youth community was voiced by someone. As that theme was picked up in the other organizations, it gathered momentum, and even in groups in which there were no radicals, voices spoke up for united action.

The movement progressed so dynamically that even some of the street gangs participated in the youth congress activity. Some of the warlords, who had previously broken up Young Communist League meetings, rode with us on the busses to Washington. Among the many young men and women who were building the Youth Congress, both Marxist and non-Marxist, were John Hudson Jones, who later became a reporter for the *Daily Worker*; Carmen and Bert Alves, who met and then fell in love; Jackie Fanning Ellis, our most courageous militant; Mercedes Peters, later to become an outstanding therapist; Alline Robbins from High Point, North Carolina; Roscoe Smith, also from High Point; and his buddy Talmadge Moore from the same town; Roscoe's sister, Florence; Everett "Teak" Thomas, a fine musical talent whom we convinced to convert to full-time organizing work; Pearl and Allan Laws, fur workers who felt responsible for the community despite their manifold activities in the fur market; Tom Jasper, an official in the Fur Floor Boys Local; Clinton Salisbury, an artist and theater lover; John O. Killens, the novelist whom I attempted to convince to give up writing and go into Marxist educational work; Ossie Davis, who also resisted our efforts to sidetrack him; Bertha Shaw, later a radio commentator in Rome; the ever-faithful Oscar James; Una Mulzac, the daughter of the first Black captain of the Liberty ship the *Booker T. Washington*, Captain Hugh Mulzac; Winifred Norman; and James Williams, who went on to become a New York Urban League executive.

There was also the CCNY student Saul Katz, who took the stand of the YCL against racial prejudice seriously in his personal life. When he fell in love with a Black woman (something very few white males allow themselves to do in our culture), he went ahead and married her (an act even fewer white males allow themselves to perform in the racist culture they are brought up in). He married Bertha Shaw, and one of his best friends, also my closest white associate, a City College honors student, Abe Dubin, also married a Black woman who was herself the daughter of a Black–Jewish interracial marriage, a stunning beauty, Yvonne Cohen. It was this kind of spirit that permeated our ranks and impressed our surrounding community of the sincerity of our purpose. We were not kidding about the things we talked about. We were serious.

These qualities among our members gave the people in the community confidence in us even though many of them thought we were crazy for risking the kinds of sacrifices that public exposure of our viewpoint often entailed. But even that crazy sort of risk-taking enlarged our reservoir of good will in the neighborhood. The slogan that most of us attempted to live up to was "close the gap between theory and practice." This was not a quality too often evidenced among the local political hacks who supported officeholders beholden to the establishment and whose election promises were honored more in the breach than the observance.

The community saw us as having no vested interests, though some, influenced by the anticommunist press, did believe that we worked for Moscow. Not all Blacks who felt that way were necessarily turned away from us. Those who were not believed that any nation which challenged the white racism in America was worth supporting. In fact, during the height of the "Red scare" of 1940, developed as part of the scenario for the passage of the anticommunist Voorhis Act, I was able to sell more than 500 one-dollar copies of the Dean of Canterbury's book *Soviet Power* in the streets of Harlem. The YCL as a whole sold more than 1,000 copies. It could be said that Harlem was not as taken in by the "Red scare" as many of those in the blue-collar white communities were. Blacks, generally, were not as easily hoodwinked about the advantages of capitalism. The Black view of the system was much more critical, probably not because of any innate acumen but primarily because of the disadvantages and penalties the system imposed on them through the institutionalized processes and norms that maintain the racist infrastructure despite all the limited democratic reforms that are made from time to time in the superstructure. On the whole, we worked in a friendly environment, and our forms of organization enhanced our political strength among the youth.

The Young Communist League had three clubs in Harlem. The Club Ashford, named after one of the very dynamic leaders of the earlier YCL in Harlem, James Ashford, was the oldest of the branches, having its main membership base among the working class and among unemployed youth in the Valley, as central Harlem was called. The second branch I organized on Sugar Hill had a newer membership with a more middle-class outlook; this was not surprising in view of the more affluent population on Sugar Hill. We also had been assigned a group of students from City College, Hunter College, and Brooklyn College who either lived in Harlem if they were Black or who had volunteered to work in Harlem if they were white, or Black students who normally would have been assigned to campus work. One of those volunteers was a brilliant young Jew, Mal Wofsy, whose father had been the district organizer of the Communist Party in Connecticut. Mal and his wife, Ida, became my closest friends. When we finished our sundry tasks of YCL organizing, we spent the precious free time we had at each others' homes playing various mind-challenging games like Charades or a juiced-up version of Twenty Questions that we called Abstract or Concrete. Mal went into the Army before me, but, unlike me, he took advantage of the G.I. Bill to finish his graduate studies, winding up as a leading contributor to the science of biochemistry. He taught me about details of organization and the importance of giving meticulous attention to assignments. His qualities undoubtedly carried over into his biochemical research and contributed to his success. One of his closest friends at City College was a high-IQ'd Black student, Clinton Oliver, who was probably the first Black to obtain tenure in the English Department at Harvard. Bob Fogel, who had married a beautiful Black YCLer named Enid, later won the Nobel Prize in economics. With such talent working for our program, we never had any doubts concerning the inevitable success of our goals.

The third club in Harlem was the Manhattanville Club, which was based in the area from 125th Street and St. Nicholas Avenue west and south to 110th Street, an area once called the Bloomingdale section of Manhattan. While the Ashford Club was predominantly Black in its composition, the Manhattanville Club was predominantly white, yet we were able to mesh the activities of these three distinctly different organizations successfully so as to contribute to the development of the Harlem youth movement.

Besides these street clubs, as we called them, we also had a more sophisticated form of organization for those members who might have had some personal stake in not making their membership in the YCL public. Security ordinances in federal jobs, as well as in police, fire department, and post office workers, put such employees at risk of losing their jobs at once if they were known to be communists. The principle of anonymity was an established American tradition—the Masons, others, and the most successful of all organizations—Alcoholics Anonymous—had used the principle of anonymity to protect their members.

Our particular form of anonymity was the organization of a closed group with its membership restricted in numbers. Most of the members had taken assumed names as if they belonged to an underground organization. We generally called such groups "mass org" groups—whenever we had a closed group of leaders who worked in a community organization—that is, any type of organization that might be attacked as communist if it were known that even one communist sat on its board of directors or acted as an official. The policy of anonymity was designed to protect not only individuals from persecution for their political beliefs but also community organizations and other institutions. The insiders who had knowledge of the membership called one another "submarines." It was a highly selective group with members on the executive boards of a number of important youth organizations in Harlem. Through these members we could get a weekly assessment of the relationship of forces on each major issue, the level of political consciousness, key and influential personnel who should be worked with, and the expected level of participation and activity of the membership in each community organization. This approach had a combat inference that appealed to the Leninists among us and expressed some of our romanticism as youth.

Submarines functioned in a number of areas. I recall one Black woman, Jesse Campbell, who served on the national board of the YWCA. She was well spoken, highly intelligent, physically most attractive, and possessed of impeccable Black bourgeois connections. She had the ability to perform as a straight bourgeois liberal without ever soiling her discussion with what some of the people in those circles might have labeled as "abrasive" language. On top of that, she had a remarkable ability to keep her cool in the most provocative and heated circumstances. In the forty years I have known her, under all kinds of conditions, I have never heard her speak angrily or raise her voice.

At the National Training School, which I attended in 1938, I had the opportunity to meet the scion of a wealthy Jewish family, Abbott Simon, who lived in a magnificent penthouse on Park Avenue. As our submarine in the top leadership of the American Youth Congress, he often regaled us with stories of his luncheon dates with the then–First Lady, Mrs. Eleanor Roosevelt. This was heady stuff for us and gave us a sense both of being in on history and having more power even short of a revolution than any of us had dreamed of. Of course, reference to positions of influence such as these were an important part of our stock-in-trade in recruiting speeches.

One of our submarines, Bob Schrank, had enormous talent as a trade unionist and went on to become a top official in the Ford Foundation, influencing the giving of grants and participating in the formulation of policy at the highest level. In 1940, I was appointed to the national board of the Young Communist League, and there I had the opportunity to meet with one of our finest submarines, Arthur Kinoy. His comments in our board meetings always had a depth and illuminating quality that unmistakably marks the exercise of a keen mind. I always looked forward to his participation in a discussion because, whatever the subject matter, he had the capacity to uncover angles of vision and nuances that quite often might otherwise have escaped us. It's no wonder one of the most effective civil rights organizations in the United States, the Center for Constitutional Rights, is his creation.

As part of my development, I was assigned to accompany Claudia and Carl Ross, as representatives of the National Board of the Young Communist League, to the 1941 convention of the Southern Negro Youth Congress. The SNYC was a model communist-led youth organization with a very dynamic leadership that included the brilliant and indefatigable Ed Strong; his wife, Augusta; Dr. James E. Jackson; and Esther Cooper, who was to marry James. Together they formed a team of four dedicated young Black revolutionaries who risked their lives working in the racist-dominated atmosphere of Birmingham. The cadre they brought forward in the South became the shock troops of the later developing civil rights movement. As noted earlier, the chief of police at that time was "Bull" Connor, later to become infamous as the organizer of the dog attacks and the use of bull prods against the civil rights marchers in the '60s.

Claudia and I had an interesting trip down on the train. When we changed trains in Washington from the Pennsylvania to the Southern Railroad, I experienced for the first time the segregation system of Jim Crow. I had heard about Jim Crow, but it was something else experiencing it on a public conveyance. I watched as all the Blacks marched into the Jim Crow coach as if by tacit consent. I would have found it difficult to believe if I had not experienced our collaboration with similar indignities at the Cotton Club. Claudia and I decided that we'd try to tackle the beast with a flanking maneuver by going to the dining car, where we hoped we could be seated without segregation. The Black porter came over to us and told us, "You two can't sit here."

We were right in the middle of the dining car. We looked at him with an assumed air of puzzlement; some folk call it the "dumb nigger" look. He pointed to the end of the car and said, "You'll have to sit at that table."

When we changed our seats, he then came over and said gently, as if to educate two northerners in a friendly fashion: "You see. This table has a curtain we can pull around you so when the gooood white folks come in, we can pull the curtain around you and they won't have to see you sitting in the dining car."

I was fit to be tied as Claudia suggested we remember that our primary mission was to get to Tuskegee for the SNYC convention, where the consultation we were to give would be a much more effective method of struggle against the system. Though it was painful to have the curtain drawn when the first white party came in as if we were some kind of lepers, Claudia was able to distract me with some stories about the idiosyncrasies of some her confrères, so things went smoothly until we finally arrived in Birmingham. Mary Southard, who came from one of Alabama's finest families, and Carl Ross, who had come down to take care of some American Youth Congress business, met us at the station, from which we were to drive down to Tuskegee through Ku Klux Klan–infested territory. They outlined a strategy for us because a mixed foursome would inevitably be stopped between Birmingham and Tuskegee.

Carl and Mary were to be a young couple who had hired Claudia and me as maid and chauffeur (I couldn't drive a wheelbarrow), and they were driving us to their estate. As luck would have it, we were stopped by a group of evil-looking "rednecks" who stared at us as if they were aching for a lynching, but they bought our contrived story without any question. Mary Southard's good looks and family credentials made our story plausible, so we arrived in Tuskegee without any further difficulty. It was stressful, but that was the territory.

The local area was in a state of great excitement because the highlight of the SNYC convention was to be a personal appearance by Paul Robeson as guest soloist with the Tuskegee Choir. One little episode while we were waiting outside the concert hall to hear Robeson made up for all the tension of the trip down from Birmingham. A young white couple, he looking like F. Scott Fitzgerald in a white linen suit and she looking like Scarlett O'Hara in *Gone with the Wind*, approached us and asked, "Do you know where the white entrance is?"

A little old Black woman wearing a faded purple Sunday-go-to-meetin' dress standing beside us overheard the question and as some Black matriarchs can do, interrupted to say, "We are all going in the same entrance today. This is Mr. Robeson's concert and it's a real American thing!"

Robeson had issued a press statement that it was his policy not to sing to segregated audiences and this had created quite a stir in this Black Belt county.[3]

Before going to Alabama, I had met Claudia on Sugar Hill. She was one of the YCL leaders who had gotten word that I was making a very favorable impression on the party organization at 702 St. Nicholas Avenue. Meetings were picking up in attendance, and some of the new participants were friends of mine who liked a good time in addition to wanting social change. At the time, most party branches were either "shop" or "street" branches. A shop branch consisted of party members who worked in the same factory, office, or other type of place of employment. This organization expressed the application of the policy of industrial concentration designed to give the party greater effect among industrial workers. Normally, shop branches were organized in separate sections from the street or community branches and had section committees that consisted of a section organizer, organizational secretary, educational director, treasurer, literature director, the branch organizers, and one or two key people who were usually co-opted for particular talents without having a specific functional role on the section committee. They developed an overview of the problems of the particular trade or union that co-coordinated the affairs and activities of all the branches.

Claudia had a slight touch of what I called later revolutionary nationalism, which manifested itself in a keen nose for racism of any kind among our white comrades. She was particularly fond of telling about her altercation with Carl Ross, who was one of our most brilliant tacticians in the American Youth Congress and also a member of the national board of the Young Communist League. She called Carl on his racist attitude at an after-meeting rap session. Carl had referred to James Robinson, later to become the minister of the Church of the Master and head of the Afram Institute, as a talented "boy." Claudia had some difficulty explaining that the term "boy" was racist with its implication that Blacks even after their maturity never really grew up. Carl, first in typical fashion, grew indignant and denied any racist intent, citing his longstanding friendship with Jim and other Blacks until he was red in the face, but he finally reluctantly agreed that if Claudia found the expression offensive he would discontinue using it. I was later added to the national board of the YCL and sat in on one meeting where I heard Carl refer to some other Blacks as "lads." Claudia was sitting opposite me at the time and she fluttered her eyes heavenward in a gesture of hopelessness that almost had me splitting my sides in laughter.

Once Claudia had selected me as a candidate for development to leadership, she was to expose me to every discussion that took place in the leading party committees on which she served. This exposure was detailed and relatively objective, though Claudia had an intriguing way of describing the presentation of viewpoints with which she did not agree. It may have been a West Indian cultural characteristic that made her gesticulations, changes of tone of voice, and facial expressions so vivid, but when Claudia got through describing a party meeting, especially if it involved some of the more pompous white comrades, it was a show—an entertaining one—that made the briefing as fascinating as if one had a video of the best quality.

Claudia was on the editorial board of the *Young Communist Review* and the national board of the YCL, and she also served on the national committee of the Communist Party. From these vantage points she had a bird's-eye view of every important discussion taking place at the most important levels in both the adult as well as in the youth movement. She often spoke in great detail of the participation of leaders like Earl Browder, Eugene Dennis, and William Z. Foster. With great wit she quoted what they had said, related how they differed, and told of some of the infighting, both political and psychological, that accompanied the debates. In this manner I received what amounted to an accelerated political education and specialized training in the process of intra-party struggle that went on at the national level. I became aware that party politics could be fierce and that the manifest unity of the party leadership developed out of intense, sometimes vicious, infighting.

As I became more indoctrinated with the basic tenets of Marxism, my estimate of the revolutionary character of the actual Black population shrank. My criticism of the Black bourgeoisie and petty bourgeoisie sharpened, and I became even more increasingly aware of how "bourgeoisified" the Black workers were. Simultaneously, my love for the party and my comrades grew. When I first entered the party, it had bothered me that Stalin's picture was hanging on the wall at the branch at 702 St. Nicholas Avenue. But he was to become a fierce and brilliant gray eagle, protecting the peoples of the world from their imperialist oppressors. I spent more and more of my time with comrades who agreed with me and less and less time with nonparty people except my dearest friends. I found later that they were learning to talk about nonpolitical subjects with me because I had become much too dogmatic to entertain the pros and cons of debate with grace. I counterbalanced this negative attitude toward the real world with a dream world in which an ideal American people and an ideal Black movement were shaping up. I lived in the "what was going to be" rather than the "what was." Eric Hoffer, in his insightful book *The True Believer*, delineated for all time the kind of unreal mental state into which the cadre of any fundamentalist organization can slide, unknowingly. I had slowly become a true believer.

After I had graduated from the National Training School, Claudia, who had been the main inspiration for my attending and had come up to Beacon to visit, showing more than comradely interest, began to pay a great deal of attention to me. We had many political discussions, furious arguments, most of which she won, and eventually, we wound up in each other's arms. She shared a couple of rooms with her sister, Yvonne, and because the place was just down the block from one of my favorite hangouts, La Marcheri, quite often after a few drinks there we listened to Jimmy Lunceford recordings of "By the River of St. Marie," "Margie," and "My Blue Heaven." (A young playboy named Malcolm Little also hung out at La Marcheri, but we didn't attach any significance to that. He later assumed the name "Malcolm X." "West Indian" Archie, who often played poker with my father, told me Malcolm had said he liked to hear me speak. Perhaps some history would have been changed if I had stopped to chat with Malcolm instead of stopping off at Claudia's farther down the block on 147th Street.) I appreciated Claudia as a YCL leader and a brilliant young Black woman, and I felt quite complimented that she saw me as a lover, but I never had stronger than platonic feelings for her, which did not make the sex any less exciting for me.

Another woman was to enter my life in the summer of 1939. By this time I had become the president of the Club Ashford, which had been meeting at 433 Lenox Avenue and represented a more proletarian membership than was the case with the Milton Herndon Branch, which I had started on Sugar Hill with its more middle-class membership. At one of our joint dances held at the Manhattanville Club, a beautiful young blonde sent one of the YCL guys over to me to ask me if I would dance with her. I did and was immediately smitten. Later she began to attend meetings of the Club Ashford, where I discovered that her name was Jean Rogers and that she had a studio in the Washington Hotel on Old Broadway in order to be near her classes at Juilliard School of Music, where she was studying the piano. This information bowled me over, being a frustrated musician myself who was always in awe of anyone who could play any instrument whatsoever. We began to see each other after the club meetings once a week and we agreed to attend the New Masses Ball on New Year's Eve. It was around this time that I found that Jean's name was her YCL name. She had ambitions of becoming a concert pianist and in the repressive atmosphere of the time, it would not have been politic to openly profess one's identity as a communist in the entertainment professions. The blacklist set up through the anticommunist publication during the McCarthy hysteria of the '50s, *Red Channels*, would prove that strategy to have been wise. It turned out that Jean Rogers was really Martha Sherman. She came from a Brooklyn family of garment workers, parents both members of the International Ladies' Garment Workers' union (a big plus as far as I was concerned) and had an equally beautiful sister, Zelda, and two brothers, Joe and Charlie. Zelda and Charlie were in the YCL.

The newly emerged Martha (having shed her Jean Rogers identity for me) had agreed to meet me at the Ball. I arrived looking in every direction for her and was bowled over when from the center of the ballroom, I saw her coming toward me with a big "Well, here I am" smile and dressed in a stunning floor-length evening gown. She was inarguably the most beautiful woman at the Ball, and I was incontestably the proudest male there.

After that event our romance accelerated, and when Martha left school to go on tour as a demonstrator of the new electrified Story and Clark piano, we kept up a fiery correspondence. But when she returned in late 1940, pressures had arisen in her family and we started a long series of talks about where we were headed. I proposed marriage and that put our relationship on a new plane.

We finally got married on March 22, 1941. Bob Campbell, the organizer of the Harlem section of the Communist Party, was a good friend of mine and arranged for our wedding at the home of Reverend Theophilus Alcantara, who had an African Orthodox Church. The attraction of having him perform the ceremony was its African ritualistic aspect in which, after taking the vows, we were bound together with a long green sash. Martha went into a giggling fit from nervousness that interrupted the ceremony. I recall the unsympathetic frown on the face of Dorothy Funn, a woman Bob had invited along from the Brooklyn Party organization. It was later discovered that Dorothy was a police agent.

I had joined the party with the expectation that at last I had found an organization which already embodied the kind of society that was free of racism and any other form of exploitation. Martha's brother Charlie had been opposed to our marriage and had gone to one of our party leaders, Johnny Gates, to ask him to intervene on his behalf. Johnny had called me into a meeting and asked me what my intentions were with regard to Martha. He had told me of Charlie's objections to our proposed union. I responded that I loved Martha and that my family supported our right to choose each other, though they felt there would be difficulties. They, as my mother said, knew I had a mind of my own and would probably do what I wanted to do regardless of their position. In hindsight, in few other organizations would there have been these kinds of discussions. In most, the interracial couple would have had to conceal their decision to marry and would have had to elope and present a *fait accompli*. In some organizations, the couple would have been expelled and ostracized. In the party, the objectors were given the opportunity to present their side of the story to a leading party person and were then told that they would not stop the marriage. This was the message I got from Johnnie, and once Martha and I were married I always felt I had his support. I believe that Johnnie, who went through with his marriage to Lil Ross, who had been the wife of Carl Ross, had been strengthened by the trials he saw Martha and me go through.

7
The War Years

The White House, Washington, D.C.
February 1940

While we were for collective security and developing a united front against fascism, our antifascism took quite a turn with the signing of the Soviet–German Nazi nonaggression pact. I was much too enraptured with the line of the party and its mythology at that time to raise serious objections to the analysis and went along with all the other Black leaders who accepted the idea that the Soviets had been forced into making a maneuver that would buy time for it to stop what had been seen as an ultimate Nazi attack on the Soviet Union. The failure of the United States and Great Britain to develop a collective security policy had turned Spain over to Franco and his fascist forces, and we saw the move of the Soviet Union as a tactic of last resort to prevent the Nazis from moving against it. Our line against fascism was adjusted to include all imperialists, and we focused on the reactionary trends in the Western imperialist nations. In the Black community, the colonialism of Great Britain, particularly in the West Indies and west Africa, was well known, and our attacks on British imperialism were well received by a community that itself was in something of a semicolonial status. Our slogan, "The Yanks are not coming!" was well received and our condemnation of Jim Crow and other forms of discrimination at home carried weight. Our sales of *Soviet Power* mounted, and we held many meetings explaining that the Soviet Union was conserving itself through

the treaty with the Nazis to further strengthen the struggle against colonialism by giving itself time to build up its armed forces and defense
industry. Britain and France through Neville Chamberlain and Édouard
Daladier, respectively, had done much worse at Munich in giving over
the Sudetenland and, eventually, Czechoslovakia to the Germans.[1]

Our own application of the united front tactic was exemplified in
one of the most popular and eventually successful campaigns we had
undertaken, the drive against Jim Crow in major league baseball. The
national board of the Young Communist League had decided to make
the issue one of our central concentrations. Lester Rodney, sports
editor of the *Daily Worker*, had been carrying on a virtually one-man
campaign for years, buttonholing baseball managers, interviewing white
ballplayers to see whether they had any objection to playing alongside
Blacks, and keeping up a steady drumfire of articles about the great Black
talent that was dammed up in the National Negro League by the segregation system. I could vouch for that personally, having seen most of the
great ball teams fielded by Blacks when my father was playing. He was no
slouch himself, being a .300+ place hitter and a flawless fielder with an
arm that could cut off a base runner from center field at home plate in
a perfect strike. He was also an exciting base runner whose antics
stealing bases anticipated Jackie Robinson's crowd-thrilling performances down the chalk lines from third base to home plate—in the
most exciting steal of them all—the run-producing one at home plate!

My father had played with the Grand Central Red Caps; the Pennsylvania Red Caps; the McConnell Giants in Montclair, New Jersey;
and finally with one of the all-time great teams, the Lincoln Giants—
forerunners to the New York Black Yankees. The Lincolns had played
at Catholic Protectory Oval between Lenox and Fifth at 136th Street
near the site of the Riverton Houses. There I had seen colorful players,
all of major league caliber—"High Pockets" Hudspeth; Satchel Paige;
Oscar Charleston; "Fats" Jenkins, also a formidable basketballer; and
dozens of others who like my father had often played off-season against
the best of the white major league players when they went on "barnstorming" tours with luminaries such as Babe Ruth, Wally Schang,
Tony Lazzeri, Earle Combs, Frankie Frisch, and others of that rank.
The Black players not only played the white teams—more often than
not they defeated them. The element of politics was very strong in these
games because the Blacks were constantly making it as clear as possible
that they were of equal rank and should not have been excluded from
the major leagues. The stakes were special because the ball field was

one of the few places (that is, in these off-season games) where Blacks had the opportunity to demonstrate their process with no prejudicial strings attached. So, it was with a strong sense of personal identification that I welcomed the decision of the YCL to concentrate on the baseball campaign and make it a success.

The baseball campaign became a major project for the Harlem YCL, and I proposed to the New York state YCL that we have a statewide mobilization of "actives" in a petition campaign for signatures outside Yankee Stadium during the 1939 World Series. We had originally thought of Yankee Stadium, because it was so close to Harlem, as an exclusively Harlem project with a turnout of a hundred members from the Harlem organization. But as we discussed the campaign, I began to express the idea that it would be an even more dramatic demonstration if we could get the participation of white youth from all over the city to collect signatures. The idea was accepted, and the mobilization resulted in more than 1,000 members, Black and white, forming an enthusiastic ring of signature collectors around Yankee Stadium. Lester Rodney had, through his connections with the Yankees, arranged for our petition drive to be announced over the PA system. We were delighted and inspired to hear it announced that the fans should give their support to the petitions being circulated outside the stadium. I spotted A. Philip Randolph entering and was proud to get his signature.[2]

At the moment that A. Philip Randolph signed my petition, I had no prescience that he would soon be denouncing communism at a historic meeting of the National Negro Congress, nor that our campaign would be victorious in a short seven years, when Jackie Robinson, who had been a member of the Young Communist League at UCLA, would be the first Black to enter the major leagues on the Brooklyn Dodgers team. Lil Gates and I were designated to represent the Young Communist League in carrying the collected signatures from the "Jim Crow in Baseball" campaign to the office of Pete Cacchione, who was then the only communist on the New York City Council and from Brooklyn. Pete was a great baseball fan, as was practically every person in the borough of Brooklyn, and he needed no argument to be convinced to introduce a resolution in the City Council calling on the New York teams—the Yankees, the Giants, and the Dodgers—to be the first to end segregation in baseball. The public receptivity to the idea was at its peak in Brooklyn, and the activities of the Communist Party in the borough of Brooklyn were probably one of the factors in the carefully balanced equation that led to the decision on the part of Branch Rickey to break Jim Crow by signing Jackie Robinson in Brooklyn as the community where his efforts would get the greatest support.

Certainly, I never anticipated that I would help organize the United Negro and Allied Veterans of America (UNAVA) and be elected National Vice Commander in charge of education along with Coleman Young, later to become the Mayor of Motown (Detroit), as National Vice Commander in charge of labor. Jackie Robinson would be the honorary chairman of the New York state UNAVA. On Jackie Robinson Day at Ebbetts Field, the first of many, I was to present him with a gift from UNAVA. It was Banner Day at Ebbetts Field.

While the Dodgers had always had Black fans who were ardent supporters, as ardent as any other Brooklynites because the love for great athletes transcends the color line, the Black attendance at Ebbetts Field had quadrupled and quintupled. Housewives, teenagers, and grandmothers not normally associated with the sport filled the bleachers. Busloads from church organizations and other community groups made the trip from Harlem down to Ebbetts Field, and the residents of Bed-Stuy had only to walk to Ebbetts Field, so Jackie Robinson Day at Ebbetts Field had at least 25 percent Black attendance.

It was more than an interest in the sport. To the Black community it was a political event of the first rank—a tribute to the first Black in organized baseball, a tribute not only to his physical presence on the team but in tribute to the courage, coolness, and superlative athletic ability he had demonstrated on this very first season of his participation in the sport at the major league level. Jackie had proven what we had contended for years—that Blacks were of major league quality; that whites would, however reluctantly, play alongside Blacks; and that the fans would support integrated teams! All of this was being demonstrated at Ebbetts Field and was much appreciated by me because I had been in the forefront of making the arguments for this viewpoint at rallies, meetings, and other forums where the question of the equality of the races was discussed. My heart was bursting with pride as I heard Bill "Bojangles" Robinson, mayor of Harlem, world's greatest tap dancer, and no small athlete himself, introduce Jackie over the PA system. (Mentioning Bojangles' athletic ability brings up a little-known fact about him. In the '20s, he had a standing bet that, running backward, he could beat any Olympic dash man in the hundred-yard dash, with a fifty-yard handicap. He successfully withstood challenges from the Olympians Charles Paddock and Frank Hussey, and he defeated even a champion race horse at a track under those conditions!)

When we heard Bo's grainy baritone ring out over the PA system he was speaking as one athlete to another, ". . . and now, ladies and gentlemen, it is my great pleasure to introduce one of the great athletes of our time—a Ty Cobb in Technicolor!—Jackie Robinson!" And the house came down with roars and screams of approval! The allusion and alliteration may have been serendipitous, but nevertheless it was poetic justice that Bojangles should tie the "Georgia Peach," as Ty Cobb was called, notorious for his outspoken racism as much as for his spectacular playing feats on the ball field, with Jackie Robinson, the first Black ballplayer, who was to surpass the Georgia Peach in most departments.

The other irony connected with the event was Jackie's co-opted appearance before the House Un-American Activities Committee (HUAC) hearings in 1949, where the archconservatives, racists, and antilabor forces all used the forum to whip up the anticommunist hysteria that had become a part of the Cold War. To cover up their racism in their attack on Paul Robeson, they'd found it necessary to get a Black of some significant reputation to testify against him. Not too many Blacks of any stature would allow themselves to be used in this fashion, but Jackie was in the major leagues only two years and my surmise is that the HUAC had access to FBI files on Jackie that indicated his former membership in the YCL and may have used that information to pressure him into doing what they could not get any other self-respecting Black to do. He was probably threatened as others were, as revealed in the published files of the CIA and the FBI with the Cointel Program.[3] So Jackie succumbed to the pressure. This alone was probably not what made Jackie give in, because he had proven his courage. It was more likely the FBI offered him permanent security as a vice president of a thriving corporation, Chock full o' Nuts.

Shortly after Jackie's testimony, according to one of Harlem's long-time journeyman reporters on the political scene, Jackie happened to be sitting in the Red Rooster eating dinner when Paul Robeson walked in. The entire place came to an abrupt dead silence as Robeson strode over to Robinson's table with Jackie looking up in somewhat suspenseful anxiety. When he reached the table, Paul smiled and bent over, saying, in his eloquent bass-baritone voice that had thrilled audiences the world over, "That's all right, Jackie, I'm sure you didn't mean it, really. You only said what you had to say."

The early part of 1940 was highlighted by a major mobilization of the youth movement throughout the country, headed by the American Youth Congress. The Soviet Union had invaded Finland to head off a threatened attack by the Finns. The official Soviet policy explanation was that it was necessary to seal the borders. As loyal Young Communists, our line was to get the United States to keep hands off. Even though it was difficult to explain the sophisticated convolutions of Soviet strategy, we valiantly tried to explain to the public at large the Soviets' every move as an advance for human progress and socialism. In our book the Soviet Union could do no wrong. It was as if the Soviet Union, and, of course, Joseph Stalin had become our God. It was very much like the expression "God moves in mysterious ways, his wonders to perform." When the Soviet Union moved in its mysterious ways its performance was always bound to do something wonderful for the world, according to our unshakable faith. Though I was only two years in the movement, I was already beginning to have the bright-eyed faith of the "true believer."

That burning faith provided us with the energy to gather all the forces of the youth movement in Harlem, and we were able to fill two busloads of Black youth for the peace demonstration at the White House, where it had been arranged for President Roosevelt to address us from the East Wing while we stood on the White House lawn. It was a gray, rainy day and very cold. We were not quite prepared for FDR's scathing attack on the Soviet Union and his seeming support for the fascist—at least, as we thought—Finnish government. I had twisted my ankle during the march down Pennsylvania Avenue and joined in the protests of the president's discourse with doubled resentment at his attacks on the Soviet Union and the pain of standing on a bad ankle.

Our booing of the president was unprecedented and hit the headlines of all the capitalist press in the United States. We considered this a triumph for our public relations. My personal triumph, however, was the significant numbers of Black youth from Harlem who had participated under the auspices of the Harlem Youth Congress, which was really my baby. More than two hundred people had been involved, and I was thinking we could go back to Harlem and utilize the heightened political awareness of the marchers to further strengthen the youth movement there. This, in turn, meant more possible recruiting into the YCL. Because of the spearheading role of the Young Communists, many of the most thoughtful youth in the HYC ultimately would become members of the YCL. When we returned to Harlem, we began to develop more organizations with emphasis on Black working-class youth through the Furriers Club, the Local 65 Club, and the Convoy Club, which was our youth center for seamen. Martha was an active member of that club, a role assigned partly to give her an opportunity to be groomed for political leadership in the YCL without taking the place of a Black youth, which, if she had continued to work in Harlem, would have been the case. It also removed her from a certain resentment and anger expressed by some of the Black women in the Harlem YCL who did not appreciate at all the intermarriages that were appearing with increasing frequency between young Black leaders developing in the communist movement and young white women eager to demonstrate their commitment to the principle of proletarian internationalism.

My position was that our movement reflected the kind of world we wanted to have in the future, and we could not accommodate ourselves to any of the prejudices of chauvinism or nationalism. Certainly, if I was going to face the FBI, the courts, the police, and the bosses themselves on the picket lines of the class struggle, I was not going to decide whom I would marry on the basis of prejudices that reflected a past we were dedicated to overthrowing.

The communist movement had declared itself opposed to political, economic, and social inequality. If its leaders were to act out lives that demonstrated political and economic equality but compromise on one of the major problems of American society, social equality, we might as well go out of business.

Grand Central Terminal, New York City
October 16, 1943

On June 22, 1941, the Soviet Union suffered a surprise attack and invasion by the Nazis. This had precipitated the Soviets' official entry into World War II against Germany. So it was that in August 1943, when I got my greetings from the president of the United States, although there was much going on that I wanted to be a part of, I felt ready to report to Grand Central for a physical on September 25, 1943. Martha had given birth to Wendy in February. We were enjoying the excitement of being parents, but my being a father did not put me in the 3A status of deferral because of hardship to dependents under the Selective Service Act.

The Young Communist League was growing, and my political activities in Harlem were bearing fruit. We had just completed a series of demonstrations and meetings protesting the police attack on the Blacks in the Detroit riot. I have strong suspicions that the FBI and the War Department made the decision to draft me because of the success of my radical activities in Harlem at that time. The War Department exercised a flexible tactic on the handling of communists during World War II. Many party members were drafted and placed into isolated noncombatant units where they were often victimized by their fellow soldiers. Others like Bob Thompson, Johnny Gates, and Irving Goff were placed in leading positions as noncommissioned officers because of their combat experience in Spain in the Abraham Lincoln Battalion of the International Volunteer Brigade. In fact, Irv Goff was assigned to the Office of Strategic Services (OSS) under "Wild Bill" Donovan, who utilized Irv's skills in training OSS cadre in guerrilla warfare. Others were not considered for the draft at all despite their eligibility.[4]

After getting my physical at Grand Central, I was to be inducted on October 16, 1943. The Selective Service Board that I reported to was on Sugar Hill, where many of the Black theater people lived—musicians, artists, dancers, and other show folks—so I wasn't surprised to see Benny Paine from Cab Calloway's Cotton Club Orchestra, Sy Oliver from the Jimmy Lunceford Band, and Russell Procope from the John Kirby Quintet at Grand Central Terminal for their physicals. They all lived on or near St. Nicholas Place or Edgecombe Avenue. Nor was I surprised later when they showed up at Camp Dix (later Fort Dix), New Jersey, where we were stationed before being assigned to permanent outfits. At Dix, Benny, Sy, and Russell were assigned to the Special Services unit, where they played in the Camp Dix Jazz Band, one of the finest musical organizations in the world, making great music for the newly arrived inductees. The band was of the highest caliber with some of the best jazz talent on the East Coast.

Someone suggested to me that I should try to get into Special Services because of my experience at the Cotton Club, with *New Faces* and the Duke Ellington Revue, but I vetoed that idea because I considered it my duty to be where the majority of the troops were. The Special Services units were something of an elite, living in isolation in a protected environment, and I did not want that to be my war record. I thought, in view of the tensions in the armed forces over the segregationist policies of the War Department, that my political talents would be more useful among the rank-and-file troops.

While the war had begun as a struggle against fascism abroad, I saw the nature of that struggle as one that would lead to further democratization of the United States. I foresaw the role that Black veterans could possibly play in the struggle against racism in the United States on their return (those who did return). I wanted a war record not only for patriotic reasons but for the political possibilities in the postwar period. So I did not exploit my show business background. My reward was to be assigned to a Quartermaster Corps Fumigation and Bath Unit at Fort Warren in Cheyenne, Wyoming. By the first week in November, we were already in Fort Warren being fitted with Arctic clothing for testing before being used in the Aleutian Islands. That the United States needed the Aleutians in World War II against a German main enemy meant to me that military intelligence was preparing, even at that time, for eventual war against the Soviet Union. Japan did not represent that much of a military threat despite its attack on Pearl Harbor. As revealed forty years later in the book *The Puzzle Palace*, Pearl Harbor would not have happened if the intercepted Japanese code revealing the Pearl Harbor attack preparations had not been filed in an outgoing ordinary mailbox when it should have been wired to Washington.[5]

Because Fort Warren was a Quartermaster Corps national training center, Quartermaster troops were the main body of inductees, and the discriminatory nature of Army assignments was flagrantly revealed for the eyes of those willing to see. Of the 16,000 troops at Fort Warren, at least 10,000 were Black! There were all kinds of incidents involving race relations, one the most despicable being the occasion when a local white prostitute claimed she was raped by a Black GI and the entire population of Black troops was subjected to a lineup, probably one of the largest in the world. It should have been in the *Guinness World Records*. More than 10,000 Black troops were forced to march in single file across the stage of the Fort Warren Theater and then stand for minutes while the prostitute would shake her head yes or no under questioning from the military and police officers with her. We never heard the outcome, but we felt brutalized as a group; all of us were presumed to be potential rapists, despite the fact that we came in all sizes, shapes, colors, or marital statuses or whether we had prison records. The Napoleonic Code was being applied in the United States; we were all guilty until proved innocent!

Cheyenne itself was a hellhole of segregation. Black troops on weekend pass were confined to a strip of bars lining one block between 16th and 17th streets. We were not supposed to patronize the bars that white troops used. But my outfit had a few northeasterners who were less accepting of these conditions than the guys from the South, so we decided one Saturday night to go into one of the white bars. When we were refused service with the raw statement "We don't serve niggers here!" we all jumped up on the bar, smashing glasses, spilling drinks, and kicking bottles off the bar until the owners had to summon the MPs to get us out. We were furious and really didn't give a damn if we were jailed, guardhoused, or whatever. The MPs, who were Black, understood and escorted us in trucks to the post, where we were allowed to return to our barracks without punishment.

The aspect of life at Fort Warren that rankled us most was the kid-glove treatment given the Nazi POWs. The winter was an exceptionally cold one with temperatures constantly below zero. With the wind chill factor added, it must have seemed 30 degrees below zero on many days. It was so cold that our guard duty was changed from two hours on and four off to a half-hour on and one hour off so that we would not suffer frostbite from lengthy exposure. Even then, it was dangerous. Quite a few of the GIs lost pieces of their lips or faces from carelessly touching the cold metal of their rifles to their skin, where it immediately adhered to the metal because of the cold. The issue with the POWs was work: We were continually being forced to stay outside doing "make-work" projects obviously designed to keep us "out of trouble" through constant activity. The assignments usually consisted of heavy loading and unloading. While we were outside "totin' that barge 'n' liftin' that bale," we could see the Nazi POWs in their nicely heated barracks laughing and grimacing at us. Evidently the rules of war did not allow them to be put to work, but we knew nothing about that and combined with the rigid segregation we faced in Cheyenne, I could understand why so many Black GIs felt that it was a "white man's war." I spent a lot of time in our barrack discussions trying to demonstrate with some difficulty that it was not.

The other source of low morale was the discovery during basic training that our primary mission was to be providing showers and clean clothes for troops in the combat zone for morale purposes. Because Black troops were not allowed combat duty, it meant inevitably that we were to go into the combat areas exposed to shellfire literally to "wash white guys' asses," as some of us colorfully put it, for "their fuckin' morale." What about *our* fuckin' morale?

For some of us, this question was answered when in March we got the new Army regulation stating that "Negro" service troops desiring to transfer to combat service would be allowed to do so at their request. I talked to most of the guys, who generally had no desire whatsoever to go into combat to demonstrate equality, and succeeded in convincing

10 percent of the battalion to volunteer for combat service. Among the volunteers were my best friends: Clyde Clory from Philadelphia; Lewis Dangerfield, also from the City of Brotherly Love; Robert Lindsay from the Bronx; Charlie Johnson from Ohio; Bill Gloster from Brooklyn; Stephen Degraphenreid from Indianapolis; Harry Walters, a former racing car driver; and "Leto" Burke from 116th Street in Harlem. We were quite a bunch and soon discovered that we were going to be assigned to the 92nd Division, the famous Buffalo soldiers, who were in training for combat at Fort Huachuca in Arizona.[6]

The change in regulations that allowed Black troops to volunteer for combat duty was not the result of a sudden acquisition of intelligence on the part of the Army high command or the bureaucrats in the War Department; it was the reluctant reaction to a splendid campaign developed by the NAACP demanding combat service for Black troops as evidence of good faith on the part of the United States that we were fighting for the "Four Freedoms" not only abroad but at home also! The campaign was also a response to the savage verbal attacks on Black troops, a regular and shamefully unchallenged barrage of slander against the competence and the courage of Black troops in long filibustering speeches by Senators James O. Eastland and Theodore G. Bilbo. These southern senators, astute politicians that they were, saw the participation of Black troops on a combat basis as a long-range threat to the deep-rooted racial arrangements that dominated the southern landscape. And above all, they were deathly afraid that Blacks who learned how to handle firearms and heavier equipment overseas might not be as tractable when they returned to the South.

Under these conditions, we embarked on a long trip to an unknown destination. Our troop train took its long, meandering journey that found us stopping off at Chicago, Kansas City, and St. Louis and losing manpower at each stop as GIs had a change of heart and decided to vote against participation in the war effort by going home. The worst stop for us, particularly the northern fellows, was a layover for eight hours in Dalhart, Texas, a "cracker" town if there ever was one. The mean-looking cowboys parked alongside the railroad tracks gave out with their rebel yells as soon as they realized that our train carried more "niggers" than they had ever seen at one time in their lives. We, aboard the train, did not like the atmosphere and, knowing we were headed overseas for combat service, were quite ready to go to war with this bunch of redneck yahoos in a minute. Our officers, all white, gave an order that we could not get off the train even though the layover was eight hours. They knew that all the materials for a major protest riot were gathered there in Dalhart.

It took another day for us to arrive at Fort Huachuca, but when we did we knew we were in different country. The field artillery was the branch of the service to which we'd been assigned from Fort Warren. Handling rifles, machine guns, bazookas, grenade launchers, and, in our battalion, the 105mm howitzers felt very different from handling the equipment, showers, and replacement clothing in the fumigation and bath units. In Fort Warren we felt like chambermaids; in Fort Huachuca we felt like warriors.

The training was hard; we arrived in June and had gotten word through the grapevine that we would be headed overseas in two or three months. At Fort Warren, our training had been for the Arctic in subzero weather—what a contrast with Huachuca. We got desert training in temperatures that averaged 110 degrees in the shade. I doubt that any other GIs faced such extremes within such a short period. But there were compensations for the rigors of the training. The old post where the permanent party was stationed had a great Special Services band that had as its leader Earl Hubbard, one of the great sidemen from the Lionel Hampton Band. Their version of "Flying Home" had us all rocking with a sound and beat that matched anything that Hamp had come up with. Larry Whisonant, the great baritone who had a crush on my sister Winnie, greeted me like a long-lost friend, and we set up a weekend bridge game with Maceo, of the Four Step Brothers, that gave us plenty of time to reminisce about the relatively carefree days of show business in Harlem. Maceo knew my other sister, Shirley, well, having met her while she was married to Prince Spencer also of the Four Step Brothers. So, way down in Arizona, we had an outpost of Harlem that helped me feel very much at home.

Weekend passes were distributed freely, so we got many an opportunity to visit Naco and Agua Prieto, two fast-and-loose border towns that seemed to be designed to supply the entire division with Mexican prostitutes. I remember my first visit to a whorehouse in Agua Prieto. It was an adobe villa with walls all around it, but inside was an open courtyard with a huge cottonwood tree in the center providing shade while a *mariachi* band played appropriate music to the swirl of continuous activity as one Buffalo soldier after another entered one or another of the bedrooms that lined the interior side of the villa facing the courtyard. Despite the beauty of most of the girls, I had taken my wedding vows seriously and simply went along with the guys to drink tequila and listen to the music. They respected me and considered that it was probably part of my overall radicalism because I had talked plenty of Marxism with most of them back in the barracks. Another feature of the visit to Naco was the bullfights, which I have never forgotten. For me, it was a symbolic drama reenacting the slaying of the father by his son, the replacement of the old with the new—the bull being the father, the matador the son.

For me, the most exciting part of Huachuca was the parades when the military bands would take off. There was just nothing to equal that rush of adrenalin when the booming sound of the bass drums and the rat-a-tat-tat of the trap drums set up the rhythm for our marching. As we strode off, a special kind of sound of leather heels hitting the turf simultaneously evolved into a highly syncopated pulse that soon evoked the inspiring rhythms of the cadence count: "Hut doo three foah! Hut doo three foah!" and then the bluesy cry in cadence: "Jody is home while you left! Jody is home while you left!" And the left feet of 200 men in each company would hit the turf with a special accent that made a music all its own. There was something elemental and tribal about it that captured the men, or at least it appeared that way to my ever-active imagination.

But things were not always poetic, especially the relations between the enlisted men and the officers—that is, the 95 percent who were white and mostly southerners because the cracker-dominated War Department felt that southern whites knew best how to handle Blacks. Tensions arose to such a point that when the news began to circulate that we were soon going overseas, various bizarre events began to take place that were expressions of the resentment and rage that had accumulated in the division that had long since come to be known by us as "General Almond's plantation." Having worked at the Cotton Club under gangster rule and control when it was known as "Herman Stark's plantation," I was not slow in connecting the character of white racism and control of Blacks by whites as a pervasive feature of our society, whether it was under the illegitimate reign of the white mobsters who controlled Harlem's nightlife or the legal authority of the armed forces, the iron fist of white authority in the United States.

The first of these bizarre events was when one entire infantry company discovered that bedwetting was considered evidence of psychoneurosis. The entire outfit intentionally peed in their beds every night for one entire week. The accumulated ammoniac odor of this particular barrack began to befoul the entire surrounding compound. Ultimately, most of the men in the outfit were discharged on Section 8s, the standard section of Army regulations for psychoneurotic discharges. The second, even more demonstrative, action took place when the members of the tank destroyer command, informed that they were leaving for overseas within the week, burned two complete Army barracks down to the ground. "Burn, baby, burn" was not a slogan initiated in the '60s; it had already been a slogan of action during World War II.

Mount Folgorito, Northern Italy
April 6, 1945

I was with the liaison section of the 599th Field Artillery Battalion of the 92nd Infantry Division of the U.S. Army Ground Forces. I was assigned to this mission by the captain of my outfit, who I strongly believe was a member of the FBI assigned to my outfit to keep me under political surveillance. I had volunteered for Officer Candidate School in response to an order that General Mark Clark of the Fifth Army had issued. Future Supreme Court justice Thurgood Marshall had visited the front and examined the conditions of segregation of the Black troops, and Clark's order was a response to a nationwide campaign that the NAACP had organized in the United States against segregation on the battlefield. Because the 92nd Division, of which my artillery battalion was a part, was staffed almost 90 percent by southern white officers, they hastily improvised an Officer Candidate School in response to that campaign. The Clark order specified that any enlisted man who had an IQ of more than 105 could volunteer for Officer Candidate School. The school would be organized close to the battlefront. They planned a six-week OCS because they figured that men who are in combat would already be battlewise and wouldn't need the same amount of training that one had to have to be an officer in peacetime. I volunteered. I was a Scout Corporal at the time, with an IQ way over 105. So, I just knew I had it made. I wanted to become an officer, because being an officer in the Army gave you a tremendous amount of power, and, being political, I could see how I could use that power. I had strong motives for becoming an officer, and the other officers probably knew it, because one week after I volunteered for the OCS they shipped in Captain Jack Hayes to replace Captain Whitlock. Whitlock was from a wealthy Texas family and his full name was Elvy Whitlock. He sort of liked me, was battle shy, and would allow me to go up and man his observation post and conduct firing. In fact, I did it so well, I would come back having completed his mission, and the guys in the battery would salute me and say, "Hi, Captain Johnson."

Captain Whitlock was transferred out and Captain Hayes came in. He was a Special Services, hardboiled, macho type and he promoted me to sergeant a week after I volunteered for OCS, to my surprise. I was supposed to leave for the OCS two weeks later. Well, within that week, my outfit was sent up to the front on a behind-the-lines mission with an Italian partisan unit and the 100th Infantry Battalion of the 442nd Nisei Regiment. They were the most-wounded and most-decorated outfit in the entire U.S. Army. The outfit was composed of Nisei—that is, second-generation Japanese who had been born in the United States. They volunteered to form this unit in order to counter the charge that all Japanese were subversive. They had very high moral and political convictions, and they were most courageous. So, despite the hazards involved, I was really proud to have been selected—Jack Hayes likely thought he was doing me in and believed, probably with 90 percent validity, that I wouldn't come back. I went on this mission in coordination with the Italian partisans. They were under the leadership of an Italian communist—at least half of the partisans were communist—so I told them that I was a member of the Communist Party in the States. We became brothers. We also called the Nisei troops brothers. I discovered that some of them were also "comrades," and were all tough cookies. We were all antifascist to the core.

I really didn't care about the risk involved. I had made my commitment when I volunteered for combat. So off we went, and it took all day, and then the rest of that night, before we penetrated the German lines through some secret passages that the Italians knew. It was in the Carrara marble area, and many of the partisans had been born in that area. They knew every nook and cranny in the mountainsides from going up and down for years. So we got through the German lines. Our mission was to open up a diversionary attack about one hour before the Fifth Army made the assault on the Kesselring line, which had been a highly fortified German position for months. The lines had never been broken through. There were political reasons why: Winston Churchill had siphoned off the British 8th Army and transported them to Greece to put down the Revolutionary Greek movement, which had driven out the Greek fascists and was about to set up a democratic republic in Greece. That stratagem took the 8th Army away from fighting the Nazis, thereby weakening the Italian front to crush the democratic movement in Greece. Of course, that put all the weight on the U.S. 5th Army on the Italian front. The final offensive was launched. We opened up our diversionary attack behind the lines, but when the Germans found that we were behind them, they turned their machine guns and mortars on us and just plastered us. During my own leadership of the liaison section our job was, if a line got hit, thereby breaking communication with the artillery, to go out and find the breaks in the lines and get them together again to reestablish contact, even under heavy fire, and I hope you don't know, but can imagine, lines getting hit by shells.

A few days before we had gone on this mission, some lines had gotten knocked out by artillery fire and some of the men were afraid to go out. It was an exposed position with shells exploding all around, so I went myself and looked for lines back to my battery. The field was just strewn with wires all over the place; there were so many contact lines from so many different outfits. I had to hunt and I finally found two pieces that looked like my wire, hooked them together, and then tapped into it—I had my own telephone that I could hook into a line to find out if it was the line to my battery, and it was. The first thing I heard was a conversation going on and the corporal in my section who was responsible to me was reporting on my activities to the captain back at the artillery battery. He was an informer who had been assigned to the outfit. I knew it was bad news and I told the other guys in the section, "Look, I don't want that son-of-a-bitch anywhere near me. I don't want to discuss anything with him and I hope you will understand what's going on. I think he's a stool pigeon!" The guys went along with it. He had been reporting on everything I said or did and was the captain's ass-licker. So we isolated him.

Now, we're up on this mountainside, and we're running, and when the Germans discovered we were there, they started lobbing these mortar shells over, and the first thing I know, about ten yards away, BOOM!! A mortar shell falls about ten yards to the left of us, and then another one ten yards to the right of us. Now, as an artillery man, I know that when you get that sequence, you're in what we call a bracket. With ten yards to the right and ten yards to the left, I knew, the third shell was going to hit right down the middle. That's the way you locate a position. You fire your first round and if it goes to the left, you just move your weapon a certain distance and fire to the right, and then you divide it in half—BOOM!!—you're right on target. I knew that within seconds, that third shell was going to drop right down on us. At that moment I hollered to Justice (the stool pigeon), who was standing a few yards away from me in that direction. He was scared shitless and had dropped his helmet. I yelled to him: "Justice, get your helmet on." He went to reach over for his helmet and just as he reached over, the third shell came down behind me; it exploded and got me. I just felt as if I had been electrocuted. The shell burst into many fragments, but as I was going down, I looked and saw one piece hit Justice right in the temple and I saw his eyes glaze. He died right there in front of me. I had been hit just after that, but fortunately, I had a pack radio on my back and it absorbed all of the fragments and kept them from any vital organs. I got it in my legs. You can actually see the outlines on my body of the area that was protected by the pack radio. No vital organs hit. I was so lucky; a piece went by me and took a stool pigeon. So the moral of that story is: Stool pigeons may not survive!

That's my April 6, 1945, story. Of course, I thought I was going to die and I looked around. A little piece had hit my ear, not my neck, because the helmet comes way down. As I was lying there, I looked down at my leg and saw my hamstring hanging out of my thigh like spaghetti; a pool of blood was running out. I felt weaker and weaker, faster and faster, and I looked and there was a medic bending over a white captain with a little scratch on his stomach. So I shouted, "Goddammit, are we going to have discrimination up here on the front lines? Come over here and take care of me, I'm dying, Goddammit!" I said, "Take care of that captain later." And the medic listened to me. He came over and started piecing me together. He managed to stop the blood flow and put me on a litter to take me down off the mountainside. That took eight hours. That was 8:30 in the morning. It was 4:30 in the afternoon when they got me down to the valley. By that time the German lines had been evaporated—blown apart—so that we had access to the road taking me back to the field hospital. The Nazis plastered the medics with small arms and machine gun fire that entire eight hours, and the medics don't carry weapons. They were dropping me on the ground every time they were exposed to the rifle and machine gun fire. My butt was damn sore from the combination of shell fragment wounds and hitting the rocks for eight hours. It felt like I must have hit the ground a thousand times. I was just one bloody, muddy mess.

Do you know, it was not until twenty-five years later, at Jimmy Wright's house at a birthday party, that I got up and danced? There was a friend of Jimmy's, a Dr. Jack Quander, a Black physician from Harlem, who watched me dance, and tears came to his eyes and he said, "Stretch, do you know the last time I saw you, you were just one hulk of mud and blood, and you were brought into my combat hospital surgical tent to be operated on. I knew you were a Cotton Club dancer and I sewed you up thinking you would never be able to dance. And I didn't recognize you until we wiped all of the mud and blood off you, and I really went to work when I discovered it." Someone who knew me was waiting there and worked on me, and that's how I got pieced together.

Now that Black troops had been admitted to combat duty, while we were going through that hell in Italy Senators Eastland and Bilbo from Mississippi kept up a running fire of criticism of Black troops. The 92nd Division was specifically charged with cowardice, desertion, and incompetence after the debacle at the Cinquale Canal just below La Spezia. I had seen the heroic conduct of Black troops on the front line, especially the engineers who had the responsibility of going out into the field to defuse mines after locating them along the path of troop movement—an especially hazardous task with the slightest wrong move immediately penalized by a violent explosion that might take off an arm, hand, leg, or head. So I wrote an angry letter to the *People's Voice* explaining what lies about Black troops were being circulated against the interests of the American people in the very halls of Congress from which leadership was supposed to come. The *People's Voice* was a radical newspaper promoted by the coalition formed around Adam Clayton Powell. He was the main publisher with the left—more accurately, the Communist Party—being represented through the participation of Dr. Doxey Wilkerson as one of the editors.

Despite the hazards of front-lines service, there were compensating activities in operation. When back at the bivouac area near Pisa, I often got an opportunity to sightsee in Pisa. The Leaning Tower and the striking architecture of the Duomo in its black-and-white colors became familiar sights to me and impressed on me the intellect and love of beauty that the people of the fifteenth century must have had. The *pièce de résistance* was the leave we had permitting us to visit Florence. The entire city was a living museum. The Michelangelo statue of David had been placed back in its historic spot near the Pitti Palace, the Ponte Vecchio had not been destroyed despite the heavy fighting near it, and for me the most thrilling of all the many spectacles there was the lectern at which Dante Alighieri had defied the nobles of Florence and read from his works. The greatest political coincidence was the fact that the Communist Party had requisitioned the building behind the lectern as its headquarters. As I stood outside, a young Italian came up to me, introduced himself as Hettore Rico, and said that he was impressed with my very evident curiosity about the lectern and the building, not typical of the general run of American soldiers, who normally spent most of their time looking for the usual exchange of *signorine* companionship in exchange for *cigaretti* when on pass. He took me into the building, which was a beehive of activity—serious-faced young women, battle-hardened partisans, and elderly scholar types passing in and out constantly—explaining that the party had had first choice on a location for its headquarters because it was in charge of the first partisan unit to enter Florence after the Nazis had been driven out and naturally had sought the best building right in the center.

Ettore invited me to his home where, it turned out, he earned his living making custom-fitted shoes. With a sly smile he explained his choice was to make ladies' shoes because he liked women and his craft gave him an opportunity to meet the most beautiful women in Florence. This is saying a lot because in my experience the most beautiful women in all of Italy were to be found in Florence and Lucca. Because Italian is the language of love, it's no wonder that the most beautiful Italian of all is the Tuscan dialect, for in Tuscany, the province that contains Siena, Lucca, and Florence, the most beautiful women of Italy are to be found.

Another friendship that was very important to my morale was that of the Possano family in Pietrasanta, the first town near which the 92nd Division was bivouacked. The father was a stonecutter with a fifteen-year-old daughter and a son about twelve. When they found that I lived in Harlem not too far from the Bronx, the father asked me if I would ask my wife to get in touch with his sister who lived in the Bronx. Martha delivered a letter for him because the Italian postal system was not yet in gear, and in short time Martha forwarded a letter from his sister that I delivered to his utter delight. It was close to Christmas and he invited me to come to their house for dinner. We had a small batch of tiny fish. It could not have been more than a pound for the five of us, his family of four and me. We also shared a loaf of chestnut flour bread. The Germans had taken all the wheat out of Italy as they fled before the advancing Allied troops. There was no butter, but there was some good red wine. We said a prayer over the candle-lit meal, then talked about imperialism, racism in the United States, the oppression of the Nazis during the occupation, and what life in Italy would be like when the war was over.

Francesca, the fifteen-year-old daughter, said she wanted to come to the United States when the war was over. The boy, Rossa, called such because of his shock of red hair, sang a fascist song for the youth, "La Giovanezzi," to which he and the other sons and daughters of radical families had put some revolutionary lyrics that ridiculed the fascists. It was a beautiful night despite the meager fare, one of the best Christmases I've ever had, especially in a spiritual sense.

One of the more unpleasant episodes came in Lucca when white officers spread a rumor among the Luccan beauties that all the Black troops were diseased. Their purpose was to monopolize the plentiful supply of gorgeous females. What they didn't understand was that the Italians loved the Black troops, in the main, because the 92d Divison had liberated Lucca from the Nazis. They thought most Americans were black or brown and that the white Americans were Nazis. When they were able to discern the difference between Nazis and white Americans, they said the whites were more like the Nazis in their attitudes and the Blacks were more like the Italians. One *paisano* explained to me that "the whites think they're up here and we're down there [gesturing with his hands]. The Blacks see the Italians as equals."

The one other episode that left an undying impression on me was upon our arrival in Pisa. The Nazis had just cleared out, leaving much of their propaganda still pasted up. On one corner, a huge poster had been put up depicting a Black caricatured with a gorilla face in the U.S. Army uniform with the 92nd Division insignia. There was no mistake and this gorilla-faced Black soldier was raping a blond Italian women. As we entered Pisa, the town was still under shell fire intermittently, so we did not take the time to tear down the posters. It's no wonder the Italians had difficulty distinguishing between the racism of the white American officers and the Nazis.

On the positive side, with regard to white troops, one of my favorite people was a trooper from the 10th Mountain Division who had been wounded on the same day as I had been and was hospitalized in Naples with me many hundreds of miles south of the casualty. He had had half his scalp blown off by mortar fire while fighting alongside us in the 10th Mountain Division. He let me know that he appreciated the valor of the Buffalo soldiers in the 92nd Division.

8
Back Home

504 West 143rd Street, Harlem, New York
January 8, 1946

My first contact with the party, on my release from the Army, was through Claudia Jones. Claudia had moved into the apartment on the sixth floor in the same building on 143d Street that Martha had found to share with Carmen Alves while Bert Alves and I were doing our patriotic duty in the military service.[1] Claudia, who had always been a hero worshipper of Earl Browder's, filled me in on the damage that his policies had done to the party even to the point of its dissolution and the setting up of the Communist Political Association. She also gave me a blow-by-blow description of the infighting that had taken place while I was recuperating at Rhoads General Hospital in Utica, New York. I used to commute in from Rhoads as soon as I was ambulatory, but my Army status—I had not yet been released—made it precarious to attend the various meetings that were furiously taking place. So all my information was filtered first through Claudia and then through Lou Burnham, or through my chief guru, Henry Winston. Because my closest associates were all African American, my view of the Browder policies was highly influenced by their interpretation of what had gone on.[2]

As a Marxist, I was very interested in the overall political questions that were being debated: that monopoly capitalism could play, as a consequence of the war alliance between the United States, Great Britain, and the Soviet Union, a constructive and positive role in the postwar world. The corollary to that perspective was the possible long-range muting of the class struggle and the achievement of collaboration between the capitalist and the working class in the joint resolution of the major economic and political problems that would ensue following the end of the war. Within this perspective, there was no longer any need for a vanguard party of a Leninist type.

A broader and looser formation was developed, and the Communist Political Association was born out of this new orientation. I had learned long before that no policy was meaningful unless it was implemented organizationally, and I could well understand that the drastic change developed by Browder had to be reflected in equally drastic organizational measures. However, in the 92nd Division in Italy, my experience of the fights against racist white officers who spread vilifying stories about Black troops among the local Italian population, of the effort to get me killed in a so-called "diversionary offensive," and, on returning back home, of the obvious signs of the pervasive white racism that American life was locked into led me to conclude that there would be no quick peace on the civil rights front. Even if the class struggle eased up, I foresaw no immediate progress in terms of the national struggle, or the struggle of the African American population for full and first-class citizenship. When Claudia, Louis, and Winston related to me stories of the way in which the party's struggle for African American rights had been blunted and in many districts the struggle for civil rights had been completely eliminated, I did not need excessive argumentation to accept their way of evaluating the negative impact of Browderism on the movement.

I had had one experience with what could later be called "Browderism" before I left for the Army. It had to do with a leaflet I wrote for the Harlem YCL on the Alexandria riots in which Black troops exploded in protest against the rigid segregation that was typical of Army installations both "Down South" as well as "Up South." The leaflet had the headline "Jim Crow in the Army Must Go!" In the text I had developed the relationship between the issue of Jim Crowism and the winning of the war. I was called in by the section organizer of the Harlem party organization, who was my dear and good friend Abner W. Berry. Berry told me, "That's a bad leaflet!" I said, "Why?" He replied, "Well, the headline with its emphasis on 'Jim Crow' might be regarded as defeatist and might demoralize youth in the community." I replied, "It seems to me that any demoralization that arises in this community is a result of the Jim Crow in the Army and in the community, not from anything our leaflet says." We, being a fast-moving group, had already distributed 5,000 copies of the leaflet in the street, calling on youth to demonstrate their protests against the mass courts-martial that were being directed against the Black troops who took seriously the war aims of fighting fascism all over the world. So, the discussion was academic, but in hindsight I saw it as an expression of creeping Browderism.

The more flagrant case of Browderism involved the party's official position against the "Double V" campaign initiated by the *Pittsburgh Courier,* one of the country's leading Afro-American newspapers. The "Double V" campaign was predicated on the assumption that the logic of the struggle against Hitlerism and fascism abroad would be meaningful for Black Americans only if it was accompanied by an effective struggle against Hitlerism in the United States that included segregation and discrimination. The party under Browder's leadership took the position that the "Double V" campaign was undermining support of the war effort by elevating domestic policy questions to the same importance as international questions. Just as Browder called on labor to give up its right to strike in the interests of unity to win the war, he called on Blacks to give up their struggle for civil rights as disruptive to the war effort. I was among the group of Black communists who did everything possible to oppose that policy. All my experiences in the Army confirmed the validity of fighting segregation and racism overseas and at home. It was because of the militant protests against discrimination toward Black troops led by the *Pittsburgh Courier,* the NAACP, and other African American organizations that the armed forces were compelled to form combat regiments such as the 92nd Infantry Division as well as mixed regiments in Europe, and open up OCS schools overseas to increase the proportion of Black officers in the combat outfits.

Winston-Salem, North Carolina
November 2, 1947

The United Negro and Allied Veterans of America (UNAVA) terminal leave campaign was based on a series of discussions between me and Walter Garland, as well as with other members of the leadership, such as George Murphy, Burt Jackson, and the late Allan Morrison. We were concerned that the fledgling organization would get off to a good start at its opening convention. We had a host of issues that Black veterans were agitated about: police brutality, jobs, voting rights, housing, dishonorable discharges, and education. Isaac Woodward had been blinded in North Carolina; the Ferguson brothers had been killed by the racist cop Joseph Romeika in Freeport, Long Island; Black families were barred from admission to the Metropolitan Life Insurance project for middle-income families in the Stuyvesant Town apartment complex in Manhattan; the Klan was active among the auto workers in Detroit; and southern veterans were returning to a plantation economy that was as relentlessly oppressive against Blacks as before the war.

The idea that democracy in America was to be an outcome of the victory over Hitler and his minions had no realization in the South. If anything, the plantation lords were tightening up their control over the returning veterans. One of the forms of their attack on the returning veterans was their denial of access to the terminal leave pay benefits due the returnees. Our estimate was that more than $300 million was being denied veterans in the South through the control of the distribution of application forms by the plantation owners.

Whatever the ideology of American Marxists in the Communist Party or whatever their dedication to the Soviet Union, the way we communists worked in UNAVA illustrated our practical activity as a contribution to the American scene. We had a number of discussions with the party leadership assigned to meet with us: Gene Dennis, Jim Jackson, and Henry Winston. We finally decided that we would try to convince the noncommunist forces at the convention that we should attempt to develop a nationwide campaign on the terminal leave pay issue. I was selected to make the main report to the convention on the terminal leave pay issue, and after an enthusiastic discussion, it was adopted as the major activity of UNAVA on a national scale.

UNAVA was an embryonic and relatively weak organization. We knew that if we were to have any impact on a national scale we would have to find ways to bring the energies and influence of other organizations to bear. George Murphy, a member of one of the oldest Black bourgeois families and owner of the chain of Afro-American newspapers centered in Baltimore, was the prime mover in connecting us with two of the most influential leaders of the civil rights movement. J. Finley Wilson, Grand Exalted Ruler of the Elks, was the first. Wilson was affectionately called "The Grand" by fraternal order people and was an imaginative organizer and inimitable orator of the old Baptist preacher school. At our first meeting with him, he had been on an extensive speechmaking tour for the Elks, and we were surprised when his wife suggested that we go up to his bedroom for the meeting. When we got upstairs, there was Finley in bed ready to talk with us. He explained:

My motto for getting a lot done is:
Don't run when you can walk,
Don't walk when you can stand,
Don't stand when you can sit,
and, for God's sake, don't sit when you can lay down.
You'd be surprised how much I get done using that technique.

We all had a good laugh at that one and then in relaxed fashion, with J. Finley participating from his bed, got down to the business of what kind of support the Elks could give us. We had two meetings with the second key person in our strategic plan, Reverend Max Yergan, a top leader of the National Baptist Convention. The second meeting was the most interesting, held as it was during the sessions of the annual convention where we got the opportunity to hear Baptist preachers talking in a session on the fascinating topic of how to preach. Reverend Jernagin got us the support of the convention, which adopted the terminal leave campaign as one of their major projects for the year. The national organization of the Elks also adopted our campaign as theirs. This represented a formidable array of organizational and political clout on our side with more than 800,000 Elks and 2.5 million Baptists as supporters.

This support was decisive because the forces lined up against terminal leave pay for Black veterans were not only powerful but were entrenched and in control of the precise areas where the majority of Black veterans lived. More than 1 million Black veterans were returning to the United States entitled to terminal leave pay. Their anticipated checks would total from $100.00 to the $300.00 maximum, and 75 percent were returning to southern towns where the antebellum mores and customs were still firmly in place, "uncontaminated" by the victory over Hitler and his totalitarian state. The racist power structure confronted more than 800,000 of the returning Black veterans under conditions very much like the Nazi control of rural areas in Germany and Italy. More than forty Black veterans who had "mistakenly" spoken up for their rights as veterans had been lynched in the South in the two-year period following V-E Day. Hands had been chopped off, eyes gouged out, and genitals burned off. This sadistic racism was meant to generate fear among the Black veterans who were returning and to force them into returning to their prewar status.

Such were the general conditions facing the movement. We convinced the party leadership that extraordinary measures would be required if the campaign were to succeed against such opposition. At the national level of party leadership, Gene Dennis, James Jackson, and Henry Winston were made responsible for mobilizing the party on a national basis. The party mobilization included a necessary orientation to establish the theoretical importance of the terminal leave campaign. I was assigned to write an article entitled "The Negro Veteran Fights for Freedom," establishing the theory behind this, for the May 1947 issue of *Political Affairs*, the party's organ. Any time an article appeared in *Political Affairs*, the rank-and-file party members knew that the subject was important. Such an article usually received enthusiastic response throughout the party organization as the voice of the national leadership. Abner W. Berry, who had also become a veteran, had changed his function from Harlem party organizer to reporter for the *Daily Worker*. He was assigned to take a trip through three of the key Black Belt counties in Alabama: Lowndes, Dallas, and Wilcox. In each of these counties, the plantation conditions were the worst. Berry wrote a series of articles after infiltrating plantations in disguise to get direct information from the veterans themselves. His articles revealed that the majority of the veterans were not getting their terminal pay.

The reason was a very simple one. In order to get terminal leave pay, the veteran had to fill out an application form. However, getting a terminal leave pay application form was not a simple matter. The forms had to be picked up at the local post office, which, in these three counties, was at the county seat. The post office was open only on weekdays from 8:00 A.M. to 5:00 P.M. and a half-day on Saturdays. The catch was that in those counties visited by Berry, Blacks could not go to the county seat without a pass or permission from their employer, which in 99 percent of the cases was the plantation boss. A Black caught in town without his pass could well be arrested for vagrancy. Because the number of veterans who could get the pass was quite small, only a handful of veterans were getting their terminal leave pay. Often after the veterans received their checks, the plantation owners would charge them exorbitant fees to cash them. The white plantation bosses would charge from 50 percent to 75 percent of the value of the check to cash it, so that the veteran would get $150.00 to $175.00 in return for a terminal leave pay check of $300.00. The operational factor in this situation was the economics of the plantation. The yearly average income for a plantation worker or sharecropper was $200.00 to $300.00. This was also the average in Dallas, Wilcox, and Lowndes counties, the three Black Belt counties visited by Berry. Of course this meant that a Black veteran receiving his full terminal leave pay check was getting the equivalent of a year's pay in one shot. This also meant having enough startup money to leave the plantation to head north to industry or whatever. Because there was a labor shortage on the plantations their owners did not want potential employees and major sources of profit obtaining this kind of financial independence, so every obstacle possible was put in the way of the Black veterans.

Given these conditions, we mapped out a strategy to bypass the well-controlled post offices in the Black Belt counties by securing an agreement with the War Department that granted UNAVA the right as a veterans organization to distribute the terminal leave pay application forms nationally, even though we had not yet obtained accreditation. The next step was to get the support of the Baptist church organization and the Elks to agree to use the local organizations for distribution, which would give us direct access to areas where an organization like UNAVA would be suspect as foreign and "new." We had a big fanfare and send-off from our New York headquarters to which the 1 million terminal leave pay blanks had been delivered quite dramatically by War Department vehicles. I was quite proud to have a picture taken alongside Lena Horne, who had starred in the film *Stormy Weather*. Lena was very gracious in taking time off from her busy schedule as a gesture to the Black veterans who had made her their number one pin-up during World War II.

The Black press gave us great publicity, and in a two-month organizing blitz through the South we had distributed the 1 million terminal leave pay applications. Our estimate was that close to $30 million reached the veterans, a sum that they would not have obtained without our efforts. One phase of our mobilization is a lesson in how easy it is when there is the right combination of issue, interest, and organization. We had set up a team for the South with George Murphy responsible for Washington, D.C., and the Baltimore area; Walter Garland was to take Mississippi and Louisiana; and I was responsible for North Carolina. Berry was named for Alabama because of his knowledge of the Black Belt. I looked forward to the assignment because I was very interested not only in organizing potentials for UNAVA. Winston-Salem was in the middle of a tobacco strike of the workers at RJR (the nickname of the Reynolds Corporation plants in Winston-Salem). RJR was the citadel of non-union tobacco, and the Food and Tobacco Workers Union had decided to crack it. A formidable Black woman had risen to leadership in the union; her name was Moranda Smith. She was a giant in size, beauty, courage, and inspiration. She was also a member of the party with longstanding ties in the RJR plant. For years the Ku Klux Klan had had enormous influence among the white workers cultivating an antilabor attitude that was as virulent as their anti-Black prejudice. A key obstacle to the winning of the tobacco workers' strike was the ability of the union organizers to overcome these anti-union and anti-Black attitudes among the white workers in order to get their full participation in the strike. The Blacks under Moranda's leadership were ready to go out. If the white workers didn't, the strike could be broken. We sat up many long nights talking over arguments, tactics, and contacts among the white workers in the party whose mission was the difficult one of getting white participation in the strike. Finally we broke through, and on the first day of the union picket line, probably the first one in Winston-Salem, there were shouts of joy and tears in the eyes of some of us to see hundreds of white workers come out at the call of the union pickets along the high shed-like walls of RJR. Another aspect of the Winston-Salem situation was that for the first time in the South since Reconstruction, a Black candidate was running for mayor, Reverend Kenneth Williams. He was a veteran and had agreed to help in the organization of UNAVA in Winston-Salem despite the rigors and demands of the election campaign. The strike came to a successful conclusion with Black and white workers, after many years of segregation at RJR, where the tobacco bosses had used the racial divisions to exploit both groups, coming together in one union with meetings for the first time with Black and white workers in the same meeting hall.

The spirit of victory and the momentum of the organizing drive carried over into the election campaign, and Reverend Kenneth Williams was elected to the mayoralty, the first Black to become mayor in a southern town since Reconstruction. The atmosphere of victory, a sense of the power of united Black and white workers, and an air of confidence greeted me in the party organization when I discussed the possibilities of organizing chapters of UNAVA in North Carolina. I was assigned two Black tobacco workers who were to take me into the Piedmont area to look for veterans who might be interested in joining UNAVA but, more important, who would be interested in organizing a chapter of UNAVA in their hometown or in a group of towns. They took me to Kinston, Greenville, and Wilcox, but we were not able to arrange even one meeting. Somewhat depressed, I headed back to Winston-Salem to plan the rest of my itinerary, which had been left to the local party organization to arrange. I did have one ace in the hole that I had not discussed with the party leaders, Junius ("Junie") Scales and Bernie Friedlander, who had done a really bang-up job on the tobacco strike and the city elections in Winston-Salem. Besides those big victories, however, the organization of UNAVA did not seem to strike a chord with them.

The party generally had been concentrating on the predominantly white veterans' organization headed up by the Social Democrat Daniel James, who was later to acquire fame as the white husband of Ruth Ellington, the sister of Duke Ellington. James was an arch and sophisticated red-baiter, and the party's line on the American Veterans Committee was to work within it, to develop influence within the local chapters, and to win leadership of the chapters and through the chapters to influence the state organizations to oppose the James policies. This approach was quite effective in many states, with the result that James was not in complete control. North Carolina was one of the states where an anti-James leadership had the possibility of being elected, and most of the party's energies on the veterans' front were absorbed in this direction. I understood this, but I did not agree with the weakness of the effort to build UNAVA. They seemed to have what I called an all-the-eggs-in-one-basket approach, when I knew the assignment of one or two forces to work on the UNAVA effort would have yielded immediate results.

To demonstrate my theory I pulled out my ace in the hole, the names of some friends and cousins of Roscoe and Florence Smith and Talmadge and Alline Moore, all of whom were from the largest furniture manufacturing center in the South: High Point, North Carolina. Roscoe and Florence were brother and sister. Talmadge and Alline were husband and wife. In fact, I had been the best man at their wedding. We loved one another, we'd had had many a great party at the YCL headquarters in Harlem or at our houses in a kind of continuous round robin of good times that was part of our YCL attraction in Harlem, and I just knew that the names they gave me were going to be live ones for organizing.

I took off for High Point in the morning, arriving there at about two in the afternoon. On the bus I met a veteran from High Point and got involved in a lengthy discussion of the purpose of my trip. He was so enthusiastic about the idea of having an organization of veterans that I asked him if he could arrange to get some veterans together to have a "rap session" on issues, such as organizing and setting up a chapter of UNAVA in High Point. I gave him the addresses of the Moores and the Smiths with the agreement that he would meet there if the Moores' friends said it was OK; if not, he should be prepared to come up with an alternative. He was to bring his friends to the address at 6:00 P.M. because I had to catch a bus going to Charleston, South Carolina, at 10:00 P.M. It was 5:00 P.M., so we had an hour to sweat out and define what the organizing possibilities for High Point were.

Well, by the time I arrived at the appointed rendezvous, there were five vets there, already eager to hear what the veterans' organizer from New York had to say. They were friends of Talmadge Moore and Roscoe Smith. By 6:00 P.M., the room was full of vets, at least sixteen. I had brought charts, pamphlets, and leaflets detailing some of the UNAVA activities so that the vets could see actual evidence of what we were doing. I spoke for about forty minutes on the conditions affecting Black veterans throughout the country, some of the victories we had won on the discrimination front, and particularly about the victory we had won with the War Department on the terminal leave pay forms. Most of them did not know anything about terminal leave pay. I had some application forms in my organizing kit and helped some of them fill out the applications on the spot. This action did more to register the importance of organization with them than anything else I said or did. Action, not words, got UNAVA over.

When I answered most of their questions satisfactorily, one of the veterans asked how they could set up an organization like UNAVA in High Point. I answered that they could organize a chapter of UNAVA that night, subject to approval by the national office, and that I was a national officer and could probably convince the national office on the basis of my first-hand experience with them that the chapter should get immediate approval. All they had to do was to sign up a minimum of ten members and pay the necessary membership dues, and a chapter could be chartered. Fifteen joined, and a new chapter of UNAVA was born, the first in North Carolina.

When I got back and told Roscoe and Talmadge about the success of their contacts in helping organize the first chapter of UNAVA in North Carolina, they grinned from ear to ear and strutted around as proud as peacocks at their organizing activity by "remote control," as we jokingly called it. For the three of us, the movement was fun and we always coined expressions, catch-words, and code language to give deeper meaning and color to our activities. From then on, any time we set up contacts or got people in touch with one another, it was called "organizing by remote control."

Returning to Winston-Salem, feeling really successful, I shared the High Point experience with Bernie Friedlander and Junius Scales, getting agreement that the party leadership in Winston-Salem would utilize the High Point model for some free-flow organizing in Winston-Salem and would guarantee a chapter of UNAVA in time for the national convention. I then moved on to South Carolina, where we successfully set up chapters in Columbia, Charleston, and Cheraw. Dizzy Gillespie's brother was the key man in organizing the Cheraw chapter. The Gillespie family had a long history of struggle against "the crackers" and helping every positive thing that took place in the community. Part of this heritage explained to me why Dizzy had always been such a great admirer of Paul Robeson and rarely spoke in interviews or even at his jazz performances without mentioning what a great man he felt Paul Robeson was.

When I returned to New York to report on my experience and compare notes with George Murphy, Burt Jackson, Walter Garland, and Bert Alves, we each discovered that the bush fire effect of our organizing efforts was universal. None of our experiences was unique. We concluded that the UNAVA concept was an idea whose time had come, and we constantly referred to Victor Hugo's statement that "there is nothing as powerful as an idea whose time has come."[3]

As our campaign gained momentum, the party assigned some of its big guns in the cultural movement to give us assistance in public relations and fundraising. Walter Bernstein, who had been a correspondent for *Yank*, the GI's magazine; Arnold Perl, another writer of radio shows and, later, a movie producer; and Millard Lampell came up one night to meet with me and Walter Garland. We decided to meet in Count Basie's jazz joint at the corner of 133rd Street and Seventh Avenue, where we plotted strategy for further development of the campaign.

One of the events we planned was a fundraiser we organized at 409 Edgecombe Avenue, the principal residence of the Black bourgeoisie living in Harlem at the very top of Sugar Hill. It came off as an astounding success, far beyond any of our dreams. The party was held at the apartment of Dorothy Spencer, the wife of the baritone Kenneth Spencer, who was being hailed on the international concert circuit as "another Paul Robeson." Dashiell Hammett, who had promised to attend the party, was ill and asked Walter and me to come down to his place in Midtown to pick up a contribution. To our delight, after we chatted with "Dash" for a half hour about the UNAVA program, he asked for his checkbook and laboriously signed a check to UNAVA for

$3,000, the largest single contribution from any source. I learned only later that Hammett, a man of great principle who'd stood up against the persecution of the House Un-American Activities Committee with great dignity and a barely concealed contempt for the American-style Nazis who had control of the committee, was suffering the effects of years of alcoholic drinking. Edgar Allan Poe, Jack London, William Faulkner, Ernest Hemingway, F. Scott Fitzgerald, Tennessee Williams, Sinclair Lewis, Thomas Wolfe, John O'Hara, Malcolm Lowry, and a host of others were all victims of the insidious disease that almost made it seem that one could not be an American writer unless one were an alcoholic. Two writers did come to the party: Dorothy Parker and her lover Allan Campbell. Dorothy's wit was as scintillating as reported and she made no bones about how much she adored tall men, casting a speculative eye at me.

Dorothy showed a keen interest in my stories about our organizing experiences and expressed horror at the story of the blinding of Isaac Woodward, who was a member of UNAVA, and the murder of the Ferguson brothers in Freeport, Long Island, by a Ku Klux Klan policeman, Joseph Romeika. She pledged ongoing support. Her commitment to civil rights causes continued even after her death, when she left her estate to Martin Luther King Jr.

The one failure I had in the preparation of this affair was my date to pick up Billie Holiday, who was singing at the Famous Door on 52nd Street. Fifty-second Street had become "Swing Alley." It was Saturday night, so traversing the block meant shouldering one's way through herds of tourists, jazz buffs, and partygoers on both sides of the street. "Swing Alley" it was! Art Tatum held forth masterfully on the keyboards at the Three Deuces. Roy "Little Jazz" Eldridge was the key attraction at Kelly's Stable. John Kirby and his quintet with Maxine Sullivan were at the Onyx Club. Coleman "Bean" Hawkins soloed before a rhythm trio across the street, and Billie was at the Famous Door.

Besides the aforementioned clubs, there were the Spotlite, Jimmy Ryan's, and The Club Downbeat. In one night it was physically possible to hear Tatum; Billie Holiday; Coleman Hawkins; Hot Lips Page; Ben Webster; Barney Bigard; Stuff Smith, a perennial fixture at the Onyx Club along with his sidekick Jonah Jones, a graduate of the Cab Calloway Band at the Cotton Club; Teddy Bunn and his Five Spirits of Rhythm with the incredible master of "scat" singing, Leo Watson; Dizzy Gillespie; Charlie Parker; Don Byas; and Frankie Newton. Years later, Sir Eric Hobsbawm, the leading British Marxist political scientist, did a book on African American classical music called *The Jazz Scene*.[4] He wrote it under the pseudonym Francis Newton. From curiosity, knowing that Frankie Newton's real name was Francis, I wrote Sir Eric asking had he used the name Francis Newton after Frankie. He replied, "Yes, because Frankie was the only Black Marxist in jazz that I know." I had spent many pleasant hours with Frankie when he had an all-star band that included my dear friend and the magnificent pianist Calvin Jackson at Camp Unity discussing the "class and the ass" struggle. I also informed Sir Eric that there were many more Black Marxists in the jazz field and mentioned that we used to call Teddy Wilson a "Marxist Mozart in Mocha" and that Al Hall, the bassist, was a longtime militant.

But enough of side trips. Billie was finishing her set with the Basie band and we had arranged to fast-taxi up to 409 Edgecombe between sets because she had to be back for another show within an hour and a half. When she came off the stand, Billie said, "Stretch, order me a double brandy while I'm cooling off and then we'll take off." I did and in two minutes she had downed it and we were out into a cab on the way up to Harlem. We joked and dished dirt on the way up, but she seemed to be going through some sort of mood swing because when we got off the elevator and to the apartment where the party was in full swing, we walked around and Billie looked at the crowd, which was conspicuously interracial, and said, "Stretch, I didn't come all the way uptown to sing for a bunch of white motherfuckers. Take me back downtown." Wanting to stay on Billie's good side, for we had been friends since I had first heard her sing at Pod's and Jerry's and then the Hotcha with Don Frye accompanying her from 1933 on, I quickly got her coat and hastened out with her to get her back downtown. I guess when Billie saw all the white folks on her home turf at an affair she thought was for the Black cause, it made her mad.

9
La Lucha Continua

Foley Square, New York City
August 18, 1949

After the Henry A. Wallace presidential campaign of 1948, the government undertook a series of actions against communists that were more damaging to democracy in the United States than anything in history. The anticommunist and antidemocratic thrust had two prongs—repressive legislation, some of it sponsored by erstwhile liberals such as Senator Hubert Humphrey's bill to outlaw the Communist Party, and the executive branch attack on the left through the Smith Act trials and the Attorney General's List of Subversive Organizations.

The impact on the United Negro and Allied Veterans of America (UNAVA) is more or less reflective of what happened to most of the one hundred or more left-led organizations on the attorney general's list. Because UNAVA was a veterans' organization, it could not function effectively as one unless it had accreditation to represent veterans' claims and other interests before the Veterans Administration. UNAVA could have continued to function as a political movement, but unless it could represent veterans' interests before the VA, it would, given the level of political consciousness that existed in the country at that time, have appealed to only the most militant and socially conscious veterans. But a number of organizations were already working in that area: the National Negro Congress, the Negro Labor Committee, the veterans' committee of the NAACP, and the Communist Party itself. UNAVA, despite having been placed on the attorney general's list, applied to the Veterans Administration for accreditation and was denied. It was the only veterans' organization that was predominantly Black and, so far as I know, the only veterans' group to be turned down simply because it was on the subversive list. The attorney general offered no proof of the nature of the group's subversion. The only activities of UNAVA had been its nationally effective campaign for terminal leave pay for veterans in the South and some local struggles against police brutality as in the Isaac Woodward case.

Most of the UNAVA members went into local organizations and played active roles in continuing their struggles as veterans in other formations such as the Deacons for Justice in Mississippi, which helped lay the foundation for the civil rights movement of the '60s in that state. Many, such as Coleman Young in Detroit, moved from positions of state legislators to become mayors. UNAVA did make a contribution, as short-lived as it was, to the training and networking of a major cadre of veterans who played an important role in the civil rights struggles of the '60s, not in the same way or at the same level anticipated, but certainly the battle experience of the vets and the international education they received on the battlefronts all around the world were an important part of the rising struggle of Black folks that needs further study in its specifics to make a more definitive assessment of their role in the postwar world.

With the shutdown of UNAVA, my activities in the veterans field ended. I became more involved in the work of the leading party committees both on the national and state levels, reducing my mass work to next to nothing. I was also advancing in leadership and after the Smith Act indictments were handed up, I was told to prepare to get ready to be a witness for the defense. Each of us was assigned to various lawyers on the legal team. My partner was George Crockett Jr., a noncommunist, fairly conservative by our standards, but a top-notch lawyer whose preparation and understanding of the law made me feel most comfortable in our consultations on what we were to expect.

I had been a student of Marxist theory, studying it under the guidance of the best teachers that the American communist movement could produce at two national training schools, both near Beacon, New York. I had been a successful New York County Educational Director, responsible for the cadre training program for the actives in the membership of more than 10,000 during the years 1946–48, then New York State Educational Director, responsible for cadre training schools, including Jefferson School of Social Science, with a student body of 6,000 enrollees per year. I was responsible for supervising the party leaflets and publications, such as *Party Voice*, the mass rallies' educational content, radio broadcasts for a membership of more than 25,000, and the National Educational and Negro commissions. Because of this training, I was considered well suited to respond to the government's attack on the alleged position of the party.

To me, it was my most important fight and I wanted to be in shape for it, so from February on, I went "on the wagon," knowing instinctively that alcohol would not be of any help to me in the sharp ideological combat that could be expected from the best of the attorneys for the prosecution that the U.S. government could produce. George Crockett had very early along in my briefing warned me about the "box," a courtroom tactic that the federal prosecution was expected to utilize to the hilt. The "box" was a method of questioning from two seemingly unrelated points of view which gradually close in so that the witness is forced into an answer that may, from a legal viewpoint, be considered incriminating, even though the witness is innocent. I wanted to have all my wits about me with no retarding factor of a "hangover" to get in the way of my best performance on behalf of the party. The objective of the government's case was to make it appear that Marxist-Leninist theory was simplistically aimed at the "forcible and violent" overthrow of the U.S. government under any and all conditions.

The trial was a monstrous charade, violating every aspect of the Bill of Rights and the Constitution under the guise of the Department of Justice's defense of the Bill of Rights and the Constitution. We spent one weekend at Camp Unity getting ready as my day of appearance neared. It was much-needed rest and recreation as the tension over my testimony rose. George Crockett and I woodshedded for hours. I spent a great deal of time going over articles and party documents dealing with such questions as "peaceful transition" to socialism, the dictatorship of the proletariat, and advocacy of force and violence.

As a matter of truth, force and violence were never advocated in the courses we had at any level of party training. Most of the "blood and thunder" stuff, including the hypothetical setting up of a Soviet republic in the United States, had been relegated to the ash cans of party history with the demise of the Third Period. The Third Period, for those who have not read about it elsewhere, was roughly the period in party history prior to the Seventh World Congress, where the Bulgarian Marxist Georgi Dimitrov made his famous (in communist circles) Unity of the

Working Class against Fascism speech. The Third Period was one in which the Social Democrats were regarded as the main enemy of the working class, and the struggle for socialism, self-determination, and a Soviet republic in the Black Belt, and the dictatorship of the proletariat were the only forms through which socialism could be achieved after the violent overthrow of the bourgeoisie. Even in the Third Period, however, American Marxists had been aware that because of the particular way in which capitalism had evolved in the United States, a peaceful transition toward socialism was theoretically possible. Moreover, the Third Period had been defined as theoretically erroneous, reflecting the strong sectarian tendencies in the international communist movement. The united front of all antifascists and the strengthening of peaceful approaches to socialism in America through transition were characteristic of the broadening of our theoretical program. The new approach would make it possible for us to enter into honest relationships with our potential antifascist friends in the development of the united front. I had joined the party after the Third Period had been discarded and Dimitrov's line had been under practical application for two years in the United States. In fact, by 1938, the Young Communist League of the United States was being cited in Marxist literature internationally as a model of exemplary implementation of the Seventh World Congress line through its work in the formation of the American Youth Congress.

Having been heavily involved in the theoretical work from 1938 on, I was ideally equipped to discuss at length what was being taught in our training schools. The government had built a great deal of its case to prove, on the basis of the content of our training schools, that the party was primarily a conspiracy to overthrow the government by force and violence. The schools were portrayed as something akin to guerrilla camps where communist functionaries were taught guerrilla warfare, street fighting, and other skills of a clandestine nature associated with terrorism. Literature, some of it pathetically lurid, from the Third Period, particularly William Z. Foster's *Toward Soviet America*, was trotted out as if it were the working program of the Communist Party in 1949, when in fact it had been discarded in 1936 as sectarian to its very core. It was not even mentioned in the training schools.

When I got to the witness stand, however, I found out just how deeply the frame-up nature of the trial was woven into all its aspects. The government had the support and collusion of the judge, Harold Medina, to an extent that should go down in the history of jurisprudence as the most judicially tainted trial in American law. What is readily apparent is the consistent overruling of all objections of the defense and sustaining of almost all of the prosecution's objections. Most of the testimony dealing with rebuttal of theoretical evidence by the defense witnesses was stricken from the record or not allowed at all. The prime tactic of the government's attorneys was to avoid any open-ended questions that would give us a chance to respond with answers that could clarify our policies. Every effort was made to put us in another type of "box" that would confine us to "yes" or "no" answers. This tactic was meant to nullify our effort to make our courtroom appearance an opportunity to educate the public on the real policies of the Communist Party.

One of the most exciting moments in the trial, for me, and one of the most humorous, for the spectators, was when an opportunity that I had been waiting for arose. One night before taking the stand, I had been enjoying a fascinating game of poker with Vito "Marc" Marcantonio, who was then the congressman from the lower Harlem 18th Congressional District, at my house.[1] My father, James Jackson, and a few other close friends sat in to share the occasion and honor of sitting in on a game with the congressman. Marc had been going with Lil Landau, who was Martha's best friend. Lil had been assigned by the party to be Marc's secretary, which put her in a position to be the party's informant on everything that went on in Marc's office. Through Lil, Marc had been introduced to my entire family, all of whom captivated him.

On the night of the poker game, the subject of the trial came up and Marc said, "One of the problems of this trial is how to get through to the press. The way Medina is helping the prosecution squelch your testimony eliminates the news value of the trial." I said, "Have you any ideas on it?" He said in his incisive, clipped mode of speaking, "Yeah, if the opportunity arises, you might hit the press by tying the frame-up with the Truman deep freezer that's all over the press."

The following Tuesday, I was informed that I'd go on the stand Wednesday. I kept Marc's comment in mind. After a series of questions on my credentials as a witness for the educational work, the attorney Frank Gordon tried to link my educational work with the picket line that had been protesting the trial. He wanted to portray the picket line as a form of violence against the government. Thinking he'd surprise me, he asked, "Isn't it true that you participated in the picket line outside this courtroom recently?"

I responded, "Yes, it is true."

Then I continued, "I considered it my duty as an American to protest this trial."

Attorney Gordon: "I object to this testimony as irrelevant and unresponsive."

The purpose of this objection was to prevent any political analysis from being made.

Judge Medina said, "Objection sustained." Then Gordon asked, "In what capacity were you on the picket line?"

I replied, "In the capacity of New York State Educational Director of the Communist Party. And my purpose. . . ."

Gordon cut me off: "Objection."

Medina: "Objection sustained." Then he said, "Will the witness refrain from giving extended answers to the questions."

I said, "Yes, your honor, but I can explain why I was on the picket line in one sentence, if you will permit me."

Gordon: "I object."

Medina looked at me and said, "If you can do it in one sentence, go on." He added, "Objection overruled."

I said, "I was on the picket line because this trial is as cold a frame-up as anything in Mrs. Truman's deep freezer."

The courtroom exploded with laughter and Medina, outraged, said, "If there are any more demonstrations of this kind, I'll clear the courtroom."

The press dashed to their telephones, and the next morning my comment was on the front pages, having linked the trial to the hot news of the day about the Truman administration's getting all kinds of gifts and benefits from government contracts. One of the contractors had given Mrs. Truman a deep freezer and a mink coat that was supposed to have been hidden in it.

But despite that and other momentary flashes of the truth that escaped the governmental straitjacket over trial testimony, the wheels of injustice ground inexorably on and the twelve communist leaders were convicted in one of the most unfair trials in American history. Our body politic has never recovered from those convictions.

During the trial, news came over the radio that the Paul Robeson concert for the benefit of the Peekskill NAACP had been attacked and broken up by a mob composed of American Legionnaires. We called an emergency meeting of the state secretariat on the question of how we should respond. Certainly, the incident could not be ignored, even though Peekskill was very conservative territory with only a small number of members of the party. The secretariat and our larger governing body, the state board, spent hours discussing the significance of the attack. We analyzed the incident as an extension of the attack on the Communist Party through the Smith Act trials to the Black community and the NAACP. Harlem was disturbed by the attack on Paul, and a group on the board argued that we should organize a counterdemonstration in Harlem at the Golden Gate Ballroom, where we would be assured of the support of a friendly community.

I was one of a small group to speak out against having the demonstration in Harlem. With all the talk about an attack against the communists being an attack against all, I argued that an attack against Robeson and the NAACP represented an attack on the left, the labor movement, and all progressive whites; therefore, it was our responsibility to mobilize the entire left and labor movement. To have the meeting in Harlem would imply that the rally was primarily a Black reaction and would not get the support that it should. The others argued that a meeting of 5,000 was a realistic and proper response. I argued that we should go all out with a major mobilization of the left, as we had for May Day or a Madison Square Garden meeting with a goal of 25,000 participants, and finally, that the proper place for the reaction was back in Peekskill itself, where the original incident had happened.

My arguments and enthusiasm caught hold and the state board adopted essentially the line that I had recommended. As a result, the strategic decision was made to have a massive concert in Peekskill itself as a counterdemonstration to the fascist attack that had been made on Paul Robeson's concert.

Mexico City
September 5–10, 1949

I was sent as one of the American delegation representing the Communist Party to the Western Hemispheric Peace Conference in Mexico City the Friday before the Peekskill concert was to be held. One of the suppositions was if an alternative outcome to the second Peekskill rally was a further attack on the left and particularly the communists with arrests for involvement in the Peekskill counterdemonstration, it would be wise to have some of the leadership out of the country at the time. The communist contingent in the American delegation consisted of Arnold Johnson, Joseph Starobin, Lloyd Brown, and me. I was nominated to deliver a speech of greetings at the main rally of the conference from the American Communist Party to the delegates.

Our flight down to Mexico City was smooth and uneventful except for a hair-raising twenty minutes of turbulence over Mississippi. Lloyd and I joked about the turbulence in the civil rights struggle below.

When we arrived, after bedding down in the Lincoln Hotel with an ample supply of tequila (all of us seemed to be heavy hitters on the Mexican booze), we were informed about a meeting among the various representatives of the communist parties of the Western hemisphere who were assembled for the conference. This was most exciting to me because I would have a chance to meet not only leaders of the communist parties from countries like Mexico, Venezuela, Argentina, and Chile but also the underground representatives of the Brazilian party and the powerful Cuban party, which was at that time the strongest party in the Western hemisphere. We looked forward to meeting these well-seasoned comrades because, with the Smith Act trials in full swing, there was a premonition among us that we might need the benefit of brother parties' experience in underground activity. Less than two years later we were utilizing their experience.

The first meeting of the group took place on the Saturday before the main rally on Sunday. We were escorted to a fairly swank section of Mexico City to the very modern apartment of the artist Octavio Paz, a handsome, squat Mexican who resembled the Indians who so often dominated the murals of Diego Rivera. Carlos Rafael Rodriguez, who was to become the minister of education under the Castro government in the Cuba of the '60s; Juan Marinello, who was to become the vice president; Roger Garaudy from France; and Paul Elouard, who was later to commit suicide after the Khrushchev revelations, attended our sessions. The most colorful of the participants at our party caucus were, however, the Mexicans—particularly, Dionisio Encinas, the Indian revolutionary, who headed the Mexican party, and the artist Alfredo Siquieros. Both Encinas and Siquieros wore pistol belts to the meetings with loaded six-shooters that they would hang over the backs of their chairs prior to participating in the discussions on tactics for the conference.

The Europeans present seemed to think that some discussion of Titoism and the characterization of the Tito regime in Yugoslavia was obligatory. At the time, Moscow had defined Tito and the Yugoslav communists not only as *persona non grata* to the international revolutionary movement but also as agents of fascism. I had nothing better to do than to make the major theme of my greetings an expression of the support that the American communists gave to the later-to-be-retracted definition of Yugoslav communism. I was selected to speak for the American Communist Party and was happy to do so, believing that everything Moscow had said about Tito was true. I spent a few hours learning some Spanish to establish rapport with the predominantly Spanish-speaking audience and practiced my pronunciation with a Cuban comrade until I had a perfectly good opening paragraph for my speech, and then I went into English for the remainder. As I recall, it was the speech that a political hack would make, but at the time I was proud to speak for the CPUSA and share the platform in the great arena with such world-famous figures and many others. After coming down from the lectern I got many congratulations for being the first speaker to identify Tito as a fascist (erroneously, as history was to prove).

The other highlight of the Western Hemispheric Peace Conference for me was the party given for all the foreign delegations at the ranch, or more properly, the *hacienda* of Mexico's foremost labor leader, Vicente Lombardo Toledano. Vicente was in many respects a Mexican version of Vito Marcantonio. Marc was a stirring, inspirational orator of the old school, pre-amplifier school of public speaking. He had the charisma and emotional power to rouse an audience to a fever pitch until he became so charged up and passionate with the feedback from the audience that his arms would start to flail, his feet would stomp, and his voice would mount into unintelligible screams and growls that the crowd would respond to with their own screams and cheers. Vicente was a similar type of charismatic orator, and he had the arena in Mexico City sounding as if it were Madison Square Garden during a Marcantonio climax. Like Marc, he was a Marxist, or at least he used a Marxist analysis of society, but was independent of party discipline. When we arrived back at the *hacienda*, servants dressed as *peons* directed us to the tables in the dining room bearing all kinds of delicious Mexican dishes. My favorite, a discovery that was part of my Mexican trip, was chicken mole, mole being an exquisitely spicy chocolate sauce.

While waiting for the entertainment after dinner, Lloyd Brown and I walked into the library with its four walls hidden by ceiling-high bookcases filled with books, all expensively bound in what appeared to be the finest Moroccan leather. Something about this obvious luxury offended my idea of how a revolutionary labor leader should live. I said to Lloyd half-jokingly and half-cynically, "I wonder if any of these books are bound in human skin." I did not realize at the time how my ambivalent attitudes about the movement were reflecting themselves in my unconscious through jokes of this double-edged kind.

The *pièce de résistance* of the entire evening was a mock bullfight performed by two of the *peons*, one of whom posed as the brave matador while the other wore a bull's head. The "bull" repeatedly charged the pseudo-matador until the actual matador had executed with an arena-like flourish the significant number of *veronicas* and passes to the approving "*Olé!*" of the audience. Then the matador performed the ritualistic movement of truth for the bull wherein the sword penetrates the medulla oblongata in the death thrust. I felt somewhat ashamed that we, a kind of left-wing royalty, needed that kind of entertainment and were participating in it. But this feeling of shame was, to some degree, wiped out by my rationalization, "Nothing's too good for the working class." Maybe that meant, "Nothing's too good for the leaders of the working class."

During the course of the conference, we heard announced over the loudspeaker two momentous events. The first was the overwhelming turnout of New Yorkers at the second Paul Robeson concert in Peekskill and the second attack on the 25,000 assembled there, organized by a collaboration of the state police and the American Legion. The second sad announcement was the arrest of that magnificent tribune of the civil rights movement for the twentieth century, Dr. W. E. B. Du Bois.

Havana, Cuba
February 12, 1950

Despite the gathering storm of the worst period of the McCarthy era, a new area opened up in my life. In the short time between my release from the army on January 6, 1946, and my participation in the New York Smith Act trial, in August 1949 I had acquired a national leadership perspective in the party. This new outlook did not diminish my concern for Harlem, my base of operations. It did, however, make me acutely aware of the impact of national policy on Harlem and Black communities throughout the nation.

This was an added dimension showing me the international importance of what went on in the United States. This understanding was transmitted to us by our comrades in the Central and South American countries as well as by our European friends, not to mention the Canadians. Joe Starobin had been assigned to cover the Popular Socialist Party convention in Cuba. We decided that it might be a good experience for me to go along to augment my Latin American education, so we got in touch with the New York state party chapters, and the national leadership approved my making the trip to Havana.

The head of the Cuban party organization, Juan Ordoqui, had arranged for one of the party chauffeurs to pick us up at the Havana airport. The Cubans liked fast driving and they liked big American cars, so our escort swooped up to us in a 1938 Cadillac convertible, and in no time at all, we were at the party headquarters. It looked as if it were under guard. We later learned that the Batista regime was more repressive than we had been led to believe by the U.S. press. Attacks on party headquarters were no surprise, so there were always six to a dozen party cadre around the porch of the Havana headquarters for security.

When we arrived, Blas Roca[2] could not see us right away, so we spent some time with Carlos Rafael Rodriguez; Juan Ordoqui, the organizational secretary; and Juan Marinello, the communist senator in the Cuban legislature. I wanted to see what swimming was like in the Gulf of Mexico in February, and I wanted to take advantage of a trip to a subtropical climate.

Part of the campaign against white chauvinism in New York had been directed against the large number of party members who went to Miami for the winter season to escape the cold of the North, and because Miami at that time was strictly "Jim Crow," I wanted to experience swimming in the winter, which I had never done. It was February. What I didn't know was that the Cubans swam only in their summer season, from June to September, even though the water was warm in February. When I was asked what I wanted to do, I replied, "Go swimming at the beach." They looked at me as if I were crazy and said, "But there'll be no one at the beach. It's February!" I said, "That's OK. I'll swim by myself!" So they humored me, and two Cubans escorted me to the beautiful Havana beach and watched somewhat incredulously while I swam in the Gulf by myself.

I had mentioned to my driver that I was a jazz fancier, and he arranged for me to meet the party member who was a member of the Havana City Council—a white Cuban who was married to a Black woman and was very fond of jazz. I spent an afternoon and evening with him talking about Duke Ellington and the Cotton Club, while he played me Afro-Cuban music, which had only recently been introduced to the states by Dizzy Gillespie. Later that evening the councilman gave me an education in Afro-Cuban music, playing many records that he then gave me to take back to the States. One of the most interesting features of the Afro-Cuban music, he pointed out, was the strong Chinese influence running throughout, which he ascribed to the large Chinese population that had migrated to Cuba at the end of the previous century. That night we wound up our tour with a trip to the Tropicana, known then as the world's most beautiful nightclub. I didn't quite believe my Cuban comrades, having worked at the Cotton Club, but I was floored by the Tropicana's overall magnificence when I walked into what appeared to be an open air garden with tall palms growing inside the club. It made the Cotton Club look like someone's outhouse. The band was Perez Prado's, the Duke Ellington of Cuba. He swung both jazz and Latin rhythms. I couldn't help but find one of the best dancers to ask to dance, and we whirled around the floor as if we were at the Savoy in Harlem. I was falling in love with Havana.

The next morning, we were assigned to attend the Popular Socialist Party convention, where the main report given by Blas Roca was noted for its prediction of the overthrow of the Batista regime. The Batista regime was typical of the authoritarian governments that the United States' financial interests used as *gendarmes* to protect their profits. In the case of Cuba, the profits came primarily from sugar. I was astounded at the level of exploitation at every corner. My guide showed me the raw sugar that the customers used in every restaurant. The sugar interests had a deal that Cuba could not refine its own sugar. White sugar was, therefore, very expensive, having to travel all the way to the Brooklyn waterfront to be refined and then sent back to Cuba.

In Havana, heroin was sold openly on the street, controlled by the same mob that ran Atlantic City and Las Vegas. I saw fifteen-year-old kids lining up for their "fix" out on the street in front of a decrepit closed-down market. The dealer would simply wipe the blood off the needle, or "spike," and inject the next youth as if it were a medic station dispensing penicillin shots.

The city was also known at that time as the "whorehouse" of the Western hemisphere. By virtue of a breakdown in communications between me and my cab driver one night, I wound up in an unbelievable situation. I asked for a place where there was dancing and girls who might be willing to dance. He drove out into an obviously middle-class section with a row of two-story white stucco houses with flower-bedecked or vine-covered walls with gates pretty much alike. We pulled up in front of one. The cab driver beckoned me to follow him, recognizing that I appeared anxious, which I was. What kind of dance hall could there be in this quiet residential neighborhood?

Dressed in the all-white garb of a nun, a walnut-colored, sweet-faced matron, about sixty years old, came to the door and bowed us into a foyer where there was a candlestand, as if it were lit for prayers, holding at least a hundred blazing candles. Before my confusion could overwhelm me, she motioned to us to proceed into the sitting room, where at least ten men were seated. She nodded and a dozen beautiful women emerged in single file in various types of fine clothing, each garment more revealing than the next. I decided to go through with the adventure and asked what the price was, having gathered that my driver had brought me not to be initiated into some suburban religious cult but to a cleverly camouflaged whorehouse operating in such a way as to not wake the neighbors.

Despite my being there, I did not want to participate in any action: I was still a model husband, not because I lacked lust, but primarily because I didn't think participating would be politically expedient. I didn't want anything to get in the way of my political fortunes. I had been a frequent confidant of party women who had been "betrayed" by party leaders. Their viewpoint made me feel that there was some male chauvinism in the party and this acted as a brake on my lustful urges. Yet I didn't want to give charity, so after finding out that the going price was five dollars per girl, or woman, I asked for two and gave our nun-madam ten dollars. Our triad was escorted into a small room with tables and chairs around a stage about three feet high, and the two girls asked me if I wanted to fuck them. I asked them to dance together and make love as if one of them were a man. They did so as a beautiful pair—one was a statuesque, finely molded African about 5'10" tall and the other was a lovely, petite but voluptuous blond from Poland with cobalt blue eyes—to my simultaneous fascination and disgust, not with anything about the women, but with myself for being a party to such exploitation. I asked them to stop, bought them a drink, and then left. After some explaining, I told the cab driver I really wanted a dance hall and we finally got to the dance hall on the beach where one of the musicians was playing like a god of the drums to my relief and delight.

The next day was my introduction to the convention of the Popular Socialist Party. The PSP was the only party that had opposed the Batista regime in any major way and, consequently, the only party that had a mass base, well rooted among the workers and peasants throughout Cuba. The PSP had two divisions in a membership of approximately 125,000 total. There was a Marxist-Leninist cadre organization of about 15,000, who were the key activists and mass workers in the various trade unions and other popular organizations, and the rest of its members, who were not Marxist-Leninists but general supporters of the Popular Socialist Party. The convention was an exciting gathering of delegates selected by vote in the various regions of the party on a provincial basis.

About one hundred delegates were from such colorful regions as Islas de Pinas, Camaguey, Oriente, and many others. I was surprised that only about 10 percent of the convention delegates were Black, most of them from the province of Oriente, which is the easternmost and also the most African of the Cuban provinces. During the slave trade, most of the slaves imported into Cuba were from the Yoruba tribe, and African religious customs still extant in Cuba have a close relationship with the Yoruban rites practiced in Nigeria.

I was brought in and seated on the dais with other visiting foreign communists, and when we stood up at the opening session I towered over most of the other delegates. A peasant delegate, in good humor, saw me as he came in and exclaimed in Spanish in a joking voice that everyone in the convention could hear, "Look, there's one man standing on top of the other!" The entire convention broke into laughter.

The most significant feature of the convention for me was Blas Roca's prediction of the overthrow of the Batista regime. He forecast the overthrow of Batista by 1954. It took place, not under the leadership of the PSP, but under Fidel Castro, in 1959. When Castro took power, the multinational corporations of the United States controlled 80 percent of Cuba's utilities, 90 percent of the mines, 90 percent of the cattle ranches, 50 percent of the public railways, almost 100 percent of the oil refining industry, 40 percent of the sugar industry, and 25 percent of all bank deposits.[3] Cuba at that time had 600,000 unemployed. Fifty percent had no electricity; 31.5 million people lived in huts, shacks, and slums without sanitary facilities; rents took 33 percent of all income; 40 percent of the population was illiterate; 100,000 persons suffered from tuberculosis; 95 percent of the children were afflicted with parasites; 11.5 percent of the landowners controlled 46 percent of the total area; and the U.S. mob controlled all drugs, gambling, and prostitution.

Underground
July 1951

After World War II, when the Cold War was opened up by President Truman with the executive order requirement of a loyalty oath on the part of federal employees, we began to talk about what kind of America would follow World War II. Already by 1949, there had been sufficient indicators that the government, with its anti-Soviet policies that were reinforced on the domestic scale by the witch hunt started in the federal government with Truman's loyalty order, would become extremely right wing. The domestic witch hunt was accelerated by the Attorney General's list of 102 "subversive" left-wing organizations that was issued at that time. This led the national leadership of the Communist Party, particularly William Z. Foster, to adopt a political perspective based on what we call the three inevitables: It was inevitable that fascism would come to the United States, it was inevitable that there would be a Third World War, and it was inevitable that the Communist Party would be outlawed. We foresaw a duplication of the German Nazi experience in the United States and decided, based on the experience of communist parties in other parts of the world where fascist governments had taken over, that we should develop an underground organization. So we divided our top leadership, of which I was a part, into three segments: One segment we called the Availables, who continued to function in the open; the second segment consisted of the Unavailables, who were linked to the Availables through a courier system; and then a third segment we called the Deep Freeze, whose members were not active at all but were just holed up somewhere in case FBI surveillance and reconnaissance exposed those who were in the Unavailable category. We also had a fourth group whose members were sent out of the country to eastern Europe and the Soviet Union. We said they were "On Ice." So we actually had four categories of leadership, which we called cadres, meaning the skeleton of an organization. I was so well known, having been in show business and everything, that it was decided I should join the ranks of the Unavailables.

With the mounting anticommunist propaganda of the McCarthy period, the execution of Julius and Ethel Rosenberg on June 19, 1953, was a pinnacle of oppression, and part of my apparatus had become exposed, so we then made a decision that it was too risky for me to function as one of the Unavailables. At this point I went into Deep Freeze in 1953. I got a different identity and functioned in areas outside of New York, where I wasn't too well known, operating under the security provision that I should never go out in daylight because I had a lot of name recognition and high visibility when I was in the open in the Communist Party. I had left my family, over my wife's objections, and believe that this was a primary ingredient in our long-term separation upon my return. She had asked me whom I loved, the family or the party. I said I loved both, but the party came first.

During the period I was underground, I wrote articles for our theoretical journal, *Political Affairs*, and I met with key personnel who were involved in the day-to-day leadership to make my particular contribution to policy formation and to be kept abreast of events as they transpired in the outside world. I also visited Cuba again, where many of the people with whom I had previously met later became the power behind the Castro throne after 1959. People like Juan Martinello, Blas Roca, and Pizarro Peña were all very prominent in the Cuban government after the Castro revolution. And I must say, my experience there in Cuba was that of all of the communist parties in the Western hemisphere, the Cuban party had stronger mass ties and a kind of flexibility and popularity among the grassroots people that most of the other parties were unable to attain. This fact was accepted by other communist parties all over the world. So it was no surprise to me that a socialist government replaced Batista when his government was overthrown. I spent many enlightening and exciting hours with the Cuban communists.

Because I was in the underground and in the Deep Freeze sector, it was decided that I should be the missionary to get an opinion on the theoretical and political debate that was going on in the leadership. This trip represented another step up the ladder of increasing responsibility in the party leadership. I was officially assigned to get Blas Roca's opinion on this debate. I was also there to arrange for the safe conduct of some American cadres who were going to be put "on ice" in eastern Europe for the duration of the McCarthy period.

From my base in Jersey City, I moved to Cincinnati, where I was to do a regular "dry cleaning," or change of identity, then go to St. Louis and from there to New Orleans before taking off on the short flight to Havana. The trip was a revelatory one for me because I had never had an opportunity to visit New Orleans. During my layover in Cincinnati, the people I lived with invited me to go out with them, joined by a lovely nurse friend of theirs. It just so happened that the place they wanted to visit was the Cincinnati Cotton Club. Duke Ellington was the main attraction that night. I felt that one night out would not jeopardize me, given that I had never been in Cincinnati before. We went and my hosts secured a ringside seat where we had a great view of the whole band, and in no time at all I was up on the floor dancing with my lovely nurse companion. Between dances, I went over to Duke and asked him to join us at our table after the set. I cautioned him that I was in town under an assumed name as part of my underground existence. Duke knew about that, having been informed about my activities during his stops at my sister Winnie's home when the band played Cleveland. Immediately catching the cue, he asked me, "What shall I call you when I come over to the table?" I answered, "I'm Bob Harris here!" At the end of the set, Duke detached himself from a score of people and came over to our table, calling me Bob frequently just to demonstrate how completely he had entered into my game, to the delight of my Cincinnati friends who had never thought that they would be in such intimate rapport with Ellington, especially in front of all their local acquaintances.

To top it off, Duke asked me if I would like to stay in his suite, while he went to Chicago to see his Midwest hairdresser. He bent his head over to show me his kitchen[4] where the naps were gathering and said, "I have to drive all the way to Chicago to get a proper treatment." Then, he said, "But you'll have to wait until I give you the signal to come into my suite because there is a fine young lady that I'm going to spend about an hour with after the show before leaving!"

I didn't even have to invite the nurse to stay over with me to see Duke's suite; she just followed me there and was more than impressed. Despite my having known Duke for twenty-three years at the time, I had never expected such intimate generosity from him, but that was the way Duke was. He never let me down in any area. There was no doubt in my mind after that episode with Duke that my adventure was launched under a good star.

My next stop was New Orleans, where I had to see Canal Street, Basin Street, and, above all, Rampart Street, the last of which was legendary as the place where the life was lived. My contact was in the longshoremen's union in New Orleans, so I got a well-informed insider's tour of the wharves where the main commodity my guide worked with was Central American bananas. He told me all about the control that the United Fruit Company had over the Central American economies and what a task it had been to organize the dockworkers. When I asked him about the nightlife I had missed during the rigors of my underground life up North, he invited me to visit one of his favorite bars and listen to a great country blues singer on Rampart Street where the banana handlers hung out.

It was most exciting when we entered the joint. The music was romping and the sounds met us in the street before we entered. Inside was a bar at least seventy-five feet long. Every inch of space was taken up by workers, most of them dockworkers, banana handlers, and seamen, but there were also many sharecroppers, plantation workers, and field hands who had obviously come into the city from nearby rural towns for their weekend. There was also a great deal of traffic to a back room that attracted my attention. My guide noticed my curiosity and asked, "Want to go back? There's gambling." He probably did not expect a party leader to have any interest in that type of activity, but, as he told me later, he was both surprised and delighted that an out-of-town party leader was interested in these worldly activities. The most exciting thing for me at that Rampart Street bar was going into the back room and playing a few hands of poker, one of my strongest games. I sat down with a novelist's assortment of roustabouts, field workers, and cotton pickers around the poker table, hearing their jokes and stories, an accompaniment to any poker game no matter where it was played, in an extraordinary medley of drawls, burrs, dialects, and Creole tongues. I almost felt like leaving the money I won in the short half hour I played on the table in return for the rich experience and cross-section of southern Black workers' life and outlook that the poker game had given me.

Of all my underground experiences, I think the time in Havana was what had impressed me the most. I remember having to wait one day before Blas Roca would be able to meet with me. When we did, it was at his house. I had the pleasure of meeting his daughters and his wife. He was obviously a very busy man but exuded an air of calm confidence that made me proud to be associated with him in the same movement. He was a very handsome man with strong features that spoke of his Indian background, resembling the 1920s Hollywood star Antonio Moreno. He gave me a big smile, having remembered me from my previous visit to the PSP convention in 1949.

On entering Blas Roca's home, I was impressed first by the atmosphere of love and concern for him that emanated from his wife and daughters. At the same time, he did not appear to accept that love as his due but showed a reciprocal solicitude for them, reflecting his gratitude and appreciation. We sat down at a small rattan table, as he offered me a seat alongside him with a dazzling smile and then asked me what I wanted to discuss. Before I responded, Blas Roca told me that I had gotten a big laugh at the convention in 1949, when, in describing the various Black organizations, I had said there were more than 800,000

members of the IBPOE (the Negro Elks headed by J. Finley Wilson).
He explained that the word for elks in Spanish was also the word (slang)
for homosexuals and it was regarded as incredible that there could be
800,000 Black homosexuals in one organization until the interpreter
explained that it was not that sort of elk.

From there, we went on to the business of my trip. I spent a half
hour describing the controversy within the leadership over identifying
the main danger in the American party. He expressed familiarity with
John Swift's articles and Foster's position. John Swift was the underground name for Gil Green, one of the more flexible and creative think-
ers among the leaders who remained within the party. The essence of
the Swift criticism of our work at that time was the need to eliminate
the deep-rooted sectarianism in our work in the trade unions. Basi-
cally, Swift was calling for greater flexibility in tactics to overcome our
isolation from the rank-and-file workers, which, of course, meant a less
rigid interpretation of a slew of theoretical questions. After hearing me
out, Blas Roca responded, quite succinctly, "For me, the main danger
in the party is the one it is not fighting."

The other question concerned the passage of some of our people
through to eastern Europe. The Cuban party had a way of arranging
safe passage for American radicals through Mexico. He delegated this
discussion to Carlos Raphael Rodriguez. Carlos was the equivalent of
the director of educational work and also editor of the monthly theoretical magazine *Gamma*. We hit it off well, and later at a party that was
held for a group of the foreign visitors he displayed a professional dance
skill in the conga and other forms of *comparse*. Lazaro Peña, the Black
leader of the Cuban trade union movement and a member of the Central
Committee, making him a combination of George Meany and Henry
Winston, was also no mean dancer. Between the two of them, we felt
that we had professional entertainment. As a former dancer myself,
I felt that their putting on a show like that was not regarded as quite in
keeping with being a party leader, but the Cubans seemed to be completely relaxed and very warm in these areas of protocol. Of all the
foreign communists I ever met, the Cubans were the warmest and most
human. You just felt the ties of the party with the masses of people, and
their relationships with one another reflected that.

One of the most moving experiences for me took place after I had
been in the Deep Freeze for more than six months. I was so far into the
Deep Freeze that it took from December 19, 1953, to January 2, 1954—a

total of two weeks—for me to get word that my mother had died. It really hurt me that it took so long for me to get the news. I felt most vulnerable, my drinking accelerated, and I began to look for the companionship of a woman in the underground. Those of us in the underground had had discussions on the subject, especially married men, and the consensus was, why not, so long as the activity did not interfere with one's party responsibilities or one's family life on return. Except for one fling in Havana on my second trip there with a beautiful *señorita* whom I had met at a dance hall, I had prided myself on my "Bolshevik discipline" and been something of a prude on such matters. In fact, I had a reputation of being something of a model of marital fidelity and heterosexuality, probably a form of compensation for guilt over my "racy" background during my Cotton Club days. Anyway, my mother's death presented me with a rationale with which I could live. Opportunity knocked in the form of a talented and highly intelligent woman who had come into the underground some time before who was also lonely. By February 8, 1954, we were in continual "delicto flagrante" and my underground life took on a new dimension.

After returning from Cuba, I found myself somewhat isolated from the New York leadership, and the Deep Freeze was not an ideal setting for me. For one whole year, I had holed up in a rented room on Madison Street in Jersey City. In that year, 1953, my mother's death in Cleveland, Ohio, where she had been staying with my sister Winnie, shook me and at the same time, my contact during some of the Deep Freeze years, who knew and loved my mother, consoled me. I believe it was her underlying empathy with my loss that opened the gates of her affection for me in spite of the fact that we were both married and she, her husband, my wife, and I were all friends. The conflicts that I had emotionally were sharpening. My drinking accelerated. I didn't want to keep bottles in the room. I was always surprised at how fast a bottle became empty when I did. It was a form of denial of my increasing enslavement to the solace that the alcohol had come to represent for me. I thought I had control of myself. Instead I found a local bar that had a back room where I could drink my fill unobserved. At that time in Jersey City, a local ordinance made it illegal for women to stand at a bar. Many bars established back rooms where a woman could come in and sit down with a friend or by herself to drink. That situation offered me a convenient way of concealing my intake. Only wimps counted their drinks. I began to drink more heavily. Hiding out in Jersey City, I had little social companionship. I began to frequent a local bar where a bunch of senior citizens were awaiting my company—Old Granddad, Old Taylor, Old Crow, Old Forester, and Old Overholt. When things began to lighten up in 1954 and I emerged from the underground experience, I had developed a critical alcohol problem.

Part III

It is better to have struggled and lost, than never to have struggled at all.

—*Pete Seeger in the film* Seeing Red

10
Starting Over

35 East 12th Street, New York
June 25, 1956

The Khrushchev revelations hit me like a ton of bricks in June 1956. We had heard rumors that changes of major import were underway in the Soviet Union since the death of Stalin, but the enormity of the charges leveled by Khrushchev against the Stalin leadership had been anticipated by no one among us.

We, in the New York state leadership, had been carrying on virtually a guerrilla war with the national leadership over a period of months. It took no stretch of the imagination for many of us to make the link to the aspects of national policy and leadership that we had disagreed with and their connection with what we had begun to regard as the Stalinist approach to policy.

With the Khrushchev revelations, John Swift's critiques of our work in the trade unions seemed mild and not far-reaching enough. Many of the white comrades interpreted the Khrushchev statement to mean that everything we had done in the struggle against white racism in the trade unions was in error. We carried on a relatively relentless struggle in the furriers' union, electrical, District 65, maritime, hotel, and furniture unions—all unions where we had had considerable influence—against white chauvinism, marked by all-night debates on the merits of advancing the party's position on the Negro question in the trade unions. The position was focused on two major issues: the advancement

135

of Blacks to positions of leadership in the trade unions and the role of communists in the trade unions in the fight against racism.

The struggles were particularly fierce in fur and District 65—precisely where we had the largest number of party members and where the trade union leaders who were communists not only were in command of the union but also controlled the party organization. Many members held their jobs as a result of the control the communist leaders had over the union employment situation. One of the bitterest opponents of the party's position in fur was Leon Strauss. His arguments that "we don't have any qualified Blacks to elevate to leadership in our union" anticipated the racist approach that emerged in the '70s against affirmative action. He left the party and later functioned as one of the major consultants to strike-breaking corporations. Not that the stance he held on the Negro question inevitably led him to that position, but the connection between his opportunism and his white chauvinism was evident at that time.

The majority of the New York state leadership took the position that our struggles in the trade unions in New York in the fight for Negro rights was the prime example of our sectarianism and, in my opinion, appealed to the sometimes not-so-subtle racism in our members who castigated the many Black comrades who had been very critical of the racism among our trade union leaders. The logic of their position led them to support the Johnny Gates grouping in the national leadership, urging a more liberal, less radical approach. This was a faction that emerged during the internal crisis of 1956, prompted by the Khrushchev revelations as well as the Russian invasion of Hungary. Black comrades in Harlem were carrying on a war against the New York state leadership of which I was considered a part at the same time that I was attempting to find some bridge between the struggle against rights opportunism and against sectarianism in the struggle against white chauvinism.

This was true, even as early as the fall of 1952, when my efforts to bridge the gap between the Black comrades in Harlem and the New York state leadership had been expressed in an article published in December 1952 and January 1953 in *Political Affairs* under the pseudonymous byline of Samuel Henderson. The article was entitled "Against White Chauvinism and Bourgeois Nationalism," and very few really wanted to deal with these questions. I was naïve. My article had been attacked by both Black and white comrades, for being too critical on both sides of the fence. The white comrades tended to focus on the nationalism of the Blacks and the Black comrades veered toward a one-sided focus on the racism of the whites. Self-criticism was conspicuous for its absence.

In my experience, the members of the party, coming as they did from every walk of American life, brought with them not only their highly motivated desire to change the system but also the whole welter of norms, behavioral patterns, mores, standards, and even the English language itself built into their unconscious. Blacks were sensitive to these racist cultural patterns and for the first time began to criticize white comrades publicly. Unfortunately, too few white comrades were sufficiently sensitive to these manifestations and rejected much of the criticism coming from the Blacks. Blacks were often charged with being oversensitive, "having a chip on their shoulder," or simply not knowing what racism was. This infuriated the Blacks and generated a confrontational atmosphere in the party rather than one of mutual discussion for joint enlightenment. The confrontational atmosphere was as much a product of the resistance of the white comrades as of sectarian approaches on the part of the Blacks. The escalation of the struggle in a negative direction was a reflection of a low level of political consciousness in the party as well as the deep-rooted, pervasive quality of racism in the American society of which we were a part despite our radical vows or intentions. The oversimplification of that period in later analysis has had a harmful effect on the development of a solidly integrated Black and white cadre in the American radical movement.

Perhaps the best illustration of the position of the majority of whites in the New York district is the comment made by Joseph Starobin in his description of the period:

> Probably the most symptomatic of this "turning inward" was the 1949–1953 campaign against white chauvinism. This was a veritable paroxysm that reflected far more than the ostensible issue of the party's relations with the Negro movement. No single experience is remembered in retrospect with such dismay, even fifteen years later, by thousands of former communists and their progressive sympathizers. Not a few have asked themselves: if they were capable of such cruelties to each other when they were a small handful of people bound by sacred ideals, what might have they done if they had been in power? The white chauvinism experience helped a great many understand the revelations about Stalinism. The underground adventure was to affect only a few thousand,

but the struggle against white chauvinism wrecked the lives of tens of thousands.[1]

George Charney commented, supporting this thesis:

Thus the most harrowing experience of our post-war history was the campaign against "white chauvinism" in which our difficulties and setbacks were ascribed to the fatal weaknesses of the white members who had not shed the prejudice of the master race and were, therefore, unable to carry out an effective struggle for Negro rights. The campaign had some of the features of the Inquisition.[2]

From my vantage point, I had never seen the problems of mass struggle as being contingent on the ideological purity of the party on the Negro question and had always raised, as the fundamental question, the mass struggle on key issues. So the criticism by Starobin and Charney seemed accurate in analyzing the excesses of the Pettis Perrys and the Betty Gannetts,[3] but they did not propose a better alternative for developing the struggle against white chauvinism within the ranks of the party, as if there were no need for such a struggle.

The gross exaggeration of the negative impact of the struggles inside the party against white chauvinism by respected former leaders of the American Communist Party such as Joseph Starobin and George Charney is reflected in their characterization of the struggle against white chauvinism as having wrecked the lives of tens of thousands of members as opposed to the decision to send people into the underground, which affected the lives of only a few thousand members, clearly an exaggeration because the party did not have tens of thousands of members.

The faulty statistics are an index of the inaccurate judgment of both Starobin and Charney, both of whom were very good friends of mine. Their inaccurate judgment was influenced by their inability to understand the centrality of the race question in the relationship of the Communist Party to the Black community and an utter inability to comprehend that the Black comrades, whatever the rudeness or lack of refinement in their expression of their criticism of the white communists, were expressing the sentiments of the Black community. The struggle in the party between Blacks and whites also, most importantly, reflected the different levels of development of the political consciousness of the white and Black populations.

During that period, I had played a major role in guaranteeing the success of the million-dollar fund drive, establishing a high level of morale as the political basis for the carrying through of the drive, which was outstandingly successful. One-half of the money was to go to the legal party organization and one-half, or $500,000, was to be put in reserve for the use of the underground organization. Part of that was set aside for the immediate use of the New York state leadership for any emergency. We were each given $30,000 to hold. I had never seen $30,000 before in my life. It was all in bundles of tens and twenties. I did not want to carry it around until I could find a safe place for it, so I asked Zelda and her husband, Leon, my brother- and sister-in-law, to hold it for me for a couple of days. They put the money in packages under their kitchen sink. At the time, they lived in the relatively cheap veterans' Linden housing projects on Pennsylvania Avenue in Brooklyn. As luck would have it, there was a heavy rainstorm that night and their kitchen was flooded, getting the money totally water-soaked.

I was asked to return the money on short notice before it had a chance to dry out. Later we had many a laugh (after getting over the anxiety of anything happening to the "party money") about the long hours that Zelda spent ironing the money on her ironing board so as to get it dry in time for my pickup.

Some others did not treat party money with such care or respect. One of the trade union leaders in District 65 who were given $30,000 to hold invested it in a business, making the money unavailable when the party asked for it. Ben Davis and I were assigned to meet with the trade union leader to tell him in no uncertain terms what would happen to him if he did not return the money in a specific period of time. He hemmed and hawed. Ben and I spent an hour discussing the various things that could happen to him if he did not deliver, including my description of my loyalty to the party and how my Army training in judo had equipped me with many ways to punish traitors. Ben added his imaginative repertoire of fundraising techniques, and the trade union leader promised to get the money in twenty-four hours, and he did. At the time, I felt like the strong arm of the revolution, but the role I played embarrassed me later. I have since made amends for that violation of Dr. King's ethic of nonviolence.

I was increasingly coming to believe that the factional struggle over policy was rendering the Communist Party ineffective. I was emotionally uncomfortable with the internecine infighting that was developing, and after my bout with alcohol, none of my Black friends in the party seemed interested in my point of view. Discouraged by the lack of any concern on the part of my white comrades who had been my closest co-workers in the previous five years, I gradually came to the conclusion that I did not have much to contribute to any of the factions. I also had reached a point at which I found nothing that could morally justify my association with Stalin's regime, having been one of its most outspoken defenders in the Black community. However, I did not want to add anything to the tide of red-baiting and anticommunist hysteria that had reached its height during the McCarthy period. I feared that any criticism I made of the party publicly would be interpreted as a repudiation of my whole past activism in the labor and civil rights struggles. I had always associated red-baiting with the most reactionary, anti-Black, and antilabor forces in the United States. My solution was to leave quietly, discontinuing my eighteen-year association with the Communist Party.

I felt that Black radicals had to form their own movement, utilizing the experiences of oppressed nationalities and colonial peoples around the world. These movements formed their own radical or Marxist associations, usually independent of European or white tutelage. Because of the impact of countrywide racism suffered by African Americans in the United States and because of my experience in the Communist Party, which I considered the most enlightened of the radical organizations in the United States, I came to believe that progressive Blacks could not develop a clear strategy and tactics for the emergence of a current in the Black community if they had to filter their policies and have approval of the majority-white left-wing organizations. I believed that radical Blacks had to form their own organizations, uniting all these currents in the Black movement with the participation of all Blacks wherever they were based in white organizations. This meant that Blacks in the Communist Party, the Socialist Party, the Socialist Workers Party, the Progressive Labor Party, the October League, the Black Panthers, the Black Liberation Army, and the Black United Front should make their primary allegiance the development of a Black movement that would unite all the avant-garde trends in the Black movement. This would not mean severance of membership in the white-dominated radical groups. Dual membership is always possible and necessary. But for clear thinking, Blacks needed their own autonomous organization or coalition of trends through which Black radical thinking could be developed, unhampered by the necessity of overcoming a white veto in a majority-white organization. I had become aware of the influence of white thinking on Blacks who were members of predominantly white organizations. I recall carefully formulating proposals I wanted to make in the party leadership with an eye to how the white comrades would respond. Sometimes, after many years of participating in party strategy meetings at the highest level, I was aware that I would censor or modify ideas in advance of presentation to adjust to what I knew to be the level of acceptance or understanding of the white comrades. So my full thinking as a Black man did not emerge in party meetings, but rather a consensus opinion that I had tailored to the level of the white comrades. Professor Terry Hopkins at Binghamton's Department of Sociology has aptly called this the "Rousseauian vote principle," wherein each individual votes the way he thinks the social consensus would vote. There is also the physical energy required to participate in any organization. Internal meetings and inner-party housekeeping require enormous amounts of time, and Black activists need more time to spend with one another and with the forces they are working with in the Black community. Therefore, the time spent with white radicals should be carefully allocated so that the white connection does not interfere with the necessary time that must be put into the Black community. There should be frequent consultation and coordination between white and Black progressives, but that should not be at the expense of their primary tasks and responsibilities. Black activists presenting themselves as leaders in the Black community would be less likely to be regarded as spokespersons for this or that white group. More respect would accrue to the movement in the Black community, which, in turn, would in conferring with white groups on policy affecting Black people give the very same Black progressives greater weight as spokespersons for the legitimate current in the Black community.

The party during that period began to fragment into three distinct segments: one group, led by William Z. Foster, whose closest Black associate was Benjamin J. Davis; another group led by Eugene Dennis, with whom James Jackson and Henry Winston appeared to be most closely associated; and a third group under the leadership of Johnny Gates, whose chief Black supporter was Herbert Wheeldin.

One of the things that bothered me about the divisions among the Black comrades in the party was what seemed to be a higher loyalty to the particular white leader or viewpoint than to their concern for the unity of the Black radicals in their work in the Black community, which was our prime responsibility. It was apparent to me that the three factions engrossed in the struggle over the general line of the party had divided over strategy for the Black community as well. The line of the Foster group, for which Ben Davis was the most articulate spokesperson, projected what could be described essentially as a class–against–class approach to the Black community. The class–against–class approach was outlined in a major theoretical way in a book by Harry Haywood, *Black Bolshevik*.[4] Haywood, like E. Franklin Frazier in his book *The Black Bourgeoisie*,[5] saw no positive features in the Negro middle class; Haywood recommended that Black workers direct their struggle against the Black middle class in order to fight racism successfully. The Gates group, most vocal in opposing the development of the struggle against white chauvinism, projected a line that was essentially assimilationist with no independent role for the Black movement beyond the nonviolent civil disobedience campaign led by Martin Luther King Jr. This policy was most clearly expressed in an article in the New York state Communist Party publication *The Party Voice* by one of the Black comrades, under the name of Montgomery, who had been added to the New York state leadership as a balance to the policies I had projected in my *Political Affairs* article. The third grouping, headed by Dennis and his main Black supporter, Jim Jackson, advocated a position that sought to conciliate the two extremes represented by Foster and Gates.

After leaving the party, I began to realize that my inability to identify with any of these groups was based on the fact that none of these positions showed a clear analysis of the problems of the African American movement. On the contrary, the three factions in the party were oriented toward dealing with Stalinism and its aftermath on an international scale. I felt alienated from all three groupings and gradually came to the conclusion that whatever line the Communist Party developed, it would not meet the needs of the civil rights or the general radical movement.

One of the thoughts that had nagged me when I was sent into the Deep Freeze was that the New York state leadership, sensing my growing conflict over party positions, might have wanted me out of the active underground leadership during the period of the intense debates on policy before the Khrushchev revelations.

Kings County Hospital Psych Ward, New York
August 19, 1956

That summer I was thrown into an emotional, psychological, political, and ideological shock that rattled the very core of my being. The Khrushchev revelations about Joseph Stalin immediately struck me as having an authenticity that could not be challenged. I had always considered myself a nonbureaucratic, nonauthoritanian communist leader. Many of the things that bothered me about the way some party leaders functioned in the United States I began to define as expressions of Stalinism in the American party. For a short period of time I felt an identification with the group of party leaders who thought there was a possibility of winning over the party to reconstitute itself as an American noncommunist socialist group. I attended meetings in which Earl Browder, Johnny Gates, and others of the Socialist Party discussed a new radical political formation. These meetings were talkfests that resulted in no new action. I was put off by those who talked of the "correctness" of American policy in Vietnam and who had nothing to say about the burgeoning civil rights movement in the South. Deep down, I was disconcerted and demoralized, and my drinking accelerated.

I didn't realize the extent of my drinking when I "came up from underground" and returned home expecting to be treated like the conquering hero. This was setting myself up for some major disappointment. Martha seemed distant. I didn't realize that my affair with Lucy in the underground had soured me on my relationship with Martha for all time. My denial system was operating in high gear. Lucy was a consuming sensual experience for me! Martha's antipathy toward me (as I interpreted her seeming coldness) expressed itself in many not-so-subtle ways. It intensified my attraction to Lucy. I did not recognize that my definition of Martha's attitude toward me was in large part a projection of my attitude toward her. Our personal relationship was also contaminated by our previous differences over the party's policies. She had opposed my going into the underground, asking questions like "How is this going to affect the kids?" and "Do you love me or do you love the party?" My response had been, "The party comes first. I'm a revolutionary!" This answer did nothing to diminish the distance between us.

After I was home for a short time, my drinking increased even more. I began to hang out at Joe's bar after I came home from work. Joe's bar was at the corner of 143rd Street and Hamilton Place. It was a low-down, raunchy place filled with hustlers, boosters (persons who steal items from retail stores and then sell them on the streets, usually at a discount), numbers-runners, and people I generally didn't associate with on a daily basis. I comforted myself with the thought that from time to time I was in the company of greats like Billy Strayhorn, who would stop in for a drink after rehearsing with the Ellington band.

Martha often had to send one of my daughters down to Joe's to beg me to come home for dinner. I regarded this as a form of harassment.

Didn't Martha know I was having a pleasant conversation with *the* Billy Strayhorn, who was on his way home from rehearsals with the Ellington band? She didn't say anything about her long talks with Agnes de Mille or Trudi Rittman that made her late coming home. I didn't realize that her advancement in the theater was affecting my self-esteem.

The reunited party was engaged in fratricidal warfare over policy. I was torn over the differences. The party seemed to be going down the tubes, and my married life had become a farce. Martha and I kept up a front of sorts for the public and our kids, but we were both unhappy with each other. I became more and more dependent on the bottle as a source of relief for my battered psyche. By the time the Khrushchev report was released in the *New York Times*, I was drinking up a storm.

The pain of the Khrushchev revelations about Stalin's misrule was more than I could bear. I went on a drinking binge practically every night. My hanging out at the bar became more frequent. I had no thought that I was going through all of the rituals of a typical alcoholic and that added to my traumatic reaction to the Khrushchev revelations were my domestic problems reflected in my relationship with Martha. She had accumulated four years of bitterness and resentment.

So I was caught between a rock and a hard place. I was unhappy at my job, and I was unhappy in my marriage. My drinking began to take on a life of its own. It provided me with an escape from the pain of the disillusionment with the Communist Party and with the unhappiness of my marriage.

In August 1956, Martha got an assignment to work in the musical *South Pacific* at the Brandywine Musical Tent in Downingtown, Pennsylvania. She was taking Wendy with her and we had arranged for Wini and Lisa to go to a girls' camp. So I was left alone. A few of my friends had told me I was drinking too much, and I decided I would stop at that time when the family was away. And I did.

The last drink I took was Sunday night, August 12. I slept fitfully Sunday night, then woke up Monday to start my vacation and carry out my resolve to stop drinking. I did not realize that the abrupt halt of my drinking would begin to affect me. The first night I began to feel irritable and uneasy. I had difficulty going to sleep. Before I went to bed, I saw some red flashes on the living room wall. We didn't have television, but I sat and watched these flashes as if I were watching a television program. I didn't know it, but I was having visual hallucinations of a fairly mild sort. I took it rather lightly and finally got to sleep, to wake up early the next day. I decided that taking a long walk would ease my state of tension. So I walked down Amsterdam Avenue all the way past the Lewisohn Stadium to the Columbia University campus.

One of my favorite walks was along Morningside Drive near the Columbia campus because it provided a nice overview of central Harlem from the heights along which Morningside Drive ran. Before 1953 and the underground, I had started taking walks there during the period when Dwight D. Eisenhower was president of Columbia and often fantasized that I might run in to him on my walks. One of the devices I used to ease my tensions was finding streets in New York that had a good collection of sycamore trees. I always identified the patchy, multicolored bark of the tree with my own multiethnic background and my war wounds. The patchy bark looked like wounds of some type. I had read Camus' novel *The Stranger,* and in it his hero takes long walks along streets lined with plane trees, which are related to sycamores. I identified with the character in the book, a feeling that I could not describe then—but that I realize now was alienation.

Wednesday night, more strange things began to happen. About midnight, I heard Eddie King's voice down in the street shouting, "He better stop messing with Serena! I'm going to kick his ass!" This continued for a half hour and I decided to call my brother Wesley to come down and see what was happening. At 1:00 A.M. he knew something was amiss, so he asked, "What's up, Stretch?"

I said, "Eddie King is out front threatening me! Will you come down and see what's going on?"

Wesley said, in his usual take-charge police voice, "I'll be right down."

I finished off my end of the exchange, "Bring your gun!'

In twenty minutes, Wesley was knocking on my door. I asked, "Did you see anything?"

Wesley answered, "Everything's quiet out there now. Why don't you go to bed and get some sleep?"

What I didn't know then, but realize now, was that I had entered a new stage of my withdrawal from the booze—auditory hallucinations! The whole Eddie King scene was a figment of my alcohol-inflamed imagination!

The situation went from bad to worse and I wound up in Kings County Psychiatric Ward in a straitjacket. I was told that I was an alcoholic and should never drink again. The national expert on alcoholism who knew me as a radical recommended that I go to AA meetings. I went, but in 1956, the health-conscious level was fairly low and by the

time heavy drinkers hit their bottom they were not very inviting speci-
mens of humanity. I didn't cotton to them as a peer group and quit
after my first meeting. I decided to deal with my drinking problem
through the medium of psychiatry. Two years of psychotherapy with a
radical psychiatrist, Dr. Leonard Frank, convinced me that a large part
of my problem with drinking stemmed from anxiety over latent homosexual tendencies. I was also concerned about playing a male role as a
father in contributing support to a family with three daughters. I had
had a number of jobs as a most unsuccessful salesman for the classified
ads at the *Amsterdam News* and as salesman and caster of the unorthodox Murray Space Shoes, both jobs that I knew were far beneath my
capabilities.

I was also extremely bitter that none of those whom I considered my
close party friends made absolutely any effort to find me more suitable
employment. I suspected that rumors were being circulated about me
in the party that my alcoholism had made me unemployable. Most of
my white colleagues seemed, even those who had also left the party,
able to hook into networks that found them comfortable employment.
In fact, a large number of them made the connections to achieve an
even higher standard of living than they had attained in the party.
Finally, after unsuccessfully attempting to get membership in the typo-
graphical union, Local Six, which became a haven for a number of
former party members, I heard through my friends Jesse Wallach and
John Devine about a job in a shop in New Jersey where one did not
have to be in the union to get a proofreading slot. And, in time, if you
met the work standards, the boss would let you get a union card. (The
FBI was right on top of the situation and visited my boss, Al Baisch,
telling him that I was a communist. Baisch told me that he responded
that I was doing my job and he saw no reason that I shouldn't keep it.)
It was an ideal place for me because there was a way to get into the
union in New York. The condition was that you had to work in New
Jersey for at least one year before applying for a transfer to New York. I
wanted desperately to transfer. First, it meant a leap in pay from $97.00
to $133.00 per week. Second, it would mean a savings of two hours a
day in travel time.

At the Publishers Typographic Service, I started on the night shift,
a most difficult one, but after a year I was transferred to the day shift,
where I got a chance to be a member of a car pool with Jack Devine
and some wonderful Argentineans who were refugees from the Peronist
terror. They were excellent printers, some of them having learned the

trade as an avocation to their regular function as lawyers, editors, or other professionals. Most of them seemed, from our conversations during the half-hour journey from the George Washington Bridge, where we met daily, to be former communists who, like me, had gone through a similar de-Stalinization process.

My best friend on the job was Joe Caulfield, a former professor of English literature at Manhattan College, a Catholic school. We had many philosophical and theoretical discussions during slow time at Publishers, and he often expressed the idea that I should get academic training. Though I had a strong identification with being a skilled worker, I also resented the status of being ordered around by a foreman and finally decided to go to school.

In October 1960 I enrolled in a writers' class at Columbia School of General Studies. Because I had never graduated from high school, I was asked to take a college aptitude test. I scored very high on the test, so high that not only was I accepted for the course but the advisor recommended that I take the validation program of fifteen credits, which, if passed, would qualify me to become a degree candidate. I must have done quite well, because Columbia was not aggressively recruiting Black students. The demand for increasing Black student enrollment had not yet swelled to the level it would in the mid-'60s. The Watts riots were not to come until four years later. Encouraged by my admission to Columbia, I decided to get a high school equivalency diploma and took the examination in December, scoring 297.6 out of a possible perfect 300. I was as proud of that high school certificate as if it had been a Ph.D. At the age of forty-five, and after the traumatic episode with the delirium tremens that threw me into a straitjacket at Kings County Hospital, this success was proof in my eyes that I was rational and capable of quality intellectual performance. Perhaps it was also an indication of how much my self-confidence had been eroded by the combination of disillusionment with the party and my disease of alcoholism.

I managed to get through Columbia in five-and-a-half years while working full-time in the printing industry. Jack Devine had transferred to New York during that time and informed me of an opening at Empire Typographers, where I worked on the lobster shift until late 1968. Being on the lobster shift (it was so named from the time that most newspapers were published on Park Row near the Fulton Fish Market, and when the papers were put to bed the printers would go for a seafood breakfast) enabled me to attend classes at Columbia in the day or evening. For morning classes I would leave immediately after work and go home and sleep from 9:00 A.M. to 4:00 or 5:00 P.M. and then go to evening classes and from there straight to work. This gave me a flexibility in choosing courses that enabled me to get through faster than would be expected.

I've often wondered what would have happened if I had not come back from World War II to party functionary status but had used the GI Bill, which would have given me a free education through the Ph.D. rather than having paid for it myself in my mid-forties. In any event, it's made me less than sympathetic toward students funded by all sorts of government subsidies who don't put in the proper kind of discipline and attention to their studies.

While I was going through this rigorous schedule, Martha was very supportive, placing few demands on me and making a major contribution to the family budget from her employment as a pianist with frequent Broadway musicals. Our daughters were growing beautifully—Wendy had been admitted to Hunter College after the School of Performing Arts, Wini had gotten into the School of Industrial Arts, and Lisa was a student at Downtown Community School, which had become popular with the children of many radical leaders because of the compassionate and forward-looking leadership of its headmaster, Norman Studer. Without DCS's tuition assistance program, we could not have paid Lisa's school fees.

Ironically, while our careers were growing apace, Martha and I were growing further apart. My drinking had been held down considerably during my studies at Columbia. I began to date fellow students at Columbia like Carol Billings, the playwright, and Ann Hitch, who was in an uncomfortable marriage with a CIA agent. The degree requirements—the readings, written assignments, and examination preparations—acted as constraints that enabled me to hold to a maximum of two or three drinks on weekends.

During this period, my studies at Columbia had made it difficult for me to be involved in the extracurricular campus activities, though for one semester I did volunteer for the editorial board of *The Owl*, the School of General Studies newspaper. I was given an assignment to interview Seymour Melman, a Columbia professor who was an authority on the military-industrial complex, and I wrote an article with great enthusiasm. The editors looked at the article and made some cursory comments about lack of space and length. I sensed that I was being dismissed because I was not a part of the student clique that ran *The Owl*, wasn't middle-class enough, wasn't liberal enough, and wasn't white enough.

I noticed also that teaching assistants in sociology, psychology, and other lab courses were always white and gave much attention and many explanations on complicated lab procedures to their fellow white students but seemed to choke up or become very succinct and impatient when I asked questions about procedures. The same was true of most professors. There was no question that an Ivy League atmosphere prevailed. It was unusual to see Black students in any courses. If there were Black students they were usually African, West Indian, or, rarely, Afro-American bourgeois. Removed from the Harlem community on both the job and the academic front, with homework making it impossible to do anything but work and go to classes, I had a strong sense of isolation. The one Black friend whom I saw regularly was Mel Williamson, who had left the Labor Youth League, after having been a national leader for a number of years, under much the same conditions under which I had left the party. We commiserated with each other over our lack of connection and tried to keep up with the politics of the day. I would say that up until I graduated from Columbia, I still identified myself as a Marxist of the nonparty variety, or, in C. Wright Mills's terminology, a "plain Marxist"—a pretty honorable group because it included Herbert Marcuse, Antonio Gramsci, Jean-Paul Sartre, William Morris, Rosa Luxembourg, Georges Sorel, Christopher Cauldwell, William A. Williams, Paul Sweezy, Erich Fromm, and probably Paul Baran, Linus Pauling, and Vito Marcantonio. Since then, my views on Marxism have changed, and from the '60s on I considered myself an independent radical.

My one connection with political activity other than my trade union activity was through my nephew Donald Martin Perry, the only son of my sister Winnie by the one-time Hollywood movie star Stepin Fetchit. Winnie and Stepin Fetchit had divorced in 1939, after Stepin, in one of his more brutal moments, had knocked Winnie down the steps of the theatrical rooming house where they lived. The house was known to all performers as "Jop's." "Jop" was the widow of Scott Joplin and had inherited two houses on what we called Strivers' Row. It was only years later that Winnie told us about this episode, knowing that we would probably have whipped Step's ass if we had been told at the time. Donald had grown up into a fine intellectual and militant, and he used me as a coach or mentor in working in the various militant groups. The strategy we had agreed on was that he was going to work with all of the groups—the Panthers, the RNA (the Republic of New Africa), the SNCC, and the NAACP—or at least keep in contact with them through his own participation or through his many friends.

We had a friendly rivalry going on as to who would finish college first, the nephew or the uncle. One of the most memorable episodes in our relationship took place in my apartment on 95th Street, when he brought Stokely Carmichael, Charles Hamilton, Sam Anderson, and some other friends by for a political discussion on perspectives. My perspective at that time was for the all-class unity of the Black movement as opposed to what I thought was a super-leftist class-against-class approach being worked out by the SNCC, the Panthers, and others of the Black militants. There was clearly a controversy between Martin Luther King's approach and that of Stokely Carmichael, who had Marxist leanings. It became known as "Martin versus Marx." I was also critical, while understanding the criticism of many of the whites in the civil rights movement, of the SNCC decision to remove whites from their staff. To me, this policy exacerbated divisions in the coalition for civil rights when unity was most needed. Donald described the interchange among Carmichael, Hamilton, and me in his dramatic literary style, as a kind of confrontation between "Black cobras" and "Black panthers" circling each other intellectually.

In view of the role that Hamilton played after he became chairman of the Political Science Department at Columbia University, I wonder if his divisive activity in the Black movement at that time was not reflective of a kind of "anticipatory co-optation" for his later rewards by the academic establishment.

Donald had had several heated discussions with me expressing our differences over an evaluation of Martin Luther King Jr. Some of the SNCC people were talking about MLK as "Martin Luther Queen." I pointed out to Donald that his attack on MLK coincided with the southern racists who were calling him "Martin Luther Coon," and the FBI reports on his bedroom activities with white women had given rise to the title "Martin Luther Kong." As FBI documents in the COINTEL program later revealed, a very-well-orchestrated campaign was emanating from J. Edgar Hoover's office to create the hysterical atmosphere that would end MLK's role by some form of political neutralization—up to and including assassination.

Donald himself was to become a victim of the very same program, arrested and killed on a frame-up charge on the Pennsylvania Turnpike by Pennsylvania state troopers. It was only after the COINTELPRO revelations that I realized the extent of the coordination of federal, state, and local government and police in the nationwide drive against the entire civil rights movement under the guise of combating "communism and Black nationalist extremism." Donald, while at Lincoln University, had been part of a radical discussion group of about twelve of the brightest students on campus. Of the twelve students in the group at least half of them have died under mysterious circumstances. The raid on the FBI headquarters at Media, Pennsylvania, by Quaker activists exposed documents indicating the leading FBI informant on names of militant students at Lincoln University, Donald Cheek, the Lincoln University Dean of Students. Coincidentally, Donald Cheek is the brother of James Cheek, the president of Howard University, who specialized in defusing militant activity on the part of Howard students during the same period.

My nephew Donald had also participated in the Newark Black Unity Conference in 1968 and the international meeting of Black activists in Montreal, where he had been admitted into the inner circle of leadership under the name Sakubeti. During that time he wrote some beautiful poetry and an excellent appreciation of Malcolm X based on a day he spent with Malcolm. He told me Malcolm had mentioned that he had listened to me speak on the soapbox in front of LaMarcheri on Sugar Hill and at Small's Paradise down in the valley and that I had influenced him in a social orientation even before he became a Muslim. However, Donald and I became increasingly estranged as he seemed to come more and more under the influence of the Black nationalist rhetoric. The question of skin color seemed to absorb him to the point that his relationship to his cousins—my daughters—cooled off. They were half-white—in fact, half-Jewish—on their mother's side and, on my side, at least one-quarter white, making them, in the carefully calibrated quantification of melanin content of the skin developed under the slave society, octoroons, or only one-eighth Black, if that. I argued with him that Blackness was a political stand, having nothing to do with skin color: that is, many very Black people supported the white power structure and many of the most revolutionary fighters against slavery were mulattos, such as Frederick Douglass and Harriet Tubman and later, against second-class citizenship, people like Lucretia Mott, W. E. B. Du Bois, and Mary Church Terrell.

To me, skin color ideology (white or Black) was a curse. I had seen it disrupt and destroy friendships among Black Marxists in the party, generate resentments in my own family, and spoil my first love affair with a next-door neighbor, Ruth Moore, because she was too dark in my father's prejudiced way of thinking. The European-inspired construct that dichotomized the world's population into two main divisions—Black and white—around which the greatest emotional tension was generated (and two less emotionally tense constructs of yellow and red) was, to me, a mythology that originally served the interests of the expansion of the slave trade. When allowed to flourish, the mythology became pathological. The idea of whiteness as a symbol of superiority triggered delusions of grandeur and represented to me a form of group narcissism of the secondary variety. The idea of Blackness as an expression of inferiority was simply the converse of group narcissism and where accepted by Afro-Americans represented group masochism. In fact, there is no such skin color as white or Black—human colors range from light pink to a purplish dark brown. The geographical reference to group identification as Europeans or Africans, the language description as French or Spanish, all seemed to make much more sense to me. My own belief was that we were all humans or terrestrials in the universe whose likenesses were much more fundamental as species-designation than the superficial differences of skin color. All these arguments were central in my discussions with Donald but were to little avail as we drifted apart, to my great regret.

When I got my Bachelor's of Science degree in Comparative Literature, I decided to celebrate my success by going "off the wagon" with the perspective of returning to Columbia within a year to pursue my studies for an M.A. degree. After I received my degree, an old party friend, Malcolm Wofsy, who had become a successful researcher in biochemistry as a result of his discovery of a component of the B vitamins, introduced me to two old friends of his, Ernest Gruenberg and Alexander Inkeles, for possible job placement. Inkeles was supervising a research project at Cornell University and Dr. Gruenberg was director of the Psychiatric Epidemiological Research Unit (PERU), which was conducting a federally funded research program on a concept developed by Gruenberg called the "social breakdown syndrome." I was attracted by the object of this study, the location of the unit at the prestigious Psychiatric Institute, and its connection with my alma mater, Columbia University College of Physicians and Surgeons, so I signed on as a graduate research assistant with PERU and received the title Documentation Specialist after Gruenberg learned of my years of proofreading and editorial experience. I could do most of the requirements of the job, which consisted of coding manuals, organizing the filing system, and supervising the maintenance of the file in the three stations or field units of the project, with one hand tied behind my back. It was typical bureaucratic paperwork and left me enough energy to continue to work full-time as a proofreader at Empire Typographers. Sometimes the two jobs would overlap as my cooperative co-workers at Empire would often set type for printed materials I needed at PERU. Gruenberg was pleased at the professionalism in the design and typography for the filing system directory and other materials that I produced as documentation specialist.

In the fall of 1967, I enrolled in graduate courses in sociology at Columbia with the intent of becoming a doctoral candidate. One of my first instructors was Terry Hopkins, who was very encouraging to me. Sam Coleman, who had been my assistant educational director in the New York state Communist Party, introduced us. Sam had been part of Bob Thompson's crew, which was captured in the High Sierras by the FBI. He, being Bob's right-hand man, was convicted on charges of being an accomplice to and aiding a fugitive from justice. Sam and I had been good friends as well as co-workers. He and Joe Starobin introduced me to a few people at Columbia who they thought might be helpful. Sam had been able to get a teaching position at Columbia despite his having served time at Leavenworth. Joe introduced me to Daniel Bell, who was something of a star at Columbia based on the response to his book *The End of Ideology.*

Despite the racism at Columbia, I felt I had significant support from key people and anticipated no major obstacles to attaining a Ph.D. there. In the spring of 1968, I had decided to attend Students for a Democratic Society meetings. Politically, things appeared to be warming up on campus. In February and March, SDS meetings were attended by twenty to twenty-five people. The discussions seemed to be most abstract, with much spouting of doctrine of a sectarian quality that the Communist Party had left behind at least twenty-five years before. We had called this type of talk "phrase mongering." There seemed to be much posturing, flamboyance, and egocentrism among the leaders and a pervasive kind of hostility with one another that shocked me. Name-calling and cursing that would have precipitated physical fights in our time were evidently acceptable. Mark Rudd and Al Syzmanski were among the most prominent and influential of the leaders I saw in action. My guess was that they could not possibly be effective and I stopped attending meetings, feeling like a Rip Van Winkle whom time had passed by. In March, I did attend a meeting where the big wheels from the Department of Sociology met jointly with the radical students to discuss some of the issues that were being debated—Lazarsfeld, Hyman, Etzione, and Merton came out in force, apparently to head off what appeared to be a collision course between the college administration and the students. They seemed to be attempting to defuse the student revolt with promises of "wait and see; the administration can be dealt with if proper tactics are used." By the end of March the student protests had reached the point where SDS leaders were speaking to a thousand or more students around the sundial at the center of the campus. From small sectarian gatherings of twenty to twenty-five students, in two short months SDS was leading, despite its sectarianism, thousands of students on campus.

I estimated that if SDS had 10,000 members nationally, it had provided the spinal column for more than 250,000 student demonstrators throughout the country, who in turn moved as a mobilizer of 2 or 3 million students in action for change. The student movement demonstrated how volatile the masses can be when the proper issues arise and where there is a well-organized minority that is highly committed to lead. Because there were no other radical student organizations, SDS with all its anarchistic, sectarian, sexist, racist, and middle-class style was able to play a major role in the wave of student revolts that swept the country. I had seen it happen on the Columbia campus. But in the first week of April, the blow that struck the heart of the civil rights movement, the assassination of Martin Luther King, sent me into a tailspin. I was shattered once again—this time, I saw little use in working for a degree. The streets were ablaze with demonstrations and rioting in most major inner cities, the Black community expressing its rage over the loss of our greatest leader of the twentieth century, if not of all American history.

I dropped out of Columbia's Department of Sociology Graduate Program, not knowing quite what to do in the difficult but continuing struggle for freedom. I had little anticipation that ahead of me were new careers, new struggles that would make all my previous activity seem like simply a preparation and apprenticeship for greater battles to come.

11

Malimwu

Fieldston School, New York
April 10, 1969

I returned to drinking and it escalated dramatically along with my extramarital activities. Yet, needing to work and still functioning fairly well, I learned that the Ethical Culture Schools were seeking a Black administrator. I decided to apply for the position and was accepted for an interview as one of sixteen candidates, following which I was invited to a second round of interviews for the four shortlisted people. I was called a week later by Dr. Dan Wagner, who told me I was his choice. He had just been hired to be director of the schools and wanted me to be his assistant. I was to wear three hats: assistant director responsible for community relations, Project Director of the Upward Bound Program of 105 disadvantaged youth from New York City high schools, and a faculty member teaching African American history.

After my first four weeks on campus, the Black students expressed dissatisfaction with the other Black faculty member who had been advisor to the Black Students Union and asked me if I would become their faculty advisor. It was spring and we had an immediate problem: the preparation of the four-week encampment. We had a bang-up four-week encampment for 30 students who would be the cadre for "role modeling" for the 125 students who attended the summer school program at Fieldston (which is one of the Ethical Culture schools), with its beautiful campus and very adequate equipment for all the courses. This

155

was a big change from the poorly equipped public high schools from which the Upward Bound students were recruited. The summer school was very successful, and 90 percent of our Upward Bound students who were seniors were recipients of scholarships to major colleges.

Nationally, the Upward Bound program had a similar high percentage of acceptances. The sad thing was that Upward Bound had been conceived as a pilot program for 100,000 youth who would be "models" for 1 million students in such programs designed to transform ghetto youth from dropout-prone high school students to college-going members of families who had never had a college graduate in their families. Imagine the impact that such a transformation would have on the youth of the ghetto and their families. But, unfortunately, no such expansion of the Upward Bound Program ever took place!

I decided to resign from the position of assistant director at the Ethical Culture schools. The schools had been so polarized by the divisions over the Black students' demonstrations that Dr. Wagner; Spencer Brown, the conservative principal of Fieldston School; and I, as advisor to the Black Students Union, were asked to resign. I considered putting up a fight to stay but decided that the situation was too polarized for me to be effective without the support of the board of governors. I then received a call from Aaron Bindman, who wanted to interview me for a possible opening in the Sociology Department at SUNY at New Paltz. Bindman had been looking for a Black faculty candidate for New Paltz. He had met Carl Marzani and John Killens on two different occasions and asked them if they knew of possible candidates. Both of them, independent of each other, had recommended me. Bindman told me of the situation at New Paltz. There was no Black faculty in sociology, the Black Studies Department had difficulty finding candidates who were qualified, and there was also the possibility that the chairperson of Black Studies, Dr. Marjorie Butler, who planned to retire, might consider me as a replacement.

Bindman asked me about my experience. I replied, "Well, I've taught dialectical materialism, political economy, the Negro question, class struggle, the civil rights movement, strategy and tactics in party training schools for ten years, supervised faculty at the Jefferson School of Social Science for four years, lectured at Columbia, City College, NYU, written for *Political Affairs* and the *Daily Worker*. That record may not get me brownie points in the academic world, but I think I might be as qualified a professor as you could find."

Bindman smiled and said, "Some of our people will object to our hiring someone with only a bachelor's degree."

I responded, "You know I have the equivalent of a Ph.D. in experience and qualification."

He said, "That's true. How about coming up to New Paltz and meeting some of the key people?"

I replied, "What kind of money are you talking about?"

He answered, "If you come in at the assistant professor level, it would start at about $13,000.00 annually."

I said, "I'm making $16,000.00 annually at the Ethical Culture schools. I couldn't take such a drop in income."

Bindman said, "It's possible that we can bring you in as an associate professor. That starts at $15,000.00 and you can supplement that teaching six weeks at the summer school, but the drawback is that you would come up for tenure in three years! If you start as an assistant professor, it would be six years before tenure would become an issue."

I said, "I'm willing to take my chances on that!"

Thinking about my years in the party, my success at helping to train and mold cadre, my problem of not being able to respond to all the requests for teaching assignments and speaking engagements, and my popularity as a figure in the movement, I felt no qualms about being able to stand up to a tenure struggle in the shortened period of time. I also had a general estimate of the caliber of most college professors and knew that I measured up favorably.

The courses sponsored by the Department of Sociology in the various correctional facilities in the mid–Hudson Valley were where my approach was especially useful. During the eleven years I taught at New Paltz, I had the pleasure of teaching at Walkill, Napanoch, Greenhaven, Coxsackie (a youth facility), and Dannemora. I found that most of the inmates had a much clearer comprehension of the exploitative structure of society and were less subject to illusions about democracy. The most exciting experience I had was meeting a group of inmates who, despite persecution by the staff at Napanoch, were able to form the first inmates' branch of the NAACP in the United States. One of them, Frank Abney, was put in "lockdown" supposedly for violations of prison rules when in fact he was attending my course Introduction to Sociology. In reality, the prison administration was led by the warden, Jack Warenetzky, a racist, who tolerated the existence of the Ku Klux Klan, to which many of the correction officers belonged. After his release from prison, Abney went to Howard University, becoming the director of an influential radio program in Washington, D.C. His courage, determination, and effective leadership ability were an inspiration to the other men in his cell block and beyond. Another inmate at Napanoch, after finishing his sentence, enrolled at New Paltz in a prison follow-up program organized by the Department of Sociology, graduated with bachelor's and master's of arts degrees, and then moved to the Midwest, where he became an official of the state organization of the NAACP. Another inmate, upon completing his sentence, returned to his home community in Brownsville, Brooklyn, where he led a most influential community organization that won major victories in the struggle against drugs and for housing rehabilitation.

Among these men, the very opposite of antisocial attitudes was manifested, and many of the college students could have used their example in their postgraduate life. By contrast with such self-rehabilitation under the guidance of a positive program, we can see how destructive an impact the criminal justice system has on the Black community, where one out of four Black males is either under probation, subject to parole, in confinement, or waiting to stand trial.

I have often said, "It only costs approximately $10,000.00 annually to send a youth to a four-year college. Wouldn't our society be better off if we invested our funds in the constructive policy of sending youth to college, instead of imprisonment at a cost of $40,000.00 annually?"

Unlike most professors, I spent a great deal of time doing community work as an example of my understanding of citizenship. The most important community activity evolved in the organization SCORE, an acronym for Strand Community Organization to Rehabilitate the Environment. SCORE was a community organization that had failed because of the extramilitant and nationalist orientation of its first leader, Jerry Moore, and two of his friends, Ed Leftwich and Bill Haley, who were interested in the possibilities of SCORE's revival. We decided to meet because of my experience in community organization.

I met with the three of them and in a short time we had generated a board of directors and a membership involving local grassroots people. I was elected chairman of the board, on which Reverend James Childs, the leading minister of the Black community in Kingston; Everett Hodges, the twenty-five-year chairman of the Ulster County NAACP; and some other representative members of the community also served. Ed Leftwich became the executive director and over the course of twenty years an estimated $3 million was funneled into the Kingston community as a result of the activities of SCORE.

Based on the success of SCORE, I proposed to a group of community leaders in the Hudson Valley that we attempt to emulate SCORE's success by setting up a Mid–Hudson Valley Minority Regional Congress that would be able to develop programs in all of the major towns of the mid–Hudson Valley—Newburgh, Poughkeepsie, Beacon, and Westchester County groups headed by Paul Redd. Most of these programs were successful, so I could say that my becoming a faculty member at New Paltz enabled me to bring my organizing ability to fruition in ways that were not possible during my party days. The least I can say is that my presence was felt in more dramatic and lasting ways. I had a special thrill in the knowledge that I was performing these activities in the hills and valleys of the Hudson River, the homeland of the Ramapo Mountain People, my mother's tribe.

By 1981, after being rehired as an adjunct associate professor every two years, a very conservative woman, Alice Chandler, was appointed president of the college. During this time, the college was directed along increasingly conservative lines and I felt less gratification teaching in the atmosphere created by Chandler. The Sociology Department was trimming its sails so that the department meetings manifested the transition from a department known for its radicalism to a department almost indistinguishable from the notoriously conservative English Department. I was past the time of eligibility for Social Security, so I decided to retire.

In the fall of 1981, however, the minority faculty of Black and Puerto Rican professors called for an outspoken conference protesting the attrition of minority faculty on the campus under the conservative rule of Dr. Chandler. They were demanding greater attention to fulfillment of affirmative action policies and issued statements indicating a major upsurge toward democracy on the campus. Because I was the only Black professor in the Sociology Department, and feeling that I might get support from the minority faculty, I decided to withdraw my retirement letter. The department refused to reinstate me despite my eleven-year record in which I had been characterized as one of the ten best professors on the New Paltz campus. It was here that I had felt most fulfilled as an educator, gratified by my students who called me *Malimwu*—"teacher" in Swahili—but I decided not to put my energies into what appeared to be a losing battle and rather turned them toward the possibility of becoming technical director for the forthcoming film *The Cotton Club*.

12

The Cotton Club Revisited

Back to Harlem
March 19, 1983

Five years before I left the State University College at New Paltz, an article appeared in one of the movie gossip columns. It stated that Bob Evans was going to produce a movie called *The Cotton Club*. I wrote him at Paramount Pictures explaining that Winnie and I had danced in the chorus at the Cotton Club in the '30s, that my father had been a waiter, that my brother Bobby had won an amateur night contest at the club, that I had seen every show from 1932 to 1940, and that as a sociologist I had done extensive research on Harlem in the '30s and '40s as part of my preparation for courses on "The Sociology of Jazz," "The Harlem Renaissance," and "The Sociology of Racism."

In the spring of 1983, I received a telephone call from Jim Siff, Bob Evans's cousin. He asked me if I would be willing to be interviewed as part of the preliminary work on the film. Without a moment's hesitation, I replied, "I think it would be useful!"

Within a week, we had taped three hours of my reminiscing, and Siff transferred the tapes to Mario Puzo, who developed a storyline for the movie, in which the Johnson family was featured. Gregory Hines was to be me, Maurice Hines was to be Bobby, and Thelma Carpenter was to be Winnie. In a later discussion, Francis Ford Coppola told me that they were going to bring in a white family whose struggles would parallel the struggles of the Black Johnson family during the Depression, and the Cotton Club would be the vehicle for both families on both sides of the color line to surmount the difficulties of the Depression.

I suggested in a concept paper that, whatever the gimmick, the film could be the occasion for Hollywood to portray the wealth of talent that appeared at the Cotton Club during its heyday in Harlem and counter the stereotypical portrayals of Blacks in the movies for the first time in a major way: Bill Robinson, Ethel Waters, Cab Calloway, the Nicholas Brothers, the Berry Brothers, Adelaide Hall, and the star of stars, Duke Ellington, and his music, which made the Cotton Club a symbol of the best in Black entertainment! It was my strong feeling that Coppola, looking for a box-office hit, after several films that had not lived up to financial expectations, would be assured a success with the Cotton Club film if he concentrated on the Black entertainment and the Duke's musical genius.

Coppola saw otherwise and opted for a build-up of violence and gangster elements in the film that was actually quite accurate in showing the mob control of the club. My friends and I called it "The Godfather Comes to Harlem." I had a parting of ways with Coppola, but one positive contribution I felt I had made was the scene that had been inspired by my family's direct experience and Winnie Johnson teaching her two brothers Stretch and Bobby dance routines in the kitchen.

After that project I continued to do some consultant work on a number of films like *Seeing Red*. It was a big circle in my life with me coming back to the theater and show business. In fact, my life seemed to be a series of big circles.

13
Martin Luther King Day in Hawaii

Honolulu
March 19, 1986

I had been in a relationship for quite a long period of time with Ann Hitch. We had broken up several times and she had gone to Hawaii and liked it very much. We had been corresponding, even though we were not together, and she invited me to come to Hawaii and see how I liked it. I liked what I saw and decided in March 1986 to investigate further. Finally I made my move and settled in, becoming a "child of the land" or *Kamaaina* in Hawaiian, and I really think that Hawaii, of all the states in the Union, is the one that has the greatest possibilities for realizing the American dream of a multiethnic, nonracist society.

Naturally, because Ann was a Quaker, my first contacts on arrival were with the Quakers. This was a small group of approximately fifty or sixty people, and I did not see myself operating within the social confines of that group. I did not feel that this group was a proper outlet for me with my experience, so I soon began to ask where I could meet people in other ethnic groups, because the Quakers are primarily Caucasian or *Haole*. I think there may have been one or two Hawaiians, a couple of Chinese, a couple of Japanese, but they're preponderantly *Haole* and I wanted to make some contact with the non-*Haole* local community.

I was very fortunate in the sense that the president of the African-American Association lived in the apartment building where Ann and I were living. His name was Umar Assan, and we had passed each other and hardly spoken, but one day he stopped me and said, "Mr. Johnson, would you like to come to an African-American Association meeting?" It was December 12, and Jesse Jackson was the guest speaker. So I went to that meeting and enjoyed it very much, saw a lot of folks who were members, and I figured that if I were going to have a base of operations, this Association would give me the opportunity to network in the African American community.

What impressed me immediately was the level of acceptance. It usually takes a while to be accepted in a community and to get to know people, but I would go out to demonstrations and introduce myself and say that I was interested in community organization, and I also formed a number of friendships with Third World people. I found that through the organization I was able to meet a number of leading people in the Afro-American community on an intimate level in numbers that in any other place would probably have taken me months or years.

After exposure to many groups, I tried to calibrate where the people were politically, and from using my own experience as a calibrator, I came up with the year 1930. I felt that the level of thinking corresponded to this period and I tried to explore why that was, and I think it was because they had not experienced the same struggles that had taken place on the mainland. They had not known the civil rights movements of the 1940s and 1960s. And as I looked at it from a sociological viewpoint, I realized that Hawaii understandably is determined by an insularity that serves as a buffer against the impact of the political and social trends that take place on the mainland. I discovered two kinds of insularity in Hawaii: the insularity of an island people with the ocean acting as a buffer, and then the insularity of the people who have been socialized into the military and insulated against participation in the civilian world; so it's kind of a double dip of insularity. Believing in self-determination, I consider it unfortunate that Hawaii is a part of the United States, yet it did not reflect the social and political outlooks that had been formulated on the mainland as a result of struggles. Of course there were the struggles of the plantation workers, but the Black community was not very much a part of that, so the trade union consciousness that permeates the Japanese, Chinese, and Portuguese communities, and to some extent the Hawaiian community, is not at the same level. Most of the African Americans appeared to me to be individual entrepreneurs or professionals with what E. Franklin Frazier called a bourgeois outlook.

Another factor that I think accounted for this awareness gap is that a large number of those who settled in Hawaii came from the military, which has a conservative impact on one's thinking. The disciplinary regimen of the Army, Navy, and the Marines is not conducive to creative thinking and free political expression, especially of a liberal or radical nature, and many veterans who are released, even though they might be militant in their response to segregation, generally have a conservative outlook on those questions that transcend the race question.

Despite difficulties in terms of the dissent and differing levels of political awareness in the Black community, I was committed to remaining in Hawaii for four or five years. What was remarkable to me is that this group, in the African-American Association, despite this background, emerged with a forward-looking effort to make the Black presence visible, so that it seems almost as if secretly and by osmosis, some of the perspectives of the '40s and '60s came through, although in a slightly different way than in the Black communities on the mainland. I wanted to see some changes made while I could look at them, and the fact that the first major campaign the Afro-American community undertook was successful with the passage of a Martin Luther King Jr. holiday bill convinced me that with the same kind of unity and energy expended in that direction, even more fundamental changes of a positive nature could be made.

In a short space of time, the Association had a spearhead project to create a Black newspaper, to help it achieve its primary goal of making the Black presence visible in Hawaii, and we saw the paper as a primary instrument in making that happen. I was asked, after a couple of false starts, to be the editor of the paper. And I agreed in March 1987. I discovered afterward that there had been a newspaper called *Harambe* that had had a short existence. If I had known this at the time the *Afro-Hawaiian News* debuted, I would have asked for it to be called *Harambe* in parentheses under the *Afro-Hawaiian News*, so the continuity would be kept. We completed a year with twelve successful issues of the paper, so, while it was not the first Black newspaper in Hawaii, it was the Black newspaper of the longest duration. Many of the editorials I wrote for this paper were noticed by the community at large and printed up and commented on in the Honolulu afternoon paper, the *Star Bulletin*. Thus I realized when working with the Association that I was not in the most advanced Black community, and despite this context, we were successful in bringing the Dr. Martin Luther King holiday to be created and observed in this state.

I went to one of the state parks that have a number of plant and flower exhibits, and the tour guide was telling us how many plants that are foreign finally take root in Hawaii and sometimes adapt so well that they threaten and endanger the native Hawaiian plants, and some of them take on the characteristics of the Hawaiian plants in their adaptation. There's one cactus plant, when it becomes indigenous to Hawaii, that gradually loses its spines so that it becomes a "friendly" cactus, and I analogize to the Black community that there is a kind of parallelism in this process in the Black community, where you find that among the Blacks there is an *aloha* spirit, and not quite as militant and spiny as on the mainland. There is a kind of softening effect that takes place, that sometimes accentuates the conservativism. Many Blacks, for example, have told me that you have to be careful how you do things here, and they say, "You don't talk stink." This attitude is close to a Japanese custom, a type of inscrutability. I have noticed that many of the Blacks have taken on these Japanese ways. I have not reached a view on whether that is negative or positive.

In my five trips back to the mainland since I moved to Hawaii in 1986, every time I returned to Hawaii I felt as if I were coming back home. As a New Yorker who lived in New York from 1933 until 1986, I really discovered that I had come to love Hawaii, and the atmosphere. We had formed a powerful coalition and marched together, talked with elected members of the state legislature, and campaigned successfully for a meaningful holiday of empowerment, recognized in January 1989, not just for the Black community but for all peoples: native Hawaiians, Japanese Americans, Chinese Americans, Philippine Americans, Samoans, Fiji Islanders, everyone.

14
Paris to Texas and Home Again

Paris, France
September 8, 1995

Stretch was not able to write the final chapter. We often talked about his plans for the book and his hopes of its being useful to others. Always the soldier, when diagnosed with prostate cancer, he was determined to fight the fight of the decade for him.

From Hawaii, in 1991 he and Ann moved to Saint Croix, where Stretch became very active as a counselor in an antidrug campaign and a rehabilitation center for young people. With the progress of the cancer, Stretch wanted to be on the mainland for treatment and closer to family members, of course. He and Ann then settled in Galveston, Texas, where they were living in a big house not too far from the Gulf. Some time after that my sisters and I went to see him. All the while documenting his disease and his angle of attack on it, Stretch had once again set down his radical roots to do work in the Black community with young people. He gave talks and was often invited for radio broadcasts. He founded an association to encourage children to continue their education. He was, no matter the place, always ready to be at the head of the march before they could run him out of town. Later I remember our going to see him at M. D. Anderson Cancer Center in Houston, Texas, where he had radiation therapy, hormone treatment, and then surgery. This radical course of action gave Stretch a remission of nearly ten years. During this time he was able to travel to Paris and see his first great-grand-daughter the day she was born. He met with Julia Wright, Richard Wright's daughter, and put his organizing skills to the service of mobilizing for the protests she was leading against the U.S. Embassy in Paris over the threat of Mumia Abu-Jamal's execution. At the age of eighty, Stretch marched again at the head of demonstrations with Julia, gathering American expatriates and French citizens concerned for the life of a militant believed to have been wrongly accused, convicted of murder, and sentenced to death. We worked together with members of the African diaspora living in Paris and African American expatriates here to foster unity through the vehicle of a cultural association we baptized Harambe, *or "unity" in Swahili. We staged events and held a Kwanzaa party in celebration of harvest, education, family, and community. Then came the time when Stretch had to return home to New York, where doctors at Sloan-Kettering helped him for the last battle. The cancer had returned and metastasized to the bones.*

Stretch died on May 25, 2000. He had so wanted to celebrate the new year and indeed he did. I was with my sisters when we joined hands with our father and he asked, "Well, girls, are you ready for this?" We were and, for someone who loved life as he did, surprisingly so was he. We are living at a time when our stories are being told. I share his story, his legacy of activism, in the hope that one of our lesser-known everyday heroes will continue to be of use to folks and that Stretch will be with us for generations ahead. In his New York Times *obituary by Douglas Martin a few lines say it well. In his glorious tap dance of a life, "Stretch had a ball."*

Notes

Foreword

1. Glenda Gilmore, *Defying Dixie: The Radical Roots of Civil Rights, 1919–1950* (New York: Norton, 2009); Danielle L. McGuire, *At the Dark End of the Street: Black Women, Rape, and Resistance—A New History of the Civil Rights Movement from Rosa Parks to the Rise of Black Power* (New York: Vintage, 2011); Erik McDuffie, *Sojourning for Freedom: Black Women, American Communism, and the Making of Left Feminism* (Durham, N.C.: Duke University Press, 2011). Also see Clarence Taylor, *Reds at the Blackboard: Communism, Civil Rights, and the New York City Teachers Union* (New York: Columbia University Press, 2011). Of all these books, McDuffie's is the one that explores in the greatest depth the Harlem communist milieu in which Johnson was active and mentions him as working with some of the women activists his book highlights.

2. Manning Marable, *Malcolm X: A Life of Reinvention* (New York: Penguin, 2011), contains the most accurate discussion of Malcolm X's experiences in Michigan, Massachusetts, and Harlem, some of which were fictionalized or exaggerated in his autobiography.

3. Marable's book, *Malcom X: A Life of Reinvention*, created great controversy by suggesting that Malcolm X may have had a sexual relationship with a wealthy white man he worked for. Johnson's matter-of-fact descriptions of his own experiences having sex with men for economic gain suggests such encounters may have been quite common in Harlem in that era. Also see George Chauncey, *Gay New York: Gender, Urban Culture, and the Making of the Gay Male World* (New York: Basic Books, 1995).

4. Detailed portraits of Communist Party organizing in Harlem during the 1930s can be found in Mark Naison, *Communists in Harlem During the Depression*

(Urbana: University of Illinois Press, 1983), and McDuffie, *Sojourning for Freedom*.

5. For more on the Communist Party's role in the effort to integrate major league baseball, see Irwin Silber and Lester Rodney, *Press Box Red: The Story of Lester Rodney, a Communist Who Helped Break the Color Line in American Sports* (Philadelphia: Temple University Press, 2003).

1. Early Days

1. Arising after the end of the U.S. Civil War, the Negro Leagues comprised several minor and major league teams made up of African Americans and, occasionally, Latin Americans. Although the baseball color line was broken in 1947 when Jackie Robinson began playing for the Brooklyn Dodgers, the Negro Leagues continued into the 1950s. See Christopher Hauser, *The Negro Leagues Chronology: Events in Organized Black Baseball, 1920–1948* (London: McFarland & Company, 2006).

2. W. E. B. Du Bois coined the term "Atlanta Compromise" to refer to the 1895 agreement between African American and southern white leaders. In exchange for the southern Blacks' working and agreeing not to press for equality and integration, southern whites would guarantee basic education and due process under the law for Blacks. The agreement was announced at the Atlanta Exposition Speech, with the principal African American proponent being Booker T. Washington.

3. David S. Cohen, *The Ramapo Mountain People* (New Brunswick, N.J.: Rutgers University Press, 1974).

4. Known in its time as the "New Negro Movement," the Harlem Renaissance was a cultural movement in the 1920s. See Nathan Irvin Higgins and Arnold Rampersad, *Harlem Renaissance* (New York: Oxford University Press, 2007).

2. Harlem and the Cotton Club

1. Langston Hughes (1902–67) and Alain Locke (1885–1954) were luminaries of the Harlem Renaissance. Locke, who became the first African American Rhodes Scholar in 1907, provided the philosophical underpinnings for the Harlem Renaissance, which at the time was known as the New Negro movement, after Locke's anthology, *The New Negro: An Interpretation of Negro Life* (1925). A towering literary figure during the Harlem Renaissance through his poetry, Hughes wrote what would become the lower-class Black manifesto, "The Negro Artist and the Racial Mountain" (*The Nation*, 1926).

2. Hugues Panassié, *The Real Jazz* (New York: Smith & Durrell, 1942).

3. Moving Up

1. *New Faces* was a series of musical revues written and produced by Leonard Sillman. Versions of the revue appeared in 1934, 1936, 1943, 1952, 1956, 1962, and 1968.

2. From a 1933 interview with Hannen Swaffer for the *Daily Herald*, quoted in James Lincoln Collier, *Duke Ellington* (New York: Oxford University Press, 1987), 4.

3. Helen Lawrenson, *Stranger at the Party* (New York: Random House, 1975).

4. The Negro People's Theater—co-founded by Dick Campbell and Rose McClendon in 1935—is not to be confused with the Harlem Experimental Theater (1928–34) or the Negro People's Theater in Chicago.

4. Show Biz

1. The Abraham Lincoln Brigade was a group of American volunteers who fought in the Spanish Civil War (1936–39) on the side of Spanish Republicans against Francisco Franco and the Spanish Nationalists. Many of the volunteers were communists, and the brigade was the first fully integrated U.S. Army unit.

5. Joining the Party

1. Joe Louis, known as the Brown Bomber, was world heavyweight champion in boxing from 1937 to 1949. Considered one of the greatest heavyweight fighters of all time, Louis was one of the first African Americans to rise to national prominence within the United States. For an account of Joe Louis's reign and its impact on the United States, see Chris Mead, *Joe Louis: Black Champion in White America* (Mineola, N.Y.: Dover Publications, 2010).

6. The Young Communist League

1. Georgi Dimitrov (1882–1949) was Bulgaria's first communist leader. At the 1935 Seventh World Congress of the Communist International, Dimitrov gave the concluding speech, entitled "Unity of the Working Class against Fascism." The speech was shortly thereafter followed by his opening speech, "Youth against Fascism," at the Opening of the Sixth Congress of the Young Communist International. A collection of his works can be found at http://www.marxists.org/reference/archive/dimitrov/index.htm.

2. Louis Burnham (1915–60) was a member of the Southern Negro League Congress during the Montgomery bus boycott. Along with W. E. B. Du Bois and Edward Strong, Burnham founded *Freedomways*, a leading African American political and cultural journal from 1961 to 1985.

3. The Black Belt refers to a region of the southern United States, so named for its thin layer of black soil. Subsequently the term took on a new meaning as a result of the region's higher-than-average percentage of African American residents. In his 1901 autobiography, *Up from Slavery*, Booker T. Washington writes, "I have often been asked to define the term 'Black Belt.' So far as I can learn, the term was first used to designate a part of the country which was distinguished by the color of the soil. The part of the country possessing this thick, dark, and naturally rich soil was, of course, the part of the South where the slaves were most profitable, and consequently they were taken there in the largest numbers. Later, and especially since the [Civil W]ar, the term seems to be used in wholly in a political sense—that is, to designate the counties where the black people outnumber the white" (*Up from Slavery: with Related Documents* [Boston, Mass.: Bedford/St. Martin's, 2002], 90).

7. The War Years

1. On September 30, 1938, Neville Chamberlain, Édouard Daladier, Adolf Hitler, and Benito Mussolini signed the Munich Agreement, which granted Germany annexation of the Sudetenland, a region in Czechoslovakia largely inhabited by German-speaking people, in exchange for Germany's promise not to engage in further military action. At the time, the agreement was controversial in Britain and France and subsequently has come to be viewed as a failed attempt at appeasement.

2. A. Philip Randolph (1889–1979) was a leader in the African American civil rights movement. A leader of the March on Washington movement, which convinced Franklin D. Roosevelt to sign an executive order banning discrimination in defense industries during World War II, Randolph subsequently convinced President Harry S Truman to issue an executive order that desegregated the U.S. armed forces.

3. The Cointel Program (or COINTELPRO) was the Counter Intelligence Program run by the FBI from 1956 to 1971. The program sought to infiltrate and disrupt domestic political organizations deemed subversive by the FBI. Targets included communist and socialist organizations, the NAACP, and prominent figures of the civil rights movement.

4. The forerunner to the CIA, the Office of Strategic Services (OSS) was established by President Franklin D. Roosevelt in 1942 to provide the Joint Chiefs of Staff with strategic information. The primary responsibility of the OSS was to coordinate foreign intelligence gathering, although during World War II, the Army and Navy had closely guarded competing intelligence operations. The head of the OSS was William "Wild Bill" Donovan (1883–1959).

5. James Bamford, *The Puzzle Palace: Inside the National Security Agency, America's Most Secret Intelligence Organization* (New York: Penguin Books, 1983).

6. The 92nd Infantry Division of World War II, also known as the "Buffalo Soldiers Division," was the only African American division to see military combat in Europe during World War II. The division served in the Italian campaign from 1944 to the war's end. The moniker "Buffalo Soldier" finds its origin with the U.S. 10th Cavalry Regiment, which was founded in 1866 at Fort Leavenworth, Kansas, and fought against Native Americans.

8. Back Home

1. Claudia Jones (1915–64), born in Trinidad and raised in New York City, became a black nationalist and political activist. In 1936, Jones joined the American Communist Party, and in 1949 her "An End to the Neglect of the Problems of the Negro Woman!" appeared in *Political Affairs*. In 1951, Jones was found to be in violation of the Smith Act, which established criminal penalties for advocating the overthrow of the U.S. government and required all non-citizen adult residents to register with the government. In 1955, Jones moved to Great Britain under political asylum, where she continued her political activism until her death.

2. Earl Browder (1891–1973) was the general secretary of the Communist Party of the United States of America during the 1930s and 1940s.

3. *Histoire d'un Crime* (The History of a Crime) [written 1852, published 1877], Conclusion, chapter X. Trans. T. H. Joyce and Arthur Locker.

4. E. J. Hobsbawm, *The Jazz Scene* (New York: Da Capo Press, 1975).

9. *La Lucha Continua*

1. Vito Marcantonio (1902–54) was an American lawyer and democratic socialist. In the late 1930s, he became a member of the American Labor Party.

2. Blas Roca was a leading theoretician of the Cuban Revolution. Originally named Blas Calderio, he changed his name to Roca (Spanish for "rock") when he joined the Cuban Communist Party in 1929.

3. See George M. Guess, *The Politics of United States Foreign Aid* (New York: Routledge, 1987), 94.

4. "Kitchen" is the back of the hairline, the most difficult place to keep straight if the hair is processed or permed.

10. Starting Over

1. Joseph R. Starobin, *American Communism in Crisis, 1943–1957* (Berkeley: University of California Press, 1975), 197–98.

2. George Charney, *A Long Journey* (Chicago: Quadrangle Books, 1968), 195.

3. Pettis Perry was a leader in the Communist Party of the United States of America. Betty Gannett, a Marxist theoretician, writer, and teacher, was an officer of the CPUSA.

4. Harry Haywood, *Black Bolshevik: Autobiography of an Afro-American Communist* (Chicago: Liberator Press, 1978).

5. E. Franklin Frazier, *Black Bourgeoisie: The Rise of a New Middle Class in the United States* (Glencoe, Ill.: Free Press, 1957).

Further Reading

Anderson, Jervis. *This Was Harlem 1900–1950*. New York: Farrar, Straus & Giroux, 1981.

Boyd, Herb. *Autobiography of a People*. New York: Doubleday, 2000.

Cohen, David Steven. *The Ramapo Mountain People*. New Brunswick, N.J.: Rutgers University Press, 1974.

Davies, Carole Boyce. *Left of Karl Marx: The Political Life of Black Communist Claudia Jones*. Durham, N.C., and London: Duke University Press, 2007.

Du Bois, W. E. B. *The Autobiography of W. E. B. Du Bois*. New York: International Publishers, 1968.

Ellington, Duke. *Music Is My Mistress*. New York: Doubleday, 1973.

Mandela, Nelson. *Long Walk to Freedom*. London: Abacus, 1994.

Maxwell, William J. *New Negro, Old Left*. New York: Columbia University Press, 1999.

Naison, Mark. *Communists in Harlem During the Depression*. Chicago: University of Illinois Press, 2005.

CURRICULUM VITAE
HOWARD EUGENE JOHNSON

EDUCATION
Doctor of Humanities, Honolulu University of Arts & Sciences, 1990
Doctoral Candidate in Sociology, State University of New York at
   Binghamton, 1982–89
M.A., New York University, Graduate School of Arts and Sciences,
   Department of Sociology, 1977
B.S., Columbia University, School of General Studies, Comparative
   Literature, 1966

EMPLOYMENT
9/86–12/89: Visiting Lecturer—University of Hawaii at Manoa,
   Ethnic Studies Program
1/84–6/85: Visiting Lecturer—LaGuardia Community College,
   Social Studies Division
3/82–10/83: Technical Advisor—Francis Ford Coppola film, *The
   Cotton Club*
9/71–8/82: Adjunct Associate Professor—Department of Sociology;
   Associate Professor—Department of Black Studies (1971–74)
3/69–7/71: Assistant to the Director—Ethical Culture Schools; Project
   Director—Fieldston School Upward Bound
2/68–3/69: Field Supervisor—Social Sciences Research Unit, Columbia University College of Physicians and Surgeons
9/66–10/67: Documentation Specialist—Psychiatric Epidemiological
   Research Unit, Columbia Univeristy College of Physicians and
   Surgeons

COMMUNITY SERVICE
Life Member of the Association for the Study of Afro-American Life
   and History
Life Member of the Military Order of the Purple Heart
Charter Member of the Afro-American Association, Honolulu, Hawaii
Life Member, NAACP (National Association for the Advancement of
   Colored People)
Member of the Screen Actors Guild
First Vice-Chairman, Hudson Valley Economic Development Dis-
   trict, 1981–82

Founded and Chaired Hudson Valley Minority Regional Congress, 1979–82

Reorganized and Chaired Strand Community Organization to Rehabilitate the Environment, Kingston, NY, 1978–82

Associate Editor, *Time Capsule*, Non-Governmental Organization, United Nations 1984

PUBLICATIONS

"Racism and Surplus Repression," *Community Review*, Volume V, Number One, Spring 1983

"Education and the Institutionalization of Racism," Resources in Education, ERIC Document, May 1976

Fieldston School Upward Bound Manual, 1971

PAPERS

"A Sociological Appraisal of Harlem Jazz in the '30s and '40s." Mid-Atlantic Radical Historians Organization Convention, Columbia University, April 1977

"Minorities and Liberal Arts Education." Crisis in the Liberal Arts Conference, SUNY at New Falls, February 1981

"Marcuse's Theory of Surplus Repression and Unconscious Racism." Eastern Sociological Society Convention, November 1982

MULTIMEDIA PRODUCTIONS

The Cotton Club. American Museum of Natural History, December 1983.

The Harlem Renaissance. American Museum of Natural History, November 1983

The Story of Sojourner Truth. SUNY New Falls, March 1981

RADIO

Produced Jazz Shows, WBAI, 1977–78

Produced *Afro-Hawaii News* Show, KTUH, 1988–89

Produced Neighborhood Support Network Program, Station WSTX, Christiansted, USVI, 1991–92

FILMS

Featured in *Duke Ellington*, PBS, *The Great Depression, The Story of Frank Marshall Davis* and *Art Blakey's Jazz Messengers,* 1987

Featured in Oscar-nominated documentary *Seeing Red*, April 1984

TELEVISION
Featured in *The Upward Bounders*, WNBC-TV, May 1970

NEWSPAPER
Editor, *Afro-Hawaii News*, March 1987 to 1989

LANGUAGES
Speak and read French

MENTIONS
Who's Who in the East, 1976–81
Who's Who in America, 1979–80
Who's Who in the World, 1990–94

WORK IN PROGRESS
Red, White, and Black: An Autobiography

REFERENCES
Dr. Ruth Bennett, Deputy Director, Institute of Gerontology and
    Geriatrics, Columbia University, College of Physicians and
    Surgeons
Dr. John O. Cato, Social Sciences Division, LaGuardia Community
    College
Dr. John Henrik Clark, Chairman Emeritus, Department of Puerto
    Rican and Black Studies, Hunter College
Dr. Barbara Ann Scott, Department of Sociology, State University
    College of New Paltz, New York
Dr. Glenn Paige, Department of Political Science, University of
    Hawaii, Honolulu, Hawaii

Index

101 Ranch, 30

Abney, Frank, 157–8
academics, high school, 23
Adler, Stella, 45
African Blood Brotherhood, 9
African-American Association (Hawaii),
    162–4
Afro-Cuban music, 122–3
Afro-Hawaiian News, 164
after-hours clubs, 30
alcoholism, 10; detoxification, 144–6;
    mother's death and, 131–2; post-
    underground period, 143–5; recovery
    from, 145–7; relapse after B.S.
    degree, 152–3
Allen, Cliff, 39
Alves, Bert, 109
American Communist Party: Availables,
    126–7; Deep Freeze, 126–7; end
    of association with, 140–1;
    fragmentation, 141–2; joining,
    53–61; outlawing, 126; White
    House demonstration, 84–5; white
    versus Black comrades, 136–40
American Youth Congress, Soviet
    invasion of Finland, 83–4
Amsterdam News, 9

Anderson, James, 8–10
Anderson, Sam, 150
anonymity, 70–1
anti-Semitism, 39
Arlen, Harold, 32
Armstrong, Louis, 33
Armstrong, Maxie, 33
Ashby, Katherine, 20
Assan, Umar, 162–3
At the Dark End of the Street (McGuire), ix
Availables, 126–7

Baker, Ralph Lenard, 21
Baldwin, Earl, 25
baseball, "Jim Crow in Baseball"
    campaign, 80–2
Bates, Lee, 66
Bates, Ralph, *The Olive Field*, 47
Batista regime, 123
Beasley, Joyce, 33
Beaux Arts Ball, 19–21
Bell, Daniel, 153
Benjamin, Robby, 26
Bernstein, Walter, 109
Berry, Abner W., 100–1
Billings, Carol, 148
Bindman, Aaron, 156–7
Black Bolshevik (Haywood), 142

The Black Bourgeoisie (Frazier), 142
Black Cat, 48–9; pocket picking with
    Marva, 51–2
Black inferiority teachings, 58
Black-owned night spots, 30
Blount, Harvey, 18, 20
"blue-eyed niggers," 10
Bonus Marchers, 54
bourgeoisie, Black population, 75–6
Boyer, Anice, 33
Bradley, Francine, 48
Bradley, Lyman "Dick," 48
Brannick, Lacy, 21
breakfast dances, 31
Bromberg, J. Edward, 45
Browder, Earl, 99–101
Brown, Lloyd, 118
Brown, Spencer, 156
Burgum, Edwin Berry, 48
Burke, Leto, 89
Burleigh, Harry T., 17
Burnham, Louis, 66–7, 171
Butler, Marjorie, 156
Butterworth, Charles, 27

Cacchione, Pete, 81–2
Calloway, Cab, 49–50
Calloway, Constance, 17, 20
Camp Wapello, 24–5
Campbell, Allan, 110
Campbell, Jesse, 71
Cape Cod Theater, 46–7
Carlisle, Una Mae, 33
Carmichael, Stokely, 150
Caulfield, Joe, 147
CCNY (City College of New York),
    Frederick Douglass Society, 66
Chandler, Alice, 159
Cheek, Donald, 151
Chez Clinton, 37–8
Childs, James, 158
Church of the Epiphany, 16–19
Cincinnati Cotton Club, 127–8
Clark, Kenny, 50
Clory, Clyde, 89
Club Ashford, 70–1
Clurman, Harold, 45
Coca, Imogene, 39

Cohen, David Stephen, *The Ramapo
    Mountain People*, 10
Cohen, Yvonne, 69
Cold War, 125
Coleman, Sam, 153
Coll, Vincent "Mad Dog," 28–9
college attendance, 147–8
Collins, Elizabeth, 21
Collins, Henry "Kid," 21
Columbia School of General Studies,
    147–8; Black students, 148–9; graduate
    program, 153–4; graduate program
    dropout, 154; *The Owl*, 148–9
Communist Party: outlaw attempt, 112;
    Scottsboro case, 59; training schools,
    113–14. *See also* American
    Communist Party
Communist Political Association origins,
    99–100
*Communists in Harlem During the
    Depression* (Naison), xiv
Connor, Theophilus Eugene "Bull," 67
Cooper, Esther, 72
correctional facility teaching, 157–8
Cotton Club: 24th Edition of the Cotton
    Club Revue, 33; artists, oppression
    and, 29–30; chorus admittance, 32–3;
    Coll, Vincent "Mad Dog," 28–9;
    family move to New York and, 27–8;
    female chorus, 33–4; "Flying
    Colors," 27; Johnson, Winnie, 26–7;
    mob purchase, 34; mobsters and,
    28–9; owners, 28; Police Benevolent
    Association, 28; Stark, Herman, 28;
    upper-class whites, xi; white
    controllers, xi
The Cotton Club (movie), 33, 160–1
Crockett, George, Jr., 113–14
"Crow-Jimism," 35
Crowninshield, Eddie, 43
Crowninshield, Ralph, 43
Cuba. *See* Havana
Cullen, Countee, 47
Curtis, Hycie, 33

Daily Worker, 68
dancing: breakfast dances, 31; the Bump,
    21; dollar bill snatching, 31; "kitchen

mechanics' night," 31–2; postwar
service, 95–6; the Shim Sham, 30;
Ten Dancing Demons, 32–3
Dangerfield, Lewis, 89
Davis, Benjamin J., 60
Deacons for Justice, 113
Dean, Elwood, 21
Dean, Viola, 43
Debs, Eugene V., xxii
Deep Freeze, 126–7; Cincinnati Cotton
Club, 127–8; identity change, 127–8;
mistress, 131; mother's death during,
130–1; New Orleans, 128. *See also*
underground period
DeFreece/Defreese family, 10
Defying Dixie (Gilmore), ix
Degraphenreid, Stephen, 89
DeGroat family, 10; DeGroat, Howard,
11; DeGroat, James, 11; DeGroat,
Vivian, 12
detoxification from alcohol (delirium
tremens), 144–6
Dennis, Eugene, 75, 102, 104, 141, 142
Devine, Jack, 146–7
Dimitrov, Giorgi, 65; "Unity of the
Working Class against Facism"
speech, 114–15
"Double V" campaign, 101
Douglass, Frederick, 8; Frederick
Douglass Society (CCNY), 66
draft notice, 85–6
Du Bois, W. E. B., 9–10; Church of the
Epiphany, 17–18
Dubin, Abe, 69
Duval, Betty, 20

Ebbets Field, Jackie Robinson Day,
82–3
Eberhardt, Bill, 25
Ellington, Duke: The Apollo, 41–2;
Blackness as a composer, 42;
Cincinnati Cotton Club, 127–8; the
Three Johnsons, 40–2
Elouard, Paul, 119
Encinas, Dionisio, 119
The End of Ideology (Bell), 153
Engels, Frederick (Enge Menaker), 47–8
eroticism, homoerotic tourism, xi–xii

Ethical Culture Schools, 155–6
ethnic background, 4
Evans, Venerable, 23

fashion, 20
Fenton, William, 17
Fieldston School, 155–6
Flegenheimer, Arthur, 28
Fort Huachuca, 89–91
Fort Warren (U.S. Army), 87–8
Foster, William Z.: three inevitables,
126; *Toward Soviet America,* 115
Four Step Brothers, 90
Frank, Leonard, 146
Frazier, E. Franklin, *The Black
Bourgeoisie,* 142
Frederick Douglass Society (CCNY), 66
Friedlander, Bernie, 109
Frye, Walter, 21
"The Fun Revue," 21–2
fund drive money, 138–9

Gaither, George, 4
gamblers' factory, 6–7
Garaudy, Roger, 119
Garland, Walter, 101, 109
Gates, Johnny, 78, 86, 136, 141–3
gay hangouts, 39–40
Geva, Tamara, 27
Gilmore, Glenda, *Defying Dixie,* ix
Gloster, Bill, 89
Goode, George, 8
Goode, John, 8
Goode, Lethia. *See* Johnson, Lethia
(Goode)
Gordon, Frank, 116–17
Grace, Emily, 48
Grace, Mary, 48
Great Depression, 53–5
Green, "Chuck," 34
Green, Genevieve, 20
Green, Gil. *See* Swift, John
Griffith, Peggy, 33
Gruenberg, Ernest, 152–3
Gypsy Rose Lee, 39

HA HA Club, 51
Hamilton, Charles, 150

Hammett, Dashiell, 109–10
Harden, Helen, 21
Hardy, Carolyn, 17
Hardy, Harriet, 17
Harlem: community spirit, 56–7; Negro culture, 57–8; riot of 1935, 55–6; tourism in, 36
Harlem Renaissance, 13; Beaux Arts Ball, 19–21; Cotton Club purchase, 34; cultural hybridization, 35; "The Fun Revue," 21–2; immigrants and, 35; nightspots, 34; Renaissance name use, 5; tourism, 36
Harlem Youth Congress, 67–8
Harriet Tubman Society (Hunter College), 66
Harris, Bob, 127–8
Harris, Burke, 23
Havana: Americans' passage to Mexico, 130; heroin use, 123; mistress, 131; Popular Socialist Party convention, 121–5; prostitution, 124; underground period, 129–30; visit while underground, 127
Hawaii years, 162–5
Haywood, Harry, 9; *Black Bolshevik*, 142
Hearst, William Randolph (Mrs.), 43
Herndon, Angelo, 60
heroin use in Cuba, 123
Heywood, Billy, 39
Hill, Dudley, 20
Hines, Jimmy, 28
Hitch, Ann, 148, 162
Hobsbawm, Eric, *The Jazz Scene*, 110–11
Hodges, Everett, 158
Hoffer, Eric, *True Believer*, 76
Hoffman, Robert, 22
Holiday, Billie, 30; UNAVA fundraiser and, 110–11
Holly, Edna Mae, 33
homoerotic tourism, xi–xii
homosexuality: casting couch, 39; clubs, 30; gay hangouts, 39–40; IBPOE (Negro Elks), 130; Moore, Clinton, 37–8; oral sex for money, 40; "rough trade," 47
Hopkins, Terry, 153
Horne, Lena, 29, 33

Hotel Woodside, 39
Hitler, Adolf, 57
HUAC (House Un-American Activities Committee), 83
Hubbard, Earl, 90
Hudson Dusters, 6
Hughes, Langston, xxii, 13, 57, 170
Huiswood, Otto, 9
Hunter College Harriet Tubman Society, 66
Hurston, Zora Neale, xix, xxii
hustlers, 5–7
hypnotic regression experience, 14–15

identity change, 127–8
inevitables, 126
Inkeles, Alexander, 152–3
interracial ancestry: mythologies, 11; Ramapo Mountain People, 10, 11–12
interracial marriage, 68–9
Italy: attitudes toward Black troops, 98–9; war years, 96–7

Jackson, Burt, 101, 109
Jackson, James E., 72
Jackson Blacks, 10, 11
Jackson Whites, 10, 11
James, Daniel, 107
The Jazz Scene (Hobsbawm), 110–11
JBS (Junior Bachelor Society), 18–19; Beaux Arts Ball, 19–21
Jefferson School of Social Science, 114
Jim Crow laws: "Jim Crow in Baseball" campaign, 80–2; SNYC convention trip (1941), 72–4; U.S. Army and, 100–1
Jimmy Lunceford Band, 50
job losses due to communist associations, 146
Johnson, Arnold, 118
Johnson, Charlie, 89
Johnson, Corinne, 10
Johnson, Emerson, 17
Johnson, Eugene, 4
Johnson, Gertrude (McGinnis), 10; family, 12–13
Johnson, Howard "Monk": hustles, 5–7; nickname, 4; sports, 4–5, 7–8, 80–1

Johnson, Howard "Stretch": academics, 23; community connections, ix–x; early socialist outlook, 23; final years, 166–7; marriage to Martha Sherman, 77–8; name origins, 4; personal issues, xiii; sports, school, 22–3

Johnson, James P. (J.P.), 14

Johnson, Lethia (Goode), 4; Douglass, Frederick, 8; family, 8–9

Johnson, Martha, 77; college years, 148; marriage, 77–8; Deep Freeze and, 126–7; interracial, 68–9; parents, 3–4; post-underground period, 142–4; *South Pacific*, 144

Johnson, Mildred, 19

Johnson, Robert "Bobby" Quentin, 15

Johnson, Shirley Gertrude, 15; the Three Johnsons, 43

Johnson, Van, 39

Johnson, Wesley Williams, 15, 145

Johnson, Winnie, 11–12, 15; abortion, 43; Cotton Club, 26–7; "The Fun Revue," 21–2; lovers, 33; male companions, xi; pregnancy, 42–3; Stepin Fetchit, 47, 149

Jones, Claudia, 99

Jones, John Hudson, 68

Jones, "Lanky," 24

Junior Branch of the NAACP, 18–19

Katz, Saul, 68–9

Kelly, Patsy, 27

Kennedy, Joseph, 43

Khrushchev revelations, 135–6; author's reactions, 142–5

King, Martin Luther, Jr., viii, xviii, xxiv, 27, 67, 110, 142, 150, 154, 162–5

Kings County Hospital, 142–54

Kinoy, Arthur, 72

"kitchen mechanics' night," 31–2

Koehler, Ted, 32

Lambright, Middleton, 34

Lampell, Millard, 109

language of insiders, 32

Lawrenson, Helen, *Stranger at the Party*, 43–4

Lawrenson, Joanna, 43–4

Lee, Canada, 34

Lee, Gypsy Rose. *See* Gypsy Rose Lee

Leftwich, Ed, 158

Lenox Club, 30

Lindbergh, Charles, 17

Lindsay, Robert, 89

Little, Malcolm. *See* Malcolm X

"Little Monk" nickname, 4

Locke, Alain, 34

Long, Avon, 32

Louis, Joe, xi, 58

Luce, Clare Boothe, 43

Luce, Henry, 43

lynch mobs during the Great Depression, 55

MacCormick, Dolly, 33

Maceo, 90

Madden, Owney, 6, 28

Majors, Harold, 21

Malcolm X, 76; Johnson's similarities, xi; Perry, Donald Martin and, 151

Malraux, André, *Man's Hope*, 47

Manhattanville Club, 70

Mann family, 10

Man's Hope (Malraux), 47

Marcantonio, Vito, 116–17

Marie of Romania (Grand Duchesse), 43

marijuana, 34

Marinello, Juan, 119, 122

marriage: Deep Freeze and, 126–7; interracial, 68–9; parents', 3–4; post-underground period, 142–4

Marsh, Bertha (Bea), 12, 13

Marsh, John, 12

Marsh, Linton, 20

Marsh, Peter, 12–13

Marsh, Sarah, 12

Marsh, Tina, 12, 13

Marshall, Arlene, 33

Marva, 50, 51

Maxwell, Elsa, party for Cole Porter, 42–4

McCarthy era, 126–7; Communist Party move to underground, xiii

McClendon, Rose, 43, 44

McDuffie, Eric, *Sojourning for Freedom*, ix

McGinnis, Albert, 12

McGinnis, Frank, 10
McGinnis, Gertrude. *See* Johnson, Gertrude (McGinnis)
McGinnis, Helen, 12
McGinnis, May, 12, 13
McGinnis, Sanford, 12
McGinnis, Theodore, 12
McGuire, Danielle, *At the Dark End of the Street*, ix
McKay, Claude, xxii, 13, 47
Medina, Harold, 115–16
Melman, Seymour, 148–9
Menaker, Bob, 48
Menaker, Enge. *See* Engels, Frederick
Menaker, Pete, 48
Meroe Society (NYU), 66
Messick, Kerchival, 17
Mexico City, Western Hemisphere Peace Conference, 118–21
Mid–Hudson Valley Minority Regional Congress, 159
Miles, Jesse, 22
Miller, Taps, 40–1
Milligan, "Swat," 12–13
Milligan Alley, 12–13
mobsters: Black admittance, 32; Black Cat, 48–9; Cotton Club and, 28–9; Cotton Club purchase, 34
Monagas, Lionel, 43
money from fund drive, 138–9
Monk Johnson. *See* Johnson, Howard "Monk"
Monroe, Jack, 50–1
Moore, Alline, 107
Moore, Clinton, 37–8
Moore, Tallmadge, 107
Moore, Teddy, 18, 20
Morris, Chick, 43
Morrison, Allan, 101
Morrows family, 17
Mount Folgorito (U.S. Army service), 92–8
Murphy, George, 101, 109

NAACP (National Association for the Advancement of Colored People), 58–9; Johnson, Mildred, 19; Junior Branch, 18–19

Naison, Mark D., *Communists in Harlem During the Depression*, xiv
Nash, Catherine, 33
National Negro League (baseball), 80–2
National Training School, 71–2
Negro culture, 57–8
Negro Peoples' Theater, 44–5
the Negro Question, 9
New Faces of 1936, 38–40
New Faces of 1937, 46
New Orleans, 128
New York City, family's move to, 27–8
Newton, Frankie, 111
Nichols, Laura, 21
NYU (New York University), Meroe Society, 66

Odets, Clifford, 45
The Olive Field (Bates), 47
Oliver, Clinton, 70
Oliver, Sy, 86
Olley, Rae, 20
Ordoqui, Juan, 122–5
Osbiny Club, 44
Overby, Irving, 26

Paine, Benny, 86
Parker, Dorothy, 110
Parker, Joe, 18
party money from fund drive, 138–9
Party Voice, 114
passing (for white), 13, 58; Ziegfeld Follies dancers, 27
Paz, Octavio, 119
Peekskill attacks, 117–18
Peña, Lazaro, 130
Peniston, Freddie, 17
Perl, Arnold, 109
Perlo, Victor, 48
Perry, Donald Martin, 149–51
phrase mongering, 153
Pickens, William G., Church of the Epiphany, 17–18
Pierce, Marian, 39
plain Marxists, 149
pocket picking with Marva, 51–2
Pod's and Jerry's, 30
poker games, 47

Police Benevolent Association, 28
Political Affairs: "Against White
    Chauvinism and Bourgeois
    Nationalism," 136–40; articles
    written while underground, 127;
    "The Negro Veteran Fights for
    Freedom," 104
Popular Socialist Party convention
    (Cuba), 121–5
Possano family, 97–8
postwar years, 99–111
pot (marijuana), 34
Powell, Adam Clayton, 34
Prado, Perez, 123
Procope, Russell, 86
prostitution in Havana, 124
Publishers Typographic Service, 146–7
The Puzzle Palace, 87

race pride, Johnson's, x
racially mixed family, Johnson's, x
racism: in Black community, 14–15.
    See also anti-Semitism
Radium Club, 30
Ragland, Rags, 39
Ramapo Mountain People, 10, 11–12
The Ramapo Mountain People
    (Cohen), 10
Randolph, A. Philip, 81
Randolph, Bertha, 18, 19
Raymond, "Do-Do," 23
Red Channels, 77
"Red scare" (1940), 69
Redd, Paul, 159
relief (welfare), 54
religion: Church of the Epiphany, 16–18;
    social mobility and, 15–17
Renaissance. *See* Harlem Renaissance
rent parties, 55–6
Rhodes, Florence, 17
Rhodes, Gene, 21
Rickey, Branch, 81–2
Rico, Hettore, 96–7
Riley, Cyril, 18
Rivera, Lino, 55
Robeson, Paul: American Legionnaires
    attack, 117–18; Church of the
    Epiphany, 17–18

Robinson, Bill "Bojangles," xi; Jackie
    Robinson Day at Ebbetts Field, 82–3;
    Johnson, Winnie and, 21–2, 26–7
Robinson, Jackie, 82–3
Robinson, Marie, 33
Robinson, Sugar Ray, 33
Roca, Blas, 123, 125, 127, 129–30
Rodney, Lester, 81
Rodriguez, Carlos Rafael, 119, 122, 130
Rogers, Jean, 77
Roosevelt, Eleanor, 71
Roosevelt, Franklin D., 54
Rosenberg, Julius and Ethel, 126–7
Ross, Carl, 72; *Young Communist Review*,
    75
Ross, Claudia, 72–5
Rothstein, Arnold, 28
"rough trade," 47
Rousseauian vote principle, 141
Rudd, Mark, 153–4
Rutherford, Tommie, 39

Scales, Junius, 109
Schrank, Bob, 72
Schultz, "Dutch" (Arthur
    Flegenheimer), 28
SCORE (Strand Community
    Organization to Rehabilitate the
    Environment), 158
Scottsboro Boys, xii, xxiii, 44
Scottsboro case, Communist Party and,
    59
SDS (Students for a Democratic Society),
    153–4
segregation: baseball leagues, 80–2; U.S.
    Army, 92–3
shades of skin color, 14
Shaw, Bertha, 68–9
Sherman, Charlie, 77
Sherman, Joe, 77
Sherman, Martha, 77–8; marriage: Deep
    Freeze and, 126–7; interracial, 68–9;
    parents, 3–4; post-underground
    period, 142–4
Sherman, Zelda, 77
Shim-Sham Club, 30
the Shim Sham (dance), 30
Silvera, Johnnie, 21

Silvera, Rennie, 18, 20, 21
Simon, Abbott, 71–2
Siquieros, Alfredo, 119
skin color ideology, 14, 151–2
Skrontch, 32
"The Skrontch," 41
Small's Paradise, 31; Young Communist
League and, 65
Smart, Jack, 39
Smith, Florence, 107
Smith, Moranda, 105–6
Smith, Roscoe, 107
Smith, Verna, 48
Smith, Willie "the Lion," 14
Smith Act indictments, 113–18
SNYC (Southern Negro Youth Congress),
67; convention (1941), 72–4
social breakdown syndrome, 152–3
social mobility, religion and, 15–17
socialism, early outlook, 23
Sojourning for Freedom (McDuffie), ix
Soviet Power (Dean of Canterbury), 69
Soviet Union: invasion of Finland, 83–4;
Nazi invasion, 85; White House
demonstration, 84–5
Soviet–German Nazi nonaggression
pact, 79–80
Sparrow, Bea, 17
Sparrow, Lawrence, 17, 21
Special Services unit (U.S. Army), 86
Spencer, Amy, 33, 49–50
sports: Jim Crow in major league baseball,
80–2; Johnson, Howard "Monk," 4–5,
7–8; polo matches, 23; school, 22–3
Stalin, Joseph, xiii, xxiii, 9, 76, 84, 135,
137, 140, 142–4, 147
Stark, Herman, 28
Starobin, Joseph, 118, 153
Stepin Fetchit (Lincoln Theodore
Monroe Andrew Perry), xi; abuse of
Winnie, 149; marriage to Winnie, 47
Stith, Burditt, 18
Stranger at the Party (Lawrenson), 43–4
Strayhorn, Billy, 143
Strong, Augusta, 72
Strong, Ed, 72
Students for a Democratic Society. *See*
SDS

submarines, 71–2
Sugar Hill branch of Young Communist
League, 70
SUNY New Paltz, 156–9
Swan and Lee (comedians), 32
Swift, John (Gil Green), 130
Syzmanski, Al, 153–4

Ten Dancing Demons, 32–3
Terhune, Albert Payson, 10
terminal leave campaign (UNAVA),
101–11
Terrell, Prince, 18
The Apollo, Ellington and, 41–2
The Theory of the Leisure Class (Veblen),
47–8
Third Period, 114–15
Thomas, Edna, 43
Thompson, Bob, 153
Thompson, Thelma, 20
three inevitables, 126
the Three Johnsons, 38–9; breakup, 40,
46; Ellington gig, 40–2; Johnson,
Shirley, 43; "The Skrontch," 41
Tilary, Albert, 17, 21
Titoism, 119–20
Toledano, Vincente Lombardo, 120
Toward Soviet America (Foster), 115
trade unions, 135–6
training schools, 113–14
tri-racial isolate groups, 10–11
True Believer (Hoffer), 76

UNAVA (United Negro and Allied
Veterans of America), 82;
accreditation, 112–13; fundraiser,
109–11; Hammett, Dashiell,
contribution, 109–10; High Point,
N.C., 107–8; Holiday, Billie, 110–11;
shutdown, 113; South Carolina
chapters, 109; terminal leave
campaign, 101–11
underground period, 126–7; Cincinnati
Cotton Club, 127–8; Havana,
129–30; identity change, 127;
marriage and, 142–3; mistress, 131;
New Orleans, 128–9. *See also* Deep
Freeze

unemployment: Blacks and, 54–5; rent parties, 55–6

unions. *See* trade unions

Upward Bound program, 155–6

U.S. Army, xiii; Jim Crow, 100–1; segregation, 92–3

U.S. Army service: Blacks in combat, 88–9; Buffalo soldiers, 89; Fort Huachuca, 89–92; Fort Warren, 87–8; injury, 95–6; Mount Folgorito, 92–8; OCS (Officer Candidate School), 92–3; Quartermaster troops, 86–7; Special Services, 86; white man's war, 88

Van Dunk family, 10–11; Pooch, 12

Veblen, Thorstein, *The Theory of the Leisure Class*, 47–8

Verwayne, Percy, 43

vibraphone, 50

Von der Doncken, Adrian, 10

Wagner, Dan, 155–6

Waiting for Lefty, 44–5

Walters, Henry, 89

Warenetzky, Jack, 157

Warren, Sadie, 9–10

Waters, Ethel, 32

Webb, Chick, 31

Webb, Clifton, 27

Webb, Elida, 27

Wells, Dickey, 30–1

Western Hemisphere Peace Conference (Mexico City), 118–21

Whisonant, Larry, 90

white chauvinism in the Communist Party, 136–40

White House demonstration, 84–5

white man's war, 88

whites: communists, xii; Cotton Club controllers, xi; Harlem homoerotic tourism, xi–xii

Williams, Alexander, 24

Williams, Kenneth, 106

Williamson, Mel, 149

Wilson, Lucille, 33

Winfrey, Claude, 13

Wing, Dan, 17

Winston, Henry, 99, 102, 104, 130, 141

Wofsy, Malcolm, 70; alcohol relapse and, 152–3

Woodruff, Kenneth, 21

World Series rigging, 28

Wright, Jimmy, 40

Wright, Julia, 166–7

YCL (Young Communist League), xii, 65–6; anonymity, 70–1; Club Ashford, 70–1; Convoy Club, 84–5; Furriers Club, 84–5; Harlem Youth Congress, 67–8; "Jim Crow in Baseball" campaign, 80–2; Local 65 Club, 84–5; Manhattanville Club, 70; organization, xiii; "Red scare" (1940), 69; submarines, 71–2; Sugar Hill branch, 70

Young, Coleman, 82

Young Communist Review, 75

Yugoslav communists, 119–20